W9-BXN-656

Newbery and Caldecott Medal Books

1966-1975

Newbery and Caldecott Medal Books 1966-1975

edited by *Lee Kingman*

with *Acceptance Papers, Biographies*
and *Related Material chiefly from*

THE HORN BOOK MAGAZINE

THE HORN BOOK, INCORPORATED · BOSTON · 1975

Printed in the United States of America

Library of Congress Cataloging in Publication Data

Main entry under title:

Newbery and Caldecott medal books, 1966-1975.
    Includes index.

    1. Newbery medal books. 2. Caldecott medal books.
I. Kingman, Lee.   II. The Horn book magazine.
Z1037.A2N48 [PN1009]   028.5'07'9   75-20167
ISBN 0-87675-003-X

Designed by Larry Webster

Printed by Thomas Todd Company

Grateful Acknowledgment

To Gerald McDermott and The Horn Book, Inc., Boston, for permission to reprint "Caldecott Award Acceptance," © 1975 by Gerald McDermott, from *The Horn Book Magazine*, August 1975.

To Imagerie Pellerin for permission to reproduce the two illustrations from *Les Maîtres Graveurs Populaires 1800-1850* by Jean-Marie Dumont. © 1965 Imagerie Pellerin. Reproduced by permission of Imagerie Pellerin, Epinal, France.

✓ ✓ ✓

We extend particular thanks to the Children's Services Division of the American Library Association for the continuing cooperation in which the Children's Services Division sponsors the Newbery-Caldecott Awards and the Horn Book publishes the Acceptance Speeches; our thanks to the authors and artists for permission to reprint these speeches here; and our thanks to the authors of the biographies which originally appeared in *The Horn Book Magazine* for permission to reprint them.

✓ ✓ ✓

The editor wishes particularly to thank those at the Thomas Todd Company who have helped so much in the preparation of this book: Ms. Terry Bremer for seeing it through production; Mrs. Aurora Cousins for copyreading and proofreading; and Larry Webster for designing the book and its jacket.

And also to thank for their helpful cooperation with deadlines and details, Ethel L. Heins, present editor, and Paul Heins, former editor, of *The Horn Book Magazine*; and Mrs. Elizabeth Halbrooks and Ms. Anita Silvey of The Horn Book, Inc.

*To the Librarians who have served
on the Newbery-Caldecott Awards Committees
and
To the Children's Services Division
of the American Library Association*

Contents

Preface

With the dedication of this book to the librarians who have served on the Newbery-Caldecott Awards Committees, and to the Children's Services Division of the American Library Association who sponsor and administer the Newbery-Caldecott Awards, the Horn Book, Incorporated, salutes their vital role in the recognition and appreciation of excellence in children's literature.

It has now been fifty-three years since the first award of a Newbery Medal and thirty-seven years since the first Caldecott Medal was presented. Other national and regional book awards come and go, too many unhappily dependent on the unpredictable fates of booksellers, critics, and newspapers. But the stature and permanence of the ALA invests the Newbery and Caldecott Medals with continuing prestige. The Medal and Honor Books constitute an impressive body of work in the field of children's literature.

For almost as many years as the Newbery Medal has been in existence, the Horn Book has also recognized and promoted, in its magazine and book publications, excellence in children's literature; and, as the publication of children's books has proliferated almost too abundantly, the Horn Book has also been concerned with the continuing application of high standards to children's books, as well as with the study of the field in general. Evaluation and criticism are implicit in study.

As discussion of the merits of books nominated for the Newbery and Caldecott Awards — and we assume it is very thorough and lively discussion indeed — takes place before and during the voting process at ALA Midwinter Conference, that discussion is not available for study by those interested in the children's book field. (For an explanation of the present Newbery-Caldecott Awards voting system, please see "Honoring the Honor Books" by Elizabeth Johnson, in this volume.) As with the three previous volumes in this series (*Newbery Medal Books: 1922-1955*, edited by Bertha Mahony Miller and Elinor Whitney Field; *Caldecott Medal Books: 1938-1957*, edited by Bertha Mahony Miller and Elinor Whitney Field; and

Newbery and Caldecott Medal Books: 1956-1965, edited by Lee Kingman), The Horn Book is striving in this book to make a variety of material relating to the creation and evaluation of each of the Medal books easily accessible to students of children's literature, authors, artists, publishers, teachers, and librarians.

The most illuminating material is undoubtedly to be found in the Acceptance Papers of the authors and artists, and further enlightenment comes through reading their accompanying Biographical Notes. But it is equally necessary, in looking at this important body of work, to consider the evaluations of their books.

The evaluation article in *Newbery Medal Books: 1922-1955* was written by Elizabeth Nesbitt, who titled it "The Test of Recollection." Her opening remark, "Opinion in the awarding of a literary prize is rarely unanimous" has been re-emphasized, in one way or another, by each of the critics who have contributed their carefully considered opinions to this series. These include Esther Averill, whose questions in "What is a Picture Book?" in *Caldecott Medal Books: 1938-1957*, would still be pertinent in awarding the medal today; and Carolyn Horovitz, whose evaluation article, "Only the Best," appeared in *Newbery and Caldecott Medal Books: 1956-1965*, in which she wrote:

"Criticism will only grow in stature and usefulness as discussions grow, perceptions will sharpen as viewpoints are shared, and sensitivities will become more acute as areas of agreement and disagreement are carefully delineated. The field of children's literature needs this exercise desperately."

Thus the evaluations in this book are offered as a means of looking seriously at those books bearing the weight, as well as the honor, of being "the most distinguished." John Rowe Townsend, a well-known British children's novelist, book reviewer, and a critic who is particularly attuned to the whole field of children's literature, has written "A Decade of Newbery Books in Perspective"; Barbara Bader, an American reviewer and critic who has concentrated her studies on the history and development of the picture book, has written "Picture Books,

Art, and Illustration." Books by professionals, chosen to be honored by professionals in their field of library work, deserve professional criticism.

In their remarks, both John Rowe Townsend and Barbara Bader make it clear that their opinions are their own; but to consider well-based professional opinion — personal though it may be and whether or not we agree with that opinion — is a useful learning process. It is important to note, too, that criticism of a text's content and style somehow seems more tolerable than criticism in cold print of a book's art work. Perhaps this just seems to be so, since we are more accustomed, as adults, to verbal interpretations than to visual ones in our present culture. Because we are apt to feel less at home in discussing a picture than a story, we are less able to separate our emotional reaction from our perception of it as art — how it achieves what it does and what it says. Yet art criticism, because it must deal with what is concentrated before our eyes and deal with all the elements that comprise it — color, form, dynamics, movement, composition, subjects, and media — needs to be plainspoken to be easily understood. Otherwise our opinions can only be subjective — what we like or do not like — and subjective reaction to books like *Drummer Hoff* and *Arrow to the Sun* can be strong.

During the years covered by this volume, the Newbery-Caldecott Awards Committee renamed the Runners-up, calling them Honor Books. We felt this change noteworthy, and particularly wanted a discussion of the Honor Books. Elizabeth Johnson, former librarian and Supervisor of Work with Children in the Lynn (Massachusetts) Public Library, has provided this in "Honoring the Honor Books." The Newbery Medal Honor Books and the Caldecott Medal Honor Books for 1966-1975 are listed in full.

We hope that this book will be provocative, and that it will enable all those concerned with the creation, use, and criticism of children's books, to see all the material — the Acceptance Papers in which the authors and artists tell how they feel about their work and what their trials and sufferings, hopes, dreams, and joys have been in creating their books; the Biographical Notes, which are perceptively informative; the Evaluations; but most of all, that it will encourage further consideration of the books themselves.

As more librarians, publishers, book-buyers, and booksellers grow in knowledge of what is truly worthy of recognition, everyone will benefit — most of all, the artists and authors and the children and young people who are reaching out to each other with the help of, and sometimes in spite of, all the people in between.

Lee Kingman

The Newbery Awards

1966-1975

The Newbery Award 1966

I, JUAN DE PAREJA

written by ELIZABETH BORTON DE TREVIÑO

published by BELL BOOKS
FARRAR, STRAUS & GIROUX   1965

BOOK NOTE

Born a slave in sixteenth century Spain, Juanico becomes the devoted and admiring servant of Diego Velázquez, helping him in his studio at home and at the Court of King Philip the IV. Juanico longs to become a painter, only to find the law does not allow a slave to be an artist; he longs to be a free man, even though he never wants to leave Velázquez. The years during which the black man grows to know a great deal about painting, about artists, about the life at court and the lonely King Philip, are full of valid and fascinating detail. The relationship between Velázquez and his black servant, whom he admires and paints as a friend, is explored with sympathy and seen clearly within the framework of the times. Use of the first person to tell the story brings immediacy to the problems, experiences, and artistic insights of the black slave who grew up to become the free man, Juan de Pareja.

EXCERPT FROM THE BOOK

He usually rose and had his breakfast by six, earlier in summer. His breakfast was always the same: a piece of grilled meat and a small trencher of bread. Occasionally he would take an orange into the studio, and there eat it thoughtfully as he planned his work for the day. He liked the early light when it was still fresh from the dew and without any dancing dust motes in it. He was always in the studio until the light went in the afternoon, but he was not always painting. He made drawings, many drawings, though he did not save them, but tossed them aside. (I was able to keep a few.) He drew so much, so easily, so perfectly, that when at last he stood before a frame of prepared canvas, he could sketch in the outlines of his subject in one moment of flashing charcoal, never having to correct more than a knife-edge of line.

And often he simply sat staring . . . now at a piece of draped velvet, now at a copper bowl, now at me.

When I felt a little more confidence in his presence, and did not fear disturbing him in one of his reveries, I asked him why he did this.

"I am working, Juanico," was his answer. "Working, by looking."

I did not understand and so I held my tongue, thinking that this was what he meant me to do with this cryptic answer. But a week or more later, he spoke to me as if I had put my question but a moment before, answering, "When I sit and look at something I am feeling its shape, so that I shall have it in my fingers when I start to draw the outline. I am analyzing the colors, too. For example, do you see that piece of brocade on the chair? What color is it?"

"Blue," I answered promptly.

"No, Juanico. There is a faint underlay of blue, but there is violet in that blue, the faintest touch of rose, and the highlights are red and bright green. Look again."

It was magical, for suddenly I could see them, the other colors, just as he said.

"The eye is complicated. It mixes the colors for you," explained Master. "The painter must unmix them and lay them on again shade by shade, and then the eye of the beholder takes over and mixes them again."

"I should like to paint!" I cried out in my joy at this revelation.

"Alas, I cannot teach you," said Master, and then he became silent again and returned to his easel.

I pondered this remark and lay awake at night thinking of it after dark, for I could not understand why he could not teach me. I decided that he had meant to say, "I will not teach you," or "I do not wish to teach you." I put this thought away deep in my memory because it made me so sad. I had begun to love him, you see, and to wish to offer him all my heart's loyalty. But these words were a little worm, gnawing away at my affection.

Newbery Award Acceptance

by ELIZABETH BORTON DE TREVIÑO

When *Kristin Lavransdatter* by Sigrid Undset came out in English I got hold of the book first. I sat in a corner with that novel and could not do anything but wash and dress mechanically, eat what was put into my hand, sleep reluctantly, and read, for two weeks. Next, my sister seized the book and she was tended, as I had been, and relieved of every household task and duty until, sighing, she turned the last page. Then my mother said, "All right, girls, take over. It's my turn." And she never moved or spoke to a soul until she had finished it. My father did not care. He was rereading, for the tenth enchanted time, the African journals of Frederick Courteney Selous, the great English hunter, and while we were in medieval Norway, he had been far away in darkest Africa, with all the wild forest around him. That is the kind of family we were.

When I was a child, I really suffered when I had to lay down my book in order to set the table or dust the parlor for my mother. My greatest reward for tasks well done was to be allowed to go to the library and browse among the shelves so laden with treasure. My father and mother peppered their conversation with quotations from Shakespeare, the Bible, Byron, and Bobbie Burns. My maternal grandmother loved poetry and could recite it, pages and pages of it, by heart; my paternal grandmother passed her last illness reading and died with a copy of my first published book in her hand. My Danish grandfather sang me to sleep with his own translations of Norse sagas.

As a young man, before he turned all his attention to the law, my father had published many short stories and poems. At dinner in our house he presided with the dictionary on his right hand and a portable set of encyclopedias on his left. Small fry were encouraged to take part in the conversation with their elders, but they were required to look up, immediately, words or facts about which they were shaky. Slang, mispronunciations, and breathless unfinished sentences were not merely bad form, they merited being sent from the table.

The joys of our winter evenings took place after dinner when, seated before the fireplace, my father read to me. We adventured with Tom Sawyer, Jim Hawkins, and David Balfour; we wept with David Copperfield and Oliver Twist; we endured with Jean Valjean.

When I started writing poetry, at age six, my father solemnly advised me about rhyme schemes. When, at age eight, I saw my first published verse in the *Monterey Peninsula Herald*, I felt my foot on the ladder I was determined to climb, though many weary trips to the post office were to take place before I ever saw another poem of mine in print.

I am recounting all this in order to make it clear that this literary award, the Newbery Medal, has been given to a person conditioned from birth and by education and taste to feel that it is the most wonderful thing that could possibly happen to her. It is a platform of achievement which will make the continuing road both easier and harder. Easier, because I will have with me the feeling of pride in the trust and confidence shown me and my work; harder, because now self-criticism must be less indulgent, for there is a higher ideal to keep in view. One cannot, one dare not, do less than his best, always, after such an award as the Newbery.

But it would be presumptuous and untrue to accept this award as if it were something earned entirely without help or cooperation. When an accolade such as the Newbery is awarded, surely it recognizes, in its implications, more than one book written in a given year. The recipient, it seems to me, accepts in the name of all the people and things, all that life has presented in its multiple experiences, which made the book possible. I am glad, I am honored, to remember and to mention many of the influences which helped me, and which to this day sustain and encourage me in my work.

First, my parents, who taught me to love books and reading. After I had begun writing, my father did many wonderful things for me. Before I had achieved any publication, he took an office for me, equipped it with a table, typewriter, and chair, and paid me a small salary. "Now," he said, "you will write every day from nine to twelve and from one to five. Writing is work. You may have Saturdays off." When I reported to him one day that I had started a novel, he commented, "Probably 5649 other persons started novels today. Chances are that 5640 have more talent than you. But honey, you can do what 5000 won't do. You can finish yours." Splendid advice; never forgotten.

Time has robbed me of my remarkable father, but I am fortunate to have still an equally remarkable and wonderful mother. She is a sensitive and stern critic, and all my work is colored by a promise I made her long ago. "Promise me," she asked, "that you will never write anything that you know would be offensive to me." With perfect confidence in her taste and judgment, I promised, and I will not.

While I was in high school and in college, several teachers took time from their busy days to draw me to one side, to help and advise me. First was Mark F. Wilcox, who taught English in the Kern County Union High School. A gifted teacher, he was the first to impress upon me the value of form and to give me a respect for craftsmanship. The mere recounting of impressions and piling on of details is not art, he taught; it is merely musing. One must master one's material, cut it into form, learn that the essence of art is knowing what to eliminate.

At the university I was taught another invaluable lesson by Professor David Grey, who taught the writing of drama. He read my efforts aloud to his classes, with malicious amusement; and since my plays were tragic and he made the class laugh at them, he sent me back to my dormitory in tears after every session. By his own words, he had been at pains to teach us all that the climate of writing is frustration and disappointment, that there will always be some people along our way who will not like what we have written. "You might just possibly," he said in his dry English way, "have the makings of a writer in you. For I couldn't make you stop writing, and essentially that is what writing boils down to. People who allow themselves to be discouraged are not for this trade."

Now I must list two newspapermen who helped form me as a writer, and I mention them with enduring gratitude. The first was the late, great Philip Hale, well-known music and drama critic of *The Boston Herald*. When he first hired me as an assistant music reviewer, he made gentle fun of me for writing poetry and dubbed me "Elizabeth Barrett Borton." But one day he summoned me by telegram, as was his custom, and told me in his tired old voice, "Continue writing poetry, please. Poetry, in its essence, reflects and awakens wonder, and the world, which I must leave all too soon, is a wonderful place. A wonderful place." Then, shouldering his green baize bag full of books and adjusting his derby, he shuffled out. I can see him to this day, reading as he walked along, traffic opening for him and closing behind him respectfully.

I give honor to George Minot, city editor of *The Boston Herald* when I went there as a reporter. Later, he became the managing editor, and although he is now retired, he continues as a columnist for the same paper. He taught me the inestimable value of the blue pencil. I used to tremble when he crossed out my beautiful words; now, remembering his advice, I rejoice at each word I can cut. "Make it accurate," he told me, "but rip out anything that has no right to be there."

My friend Dr. Isaac Goldberg was the next person to give me counsel that has made my life as a writer possible. I was asked to write a book to continue the Pollyanna series, the original author having died. Though I was longing to see my name on a published book, I was young and arrogant and I chanted all the sophisticated clichés of my day. I was appalled at the idea of writing a *Pollyanna!* I asked Dr. Goldberg what to do.

"If you want to be a professional writer," he advised me, "take every commission that you can get and do the best possible job with it. And write all the time, besides. The world is bursting with material, and no material is too high or too low for a writer. *Transfigure* it; that's what writing means."

I must tell of a lesson I learned all by myself. It happened when I accepted the first Pollyanna commission and was obliged to reread the Pollyanna books, which I had been so sure I was too intelligent to write. But as I read, I began to remember how I had felt when, as a child, I had read about Pollyanna. I recalled that all the veiled contempt and skepticism in the scorn of Pollyanna had not been mine; on the contrary, I had loved Pollyanna for being glad she did not have to use the crutches in the missionary barrel; I had rejoiced when she patched up quarrels and made people love each other once more. She represented courage — the English stiff upper lip, but a lip with a smile on it, the best kind after all. I returned, right there, to the child's belief in the world as a good place, which can be made pleasant and happy for everyone; to a child's optimism, trust, and hope. I subsequently wrote four more *Pollyannas*, and I have never forgotten what I had rediscovered in myself — that children love justice and the triumph of the right. Cynicism, after all, is an adult invention.

A few more names, out of many that swim into my memory, of people who encouraged me. First, my loyal agent, Virginia Rice, to whom I dedicated the book which you have honored with the Newbery Medal. Through many years she has been, besides a treasured friend, a gentle guide, or a very rock of staunchness when I needed her backing on something I felt I *must* do.

Editors, too, have been my teachers, each one showing me some valuable lesson of technique, point of view, or attitude. I want to thank them all. Margaret Cousins, with her great gifts of sympathy and of empathy, bought my very first short story and is now my editor for adult books. Elliott Schryver took a chance on an unknown and intense little Mexican señora named Treviño, who descended on him with a reticule full of ideas for great novels. He encouraged her, instead, to tell the simple story of her life in Monterrey. She did, and the book that resulted, *My Heart Lies South*, is still in print after fourteen years! Others who are not forgotten are William Poole and Elizabeth Riley, sensitive and expert, both; Hal Vursell, the imaginative and helpful editor of children's books at Farrar; and lastly, Clare Costello, so warmly understanding and responsive, who guided me in my recent children's books, including the one you are honoring today.

I cannot leave out my family, which endures me through the vagaries and struggles of my writing life and which makes excuses for me when I neglect my household duties, or when, in the heat of composition, I forget even my name.

And the many friends and readers who write me, commenting on my work, helping and encouraging me. I can never forget the letters which come to me from strangers, written out of a sense of kinship and friendship; what more could an author ask? To be sure, I sometimes receive strange missives. One I got lately was a flagrant case of plagiarism. It read: "Dear Mrs. Treviño, Rose are red, vilots are blue, suger is sweet and so are you. Do you like my poem? Love, Sonia." And there was one fan letter which I keep close to me at all times, for the good of my soul, to remind me to be humble and grateful for small favors. It says: "Dear Mrs. Treviño, I don't like to read because the stories are so silly. But the teacher makes us. She makes us write to authors, too. That is why I am writing to you. She made me read *Nacar, the White Deer*. It was prety good."

I, Juan de Pareja tells a story I learned, loved, and researched many years before it was written. The Newbery Medal really goes to the two protagonists who lived the lives I told about. If there had not been a noble and generous Velázquez and a loyal and loving Juan de Pareja in real life, there would have been no book to tell of their friendship.

And so, because "no man is an island" but we are all "part

of the main" — and this applies to the writer of books especially — I have told about the many people, living and dead, present or far away, who have helped me write *I, Juan de Pareja*. In their name, in the name of all who have been close to me, friends and teachers, librarians and editors, family and kin, it is with deep gratitude and respect that I accept the Newbery Medal.

✦ ✦ ✦

In a note written in 1974, after some years in which to gain perspective on the Newbery Award and her book, Elizabeth Borton de Treviño adds: Everything I have ever written deals with some form of love. And just as some physical defect occasionally produces a genius of the dance, because of over-compensation, so the difficulties of love across racial barriers can give rise to strong and loyal devotion. This was the theme of my story, *I, Juan de Pareja*. Precisely because men had denied brotherhood and friendship between the races for so long, it seems to me that now we can appreciate each other more fully.

The longer I live, the more I am convinced that every child is born with a deep need to love and be loved, and that this longing accompanies us through life, passing through many metamorphoses, but always at the root of all our actions and hopes. It has been my joy to learn, through many letters from readers, juvenile and adult, that the gist of my message has been perceived and appreciated. I could not ask for greater reward.

Louis Mélançon

Elizabeth Borton de Treviño

by ROSS PARMENTER

Elizabeth Borton de Treviño came by the foreign-sounding part of her name when she married Luis Treviño of Monterrey, Mexico. The "de" in her name is a result of one of the advantages Mexican wives have over wives north of the border. They can and do maintain their maiden name merely adding their husband's name to their own, with the linking preposition "de" standing for "wife of."

How Miss Borton met Señor Treviño is attractively told in *My Heart Lies South*, the book that first brought the author to wide American attention. The year was 1934, and by this time Miss Borton was already a newspaper reporter of seven years' experience. She was assigned by her paper, *The Boston Herald*, to go to Mexico for interviews with outstanding personalities. In Monterrey, the good-looking young Luis Treviño, because he spoke English, was assigned, in turn, to be Miss Borton's guide, interpreter, and explainer of all things Mexican — a task for which he was well qualified because he knew the ways of both countries, his family having been obliged to seek refuge in the United States during the worst years of the Mexican Revolution.

The visiting newspaperwoman turned out to be blonde, vivacious, intelligent, *simpática,* and pretty, with large gray-green eyes with flecks of amber in them. They were married fifteen months later.

The romance was in sharp contrast with an earlier one in Miss Borton's life. The one in question was a decidedly one-sided affair which took place while Elizabeth was an undergraduate at Stanford in her native California. At that time she had a fixation on all things intellectual. Her suitor, another student, did not live up to the intellectually severe standards she was then demanding. One day she was telling her father, wise old attorney-at-law Fred Borton of Bakersfield, what an impossible mate the young man would be. To clinch the matter of his obvious unsuitability, she said, "Why he's even foolish enough to believe in love at first sight."

Her father surprised her, for he shook his head and said quietly: "Honey, there just isn't any other kind."

I do not know to how many people Elizabeth has told that story. She has such a rich store of anecdotes that this may have popped suddenly from her past just because it happened to be apropos of something I had been saying. She told it to me as we were sitting on a terrace, looking through the trees into the steeply sloping garden of her home in Cuernavaca. An oval swimming pool and the new extension of the house were at our backs. And it was a joy to hear her merry laughter as she told this story about her own foolishness as a girl.

To one who knew how hard she had worked to get that garden and who had enjoyed her friendship since his second visit to Mexico in 1947, it was also a joy to hear her tell it in such surroundings. And on many levels it was revealing of her life and character. A few characteristics it revealed will be brought out later, but let me continue here with the most obvious one: her love of telling stories about her father's wise ways.

One story in particular convinced me that he was indeed a remarkable man, for he did one of the wisest things I ever heard of a father doing when confronted with a child announcing the desire to be something so insecure as a writer. Originally, Elizabeth had gone to Boston to study the violin, but there she had got a job on *The Boston Herald*, a job which, to her dismay, was cut from under her by the Depression. She was back home in Bakersfield, frustrated and idle. I may not have her father's exact words as Elizabeth quoted them, but this, in effect, is what he said:

"So you want to be a writer. All right, I'll go along. But on this condition. You are too inexperienced to be able to earn much by writing. And I don't much like the idea of a newspaper life for a woman. I'll tell you what I'll do. To become a writer, one has to work at it — like any other job. If you promise to keep regular office hours and write every day, I will take a little office for you and pay you a small salary."

The determined young daughter liked the fairness of that. She agreed to the terms and went to her office each day. But in 1931 *The Boston Herald* called her back. She has made friends wherever she has been, and one of the friends she made in Boston was Philip Hale, the *Herald*'s music critic. Because of her musical training, he let her cover some of the minor events that he could not get to. This led to a steady job as an entertainment reporter, and later she was promoted to the *Herald*'s city staff. She wrote many feature stories as well as routine ones, and she loved the gregarious, knockabout, exciting atmosphere of the city room of a metropolitan daily.

When I had my letter of introduction to a stranger called Mrs. de Treviño, her days as a full-time reporter were over. So were the years of her life in Monterrey, which she was to describe in *My Heart Lies South*. As most members of the Mexican intellectual community do sooner or later, she and her husband had moved to Mexico City. And it was because of the job she had there that I had my letter. I was a New York music reviewer and she was the secretary of Carlos Chávez, Mexico's most famous composer.

The address on my letter was incorrect and I had quite a time finding her office, including climbing to the top floor of the Palacio de Bellas Artes, the mammoth white marble opera house, in the center of the capital. She was all smiles when she appeared, and she extended one of her tiny hands for a surprisingly firm handshake. When I told her of having traipsed over to Calle Isabel la Católica, she thought it was funny.

"Oh that's the old address!" she said lightheartedly. "Poor dear, you must be tired, and climbing all those stairs too! Do sit down and make yourself comfortable."

Her hair was almost straw colored, parted in the center, drawn back over her head and surmounted with a crown made from her long braid. Her small nose made her large eyes seem even larger, and I saw there was sadness in those striking eyes, in spite of a naturally cheerful nature. Her skin was white and she looked rather delicate, but I noticed she filled her rather tight skirt with a comfortable roundness.

After she had arranged for the concert tickets I was after, she asked how long I was staying. When she saw that there was time enough, she said: "Then we must have a little party. I'll ask some friends whom I think you would find congenial. Could you make it for supper on Sunday night? We live in San Angel, on a side street with pepper trees down the middle."

Thereafter I went back to Mexico every September, and that was the first of many happy visits to Desierto 31 in the Mexican suburb where she lived for so long in the house and community that she has written about in *Where the Heart Is*, her other autobiographical book. After she left Bellas Artes, she had other offices, for she took a variety of jobs to help Luis keep the family breadbasket well filled for the two sons, Luis Jr., the fair-haired, moody older boy with the talent for painting, and the more ebullient Enrique, who is now a Mexico City lawyer.

Publicity jobs, newspaper articles, writing letters in English for Spanish-speaking Mexicans, baking gingerbread – there was almost no type of job she was not willing to take if it brought in some honest pesos. And all the time she went on doing her serious writing — short stories mostly, though her head also teemed with ideas for novels. Virginia Rice was her loyal agent, and every now and then they made a sale, the first big break coming with Crowell's acceptance of *My Heart Lies South* in 1953.

The fact that I was also trying to win acceptance of manuscripts was one of our great bonds in common, as was my growing love of and interest in her adopted country. A third, of course, was music. Another was religion — though I am not a Roman Catholic as she is, and when I heard, before I met her, that she had been converted to Catholicism, I felt it might even be a stumbling block in our relationship.

When Elizabeth became a Roman Catholic, she did not change her faith, for the freethinking Borton children — she has a sister and a brother — were brought up without church affiliations. In assuming one, Elizabeth was motivated, in part, by a realization that life in a Catholic country, married to a Catholic, with children to be brought up as Catholics, was likely to be more harmonious and balanced if she became a Catholic too. When I first met her she was not particularly devout.

But one September when I made my annual visit I immediately sensed a profound difference in her attitude. The change, which might have had the opposite effect, actually strengthened our friendship still further. She had moved more deeply into the heart of her religion through having the mystical experience that is known as the Sense of the Presence of God. My own life had been governed for a number of years by consciousness of the Indwelling Presence. So we shared something precious, and differences on doctrinal matters were less important than ever.

Ever since, Elizabeth's Catholicism has informed her books ever more deeply. Her faith is at the core of *A Carpet of Flowers*, the first of her children's books written under the new dispensation. It is about a blind Indian boy whose sight was restored by a miracle because he had grown the pansies that served as the eyes of the Virgin in the carpet of flowers that his town of Huamantla had prepared.

Her faith is important, too, in her first adult novel, *Even as You Love*, which describes the impact of a Catholic Mexican family on a young Protestant woman, who visits Mexico after the shattering experience of a divorce. There is much about the Catholic faith, too, in *The Greek of Toledo*, her first historical novel, which is about El Greco. In dealing with a Spanish artist, it paved the way for the Newbery-winning *I, Juan de Pareja*, which tells a good deal about Velázquez by showing him through the eyes of Juan, his Negro slave.

Between the two books about painters came another children's book, *Nacar, the White Deer*. This one, too, has a historical background, but in the forefront is a peasant boy's love of an animal and his journey with it through Mexico. The countryside is wonderfully evoked. For me, this is the most artistically perfect of her books and the one I like best.

Her hope is to alternate between books for young people and adult novels; and she followed *I, Juan de Pareja* with *The Fourth Gift*, a sometimes grim novel about the *Cristeros*, who fought against government attempts to suppress Catholicism in Mexico in the 1920s. It suggests Thornton Wilder's *The Bridge of San Luis Rey* in that it chronicles the individual stories of seven persons involved in the same sequence of events. Her growing powers as a novelist are apparent in the book, which, like everything that she has written, is physically vivid, both in its scenes and in its characters.

I hope the phrase "new dispensation" was noticed earlier. I used it because one of my surprises, while browsing in the Treviño library one year, was coming upon *About Bellamy*, a children's book that caught my interest because the author's name was Elizabeth Borton. It was a sad story about a little girl who was studying to be a ballet dancer and whose father, a Russian violinist, was so poor he had to sell his violin. Since Elizabeth had never said a word about its existence, I asked her why she did not generally list it among her publications. Harper had let it go out of print, she said. And then I learned that she had written seven other children's books under her maiden name for Page and Company. She did not list these, she said, because, as they were commissioned books, some of the characters were given to her ready-made.

The late Eleanor Parker's famous Pollyanna was one of the characters whose life story she was commissioned to carry on. While still a newspaper writer in Boston she turned out *Pollyanna in Hollywood*, *Pollyanna's Castle in Mexico*, *Pollyanna and the Secret Mission*, and *Pollyanna's Door to Happiness*. (She also provided Page with two of its Little Cousin series: namely, *Our Little Aztec Cousin* and *Our Little Ethiopian Cousin*.) It was after moving to Mexico that she wrote *About Bellamy* and then her fifth and final Pollyanna book, *Pollyanna's Golden Horseshoe*.

In appearance, Elizabeth has changed remarkably little over the years, and last December I could hardly believe it when she told me that sixty was a watershed she had crossed the year before. Her hope is that in the years that lie ahead her recently completed home in Cuernavaca will give her a new period of tranquillity in which she can use her strength to best advantage to set down the many stories she still wants to write. At present, she is working on a third novel with a Mexican setting.

My own hope is that one of these days she will write a book about the Bakersfield childhood and youth that she talks about so vividly. For her mother, Carrie L. Borton, has been as important to her as her father, and she also tells lively stories about her mother's homely wisdom. The alliance of affection and respect between mother and daughter is so close that a daily letter to each other seems as natural as breathing.

As a writer, I have been uncompromising in taking up only the projects I want at the time that I want to write them. Elizabeth has been more humble, and she has listened carefully to Miss Rice's judgment as to which of her projects her agent felt she could place. And when reading a definition of art in *The Fourth Gift* — "Art requires thirty per cent talent, thirty per cent very hard work, and forty per cent character"— I felt I could hear Elizabeth's own voice.

All those aware of her character — she is very strong despite her sweetness of manner — and of how hard she has worked have rejoiced in the fact that the American Library Association, in giving her its Newbery Medal, has helped to bring wider recognition to her talent.

Perhaps by now there is no need to labor the things revealed in her story about herself when she was a blue stocking. Her wit, her humor, her family feeling, her memory, her gift as a raconteur, her enjoyment of an incident that illustrates a serious truth, her feeling for character, her self-perspective, her capacity for change — all these, I hope, have emerged. But I would like to underline one thing the story illustrates: her life has been a pilgrimage towards a belief she now holds deeply, but which she did not always hold — belief in the wisdom of the heart.

UP A ROAD SLOWLY

written by IRENE HUNT

published by FOLLETT PUBLISHING COMPANY 1966

BOOK NOTE

Julie Trelling, a seven-year-old who has just lost her mother, is sent to live with Aunt Cordelia, a maiden schoolteacher, in the country. As a teen-age girl she chooses to stay with her aunt, even though being there limits her friends and experiences during high school. Her development during these years makes the stuff of this story, which is observed and written about with a mature point of view. Although what Julie does may be immature and typical of a questing, sensitive child, the incidents and characters are seen as part of a larger pattern: the aunt she did not realize had been a beautiful girl; the adored sister, Laura, whom she believes has allowed a husband to usurp Julie's place in her heart; the abstracted professor father, who marries again and suddenly is seen as a man; the stepmother, also Julie's English teacher, which makes a complicated relationship; the spoiled handsome boy, Brett, who flatters Julie into doing his school work; the faithful Danny; and a beautifully stated character, Uncle Haskell — a self-deluded writer and dignified alcoholic. The quality of all these relationships is presented with maturity and honesty, which also permeates the writing.

EXCERPT FROM THE BOOK

Down in the kitchen Aunt Cordelia was preparing breakfast; the aroma of coffee and Canadian bacon and hot, buttered toast met me as I ran downstairs, and I, who for weeks had been growing thinner as I picked indifferently at my food, was suddenly famished and eager.

We often ate our breakfast in a sunny corner of the kitchen, and Aunt Cordelia had placed two blue bowls on the table, two of Grandmother Bishop's best china bowls, and they were filled with raspberries picked only that morning and still frosted with dew. I was especially perceptive to all things beautiful that morning — raspberries in blue china bowls were enough to make the heart sing.

Aunt Cordelia glanced up from her work as I entered the fragrant kitchen, and I saw a light come into her eyes. She liked seeing me carefully dressed of a morning; she was relieved too, I am sure, to see that I had emerged from the despondency that had weighed upon me for weeks. I smiled at her and hurried to pour the coffee.

"Aunt Cordelia," I said in the tones of a Biblical proclamation, "I have been visited by a miracle."

The light in her eyes was clouded instantly, whether in concern over my sanity or recognition of the fact that miracles could sometimes be embarrassing to a family. She let a circle of pink bacon fall back into the frying pan, and stood looking at me. I laughed at her expression and poured the coffee so recklessly that it overflowed one cup and filled the saucer.

"There are miracles and miracles, Aunt Cordelia; this one has just given me a new outlook on life. I went to sleep last night still feeling hurt over Brett; this morning I am completely free of him. He no longer matters. It's all over."

She was relieved, there was no doubt about that, but she took her place at the table as sedately as always. "Love is not love which alters," she quoted as she passed a basket of toast to me, "when it alteration finds."

I knew then that she was happy. Aunt Cordelia was likely to be in one of her better moods when she felt like quoting Shakespeare.

As we sat together at breakfast that morning I thought that food had never before tasted so wonderful.

"You know, Aunt Cordelia, there will come a time when I'll eat berries like these some morning, fresh, dewy berries like these, and I'll think, 'What's the matter? These are not like the ones I ate with so much pleasure long ago.' And then I'll tell myself, 'Of course not, for where is the sunny kitchen overlooking the woods, and where is the beautiful room upstairs where you awakened that morning, where is the aunt who quoted from one of Shakespeare's sonnets and above all, where is the sixteen-year-old girl who had just experienced a miracle?' It will never be the same, Aunt Cordelia; I'll never eat raspberries like these again."

Aunt Cordelia just smiled gently. "Maybe not," she said.

Books and the Learning Process

by IRENE HUNT

I do not suppose that any writer who has received the honor of the Newbery Award has been less than delighted by so high and worthy a token of recognition. I am no exception. I am honored and delighted and happy. I do not know how one could feel otherwise.

I am aware, however, in the midst of my pleasure that many other fine books were written in 1966, books of distinction which have given all of us in this field great pleasure in reading. Then, too, I remember the many books that have enriched your childhood and mine, books that were published long before there was a Newbery Award. If there are moments when my spirit seems to be soaring a little too high, I remind myself of the caustic chuckle with which old Mark Twain might greet my euphoria or the raised eyebrows of that idol of my ninth year, Louisa May Alcott, if she should suddenly materialize.

And so tonight I shall not talk much about my own book — if I can help it — but of books in general and of the role I have watched them play in the learning process.

The learning process is very close to me, since I have been a teacher or a counselor or a "helper of other teachers" for many years; I have watched books bring new dimensions of happiness, of confidence and enlightenment, to young people from the age of three on up. I have respected writers of books for a long time; it is only recently that I have known the pleasure of being one.

When I was young, my fellow teachers and I were often visited by a somewhat austere supervisor, a woman completely dedicated to the relative heights of the letters of the alphabet and to the proper grasp of a pencil. We used to pass rather saucy notes to one another on the days when one of us knew of her approach. A note might run like this: "Madame X is in the building; look to it that your kiddies are not pinching their pencils!"

I have told this anecdote to young teachers to point up the fact that times and the philosophy of counseling have changed considerably since those days. One girl told me, however, that she intended to warn others of *my* approach with a note which would read: "Irene is in the building; it would be a good thing if she finds you reading aloud to your class!"

And it would be and *is* such a good thing. Of course, I am quite tolerant of math and science, of music and art, and all the other areas of learning. But real satisfaction for me is to step into a room where teacher and children are off together in another world, bound together by a bond made possible through the magic of a well-loved book.

I think there is no way in which a teacher can become so close to her class as through this shared satisfaction of a book. The great pity is that many teachers are hagridden by a sense of guilt, a puritanical hangover which has for its basic premise that anything full of joy *must* be a waste of time: it is not painful enough to be worthwhile!

But little by little teachers' attitudes are changing. Teachers are beginning to realize that children are not created fully equipped with such values as courage, compassion, integrity, and insights into the motives and needs of themselves and of others. These attributes they learn from the people around them; they are often learned from the behavior of the characters who people the books they read. We adults may preach the values we wish to instill, and the children will turn away from our sermons; but a book, a fine book that mirrors life accurately and honestly — there is the effective substitute for our ineffective sermons.

Children in general are not exactly panting to learn English grammar or rules of punctuation. They are actually predisposed to resist such learning, and often the young or shy teacher is met with hostility when he tries to overcome that resistance. Such hostility can be a formidable thing. That is one of the specific times when I counsel the teachers to throw aside all formal aspects of English for a while and turn to a good book.

I recommend what I call sure-fire books at first. Sometimes it is a former Newbery Award winner, Emily Neville's *It's Like This, Cat*. Children of junior-high age identify completely with Mrs. Neville's young protagonist. He is a little older than they are and he is a city boy who loves cats — both good points — and he is, at times, considerably wiser than his father — a deliciously gratifying point for a thirteen-year-old! Then I recommend *Old Yeller* or *Rascal* or *The Incredible Journey*. After that they are ready for *Call of the Wild*, for *Island of the Blue Dolphins*, for *Onion John*, and for dozens of others. Before half these books are finished the children are on the teacher's side; gerund clauses and predicate nominatives can be borne if later you get to hear a chapter from *Treasure Island*.

Frequently in counseling young people I have found that troubled children are often in a state of guilt. They see themselves as wicked or unclean, hateful to themselves and to others. One can say to them: "You are not unique; there is in all of us only a thin veneer of civilization that separates us from the primitive." But these assurances are only the words of an adult, and children are confident that no adult has been around enough to understand. It is in books that an identification can be made which constitutes a wholesome therapy. (The children overlook the fact that books are written by adults!) It is in books that one finds there are other cowards in this world, other youngsters who are ashamed of their environment, other people who have had strange, dark thoughts, who have had experiences too ugly to admit. Julie, in *Up a Road Slowly* is not set apart by virtue of her high-mindedness or moral values. But for a watchful family she might well have stepped into the same trouble in which some of her young readers may find themselves. *Her* young body could speak more loudly than her reason too.

Books enrich so many areas of learning that might otherwise be deadly dull. I have seen the drab facts pertinent to the impeachment and removal of an elected official from office suddenly become dramatic and real when a teacher has opened *Profiles in Courage* and has read to the class the exciting story of Senator Ross of Kansas, whose one vote prevented a president from being removed from office and the constitution of a country from being forever weakened.

I have heard the story of *Johnny Tremain* giving new life to a study of the American Revolution. I have heard Margaret Coit's superb book *The Fight for Union* discussed by children who were beginning to understand the forces that for forty years had been leading to the great conflagration of 1861. I have heard Bruce Catton's *Banners of Shenandoah* being read to children who probably could not have read it on their own but who sat in spellbound silence as the boy who served with Phil Sheridan told his story. And I have not protested when a teacher has tried to present the issues, a way of life, and a tragic leaf of history by reading my own book *Across Five Aprils.*

It is difficult to measure the effect of books upon learning, upon attitudes and insights. Difficult as it is to measure, I do know that through some of the books I have offered children the conscience and feelings of a few have been touched.

Just before Christmas last year I took Rebecca Caudill's book *A Certain Small Shepherd* into many junior-high classrooms. I said, "I am bringing you a Christmas gift, a beautifully written and very tender story which I want to share with you." Then I read to them the story of mute little Jamie, who so completely lived his role of a small shepherd in the school Christmas play that when he found a modern Mary and Joseph and

Baby, a miracle occurred: for the first time in his life he was able to articulate the words that were so clear in his mind and heart.

You all know how bigotry stalks the streets of our cities. These children — not all of them, please believe me, but many of them — were familiar with bigotry of the most vicious kind. They listened in perfect silence as the story progressed. Then when I had finished the reading we discussed various aspects of the story, finally coming to the question of why the modern Mary and Joseph should have been turned away from many homes in the mountain community. Would it not take a very hard and callous person to send them out into a killing blizzard when it was obvious that the woman was about to have a baby? Gravely they thought about it; they could not find a satisfactory explanation, and it was plain that they were concerned.

Then I opened the book to the next-to-the-last illustration. There had been no word in the text to describe the couple, but in this illustration, the young father's face is in full view. He is a Negro.

I did not know what might happen, but this is what I found, and in every room it was the same: there was a low murmur of surprise, and only that. They studied the picture soberly, and there was not one bigoted remark, not one smart-aleck word or look. These children, touched by the love of a little boy who after years of muteness could say, "Here is a gift for the Baby," had discovered something new. They had found that one cannot sneer at Mary and Joseph in the presence of a miracle, that a few shades of difference in skin color do not matter.

Rebecca Caudill had spoken to these children. I should like to tell you of a time when Carl Sandburg spoke to another group.

Each year, just before they finish elementary school, children from all over the state of Illinois make a pilgrimage to the capital at Springfield. Here they visit the old home of Lincoln; in nearby New Salem they see the reconstructed village looking much as it did when young Lincoln lived there; and in Woodlawn Cemetery they visit the tomb where the body of Lincoln lies.

Outside the tomb there is a great bronze bust of Lincoln, corroded — all except the nose — by the elements until it is quite black. Thousands of school children have leaped up to touch that nose (for good luck, they say), and it has been rubbed until the bronze shows through, giving a grotesque appearance to that sad, magnificent face.

I spoke to the group I was taking to Springfield about the fact that though the gesture was neither illegal or wrong, it did show a lack of taste, a certain gracelessness and disrespect. But I was an adult preaching, and the efficacy of preaching against something perceived as fun is very slight. So I said no more and turned to Carl Sandburg.

During the week before our trip I read many chapters from *Abraham Lincoln: The Prairie Years.* The children loved the book. They borrowed it and reread some of the chapters. They caught the heartbreak of Sandburg when he writes of Lincoln. Sometimes there were a few tears.

Then one bright morning we climbed into buses and rattled down the highway toward Springfield. We were as gay and boisterous as any group of thirteen-year-olds; there was joking and yelling, singing and squealing. It was a holiday.

Once arrived we made our tours: the Capitol, the old Lincoln Home, and then the visit to New Salem, where Lincoln once clerked in a store, where he may or may not have fallen in love with Ann Rutledge, where he began reading his law books and dreaming his long dreams. Finally at the end of the day, we visited the tomb.

I was anxious as those children walked up the steps toward the entrance. There was the great bronze bust, there was the nose that thousands of other children had touched for good luck. But I need not have worried. Those kids marched straight past that bust, eyes ahead, faces very stern. Oh, I think a few hands may have itched a little, a few arm muscles may have twitched a bit, but the owners of those hands and arms were in control. We went inside the tomb for our little time of respectful silence; then we filed out, climbed into our buses, and started back toward Chicago.

Many children gathered around me as we rode back, eager to be praised for their exemplary conduct, and praised they were, with real sincerity. Then, when the others were gone, a boy, a typical boy who would rather have been found dead than polishing an apple, came over and sat beside me. Obviously he had something to say, but he hesitated and stammered a little.

Finally he handed me a crumpled piece of paper which he had taken from his pocket. "I was reading this a while ago when we were at the tomb," he told me almost sheepishly.

I recognized the writing immediately. He had copied a paragraph from Sandburg's *Abraham Lincoln: The War Years*, a paragraph in which Sandburg describes the living death of the President at the moment the bullet entered his brain. It begins: "For Abraham Lincoln it was lights out, good night, farewell and a long farewell to the good earth and its trees, its enjoyable companions, and the Union of States and the world Family of Man he had loved."

I was not able to speak when I handed the paper back to him. The boy seemed to feel that he needed to explain. "I thought . . . I just had a feeling that when you stand at the tomb of Abraham Lincoln, you ought to have beautiful words to think about." After that explanation, he got back to a group of his peers as quickly as possible.

And so, you see, they can be reached, these youngsters who cause us so many anxious moments. There was no preaching here; only the kind of beauty which the name of Abraham Lincoln evokes for a writer like Sandburg. Great books do not have to preach. But they do speak to the conscience, the imagination, and the heart of many a child. And they speak with very clear and forceful voices.

Aunt Irene

by WENDELL BRUCE BEEM

"Here is Edward Bear coming downstairs now, bump, bump, bump, on the back of his head, behind Christopher Robin."

These words are A. A. Milne's introduction to Edward Bear, who gained fame in the world of children's literature as Winnie-the-Pooh. In my case they were also a personal introduction to my Aunt Irene, who gained literary fame in the world of children's literature as Irene Hunt.

On the occasion of that meeting she had just presented me, in commemoration of my attaining the age of three, Milne's classics, *Winnie-the-Pooh* and *The House at Pooh Corner*. I have a recollection of sitting beside Irene on a davenport, my short legs stretched out to full length but still not reaching the edge of the cushions, and listening with glee as she read of the predicaments into which dear old Pooh had got himself.

Not the first time we had met, it was, nevertheless, the first meeting that stands out in my memory. Maybe the reason is because Irene and I took many a circle about her living room that day, hands clasped behind our backs, bodies bent forward, eyes glued straight ahead as we searched for heffalumps in the manner of Pooh Bear. The adventure was fascinating and a little frightening, too, for I was more than half convinced that there was a possibility of a sizable and savage heffalump darting out at us any minute. It was great fun, though, and Irene, Pooh, and I became adoring friends that day and have remained so ever since.

About this era the strawberries-in-January incident occurred, an incident that Irene sometimes mentions when my logic begins to show strains at the seams. I had gone shopping with my aunt on this occasion and at the food store I had become interested in a display of fresh strawberries just up from the South.

"How about strawberries for dessert?" I asked, anxious to be helpful and to get my favorite dessert at the same time.

"They're awfully expensive right now," Irene told me.

"Are you out of money?" I asked solicitously.

"Oh, I have a little money," she answered, her mind evidently on other things.

"Well, what do you say we buy just a *few* strawberries?" I asked.

I remember her laughter and something about being "overwhelmed by such logic." I also remember that we (or at least I) had strawberries for dessert that evening.

I used to spend many hours cutting pictures from the comic strips and mailing them to Irene. Her letters were always gratifying. "I am so pleased with those exquisite pictures of Daisy Mae and Fearless Fosdick," she would write in her letter of thanks. "You *do* cut out pictures so beautifully. Did someone teach you or does it just come naturally?"

I remember feeling like a kitten well fed with cream when Mother read those letters to me.

Throughout the years I have enjoyed eating at Irene's. She is a very fine cook with a flair for sauces and the use of condiments, which can be most satisfying, although I admit that at times she is a bit heavy-handed with the garlic.

Irene and I have been very close during my years of growing up. We have haunted libraries together in search of material for many of my high-school term papers; we were together on my first jet flight to Washington, D. C., where we spent many pleasant hours reliving history. In recent years, each of us has proudly shown the other the pictures we have taken in European cities and byroads. We share a love for books and music, beautiful well-written books and beautiful very-loud music. At times we like to blast the roof by means of our stereos, and once in a while we have made ourselves obnoxious to more sedate souls.

One area in which Irene shows a lack of appreciation, a startling lack of understanding, is in the field of sports. My sister and I, both avid baseball fans, have tried to teach our aunt some of the more elementary points of the game with notable lack of success. She seems to try to find interest in the game occasionally in order to please us, but nine innings of baseball is too much. Our approval is hardly worth that much to her.

"I can convince myself that I'm interested for an hour, maybe, but a full afternoon of this monotony is more than I can take," she has told us, intimating that scrubbing the kitchen floor is pure joy in comparison.

She *does* give lip service to football and will sometimes join us to watch on television a college game, but even then I have an idea that she is dreaming of autumn skies and colors, of big chrysanthemums and college pennants, of the sound of several hundred male voices singing a certain varsity song and that she is not really attending to first downs or yardage gained.

I have known all my life that Irene liked to write. She was always writing. Most of the time when she is alone, her kitchen table is piled high with reference books, reams of paper, typewriter, and sharp-pointed pencils. (She bought a desk for her den so that she would have a proper place to work, but she told me that the desk is much too proper, and so she goes back to the kitchen table.) I have heard her typewriter clicking away late at night as she prepared a manuscript for what she calls "its virginal rejection," and I have seen the hurt look that was hardly disguised by her grin when the manuscript came back. I used to want to punch somebody when I saw that look. What I did not realize was that she was learning with each manuscript she wrote. Slowly and painfully she was learning to work with words, with ideas, with the creation of characters who were real and believable.

Her efforts have paid off. Her first novel, *Across Five Aprils*, won the Charles W. Follett Award and was runner-up for the coveted Newbery Award. Now, as if to prove that her first book was not merely a happenstance, Irene has followed it with *Up a Road Slowly*, the recent recipient of the Newbery Award.

When I read her books I attempted on both occasions to divorce myself from my nepotic position, for I did not wish to view them with a prejudiced eye. In each case, upon completion, I feared that I had not been objective enough. In the case of *Across Five Aprils*, objectivity was most difficult to maintain, for the book seemed to be especially mine. I first read it when I was experiencing the dubious joys of boot camp, and I identified completely with her Shadrach Yale, who was a soldier because of necessity and whose personal dreams were far from the field of guns and killing. I also saw myself in other incidents: *I* was the baby who rolled out of his cradle (I had a crib) when someone rocked too vigorously; *I* was the sober little boy whose throat grew tight with longing to keep forever the color of autumn woods or the whiteness of dogwood against a purple twilight. And reading *Up a Road Slowly*, I remembered hearing how a bewildered and frightened little girl once crawled away into a closet in order to be alone with her grief, and I could well imagine how a somewhat older little girl might have wandered off into the woods, repeating Millay or Shakespeare or just telling the Divine Presence exactly how some particular trouble had come about.

Because the books were so close to me, I was gratified later on when librarians, publishers, and critics all acclaimed them for their excellence; the blood of kinship had not beclouded my personal critique.

It is clear now that, whereas in the early forties Irene was reading to one small child whose legs did not reach the edge of the couch, she is now speaking, through her books, to children whose joined hands would reach across the country. And that is wonderful.

On my own bookshelves, enriched by volumes received from Irene on numerous occasions, stand four very special books, side by side. Two, somewhat aged now, are Milne's tales of Pooh; the other two are newer and both written by a very dear friend of mine, Irene Hunt.

FROM THE MIXED-UP FILES OF MRS. BASIL E. FRANKWEILER

written by E. L. KONIGSBURG

illustrated by E. L. KONIGSBURG

published by ATHENEUM PUBLISHERS 1967

BOOK NOTE

Claudia Kincaid, almost twelve and the oldest of four children, lives a comfortable suburban Connecticut life. But she is chafing from the need to do something: to run away — and to return home feeling that she has somehow become different. Liking comfort, she runs away to the luxurious facilities of the Metropolitan Museum of Art in New York City, and takes along her nine-year-old brother, Jamie, chosen for his adventurous company and his useful savings. Their ingenuity in eluding guards, sleeping and bathing in the museum, along with Claudia's intense program of education (she plans to do the entire Italian Renaissance in one morning) makes living in a museum seem ludicrously practical. Claudia and Jamie seem resourceful beyond their years. When they attempt to solve the mystery of whether a marble statue, Angel, was really sculptured by Michelangelo, their resourcefulness leads them to Mrs. Basil E. Frankweiler, a wealthy woman who once owned the statue. It is she who extracts the details of their escapade and is the narrator of the book. The story balances wit with fun, intelligence with childlikeness, and with true art manages to make the unbelievable totally believable.

EXCERPT FROM THE BOOK

They wandered back to the rooms of fine French and English furniture. It was here Claudia knew for sure that she had chosen the most elegant place in the world to hide. She wanted to sit on the lounge chair that had been made for Marie Antoinette or at least sit at her writing table. But signs everywhere said not to step on the platform. And some of the chairs had silken ropes strung across the arms to keep you from even trying to sit down. She would have to wait until after lights out to be Marie Antoinette.

At last she found a bed that she considered perfectly wonderful, and she told Jamie that they would spend the night there. The bed had a tall canopy, supported by an ornately carved headboard at one end and by two gigantic posts at the other. (I'm familiar with that bed, Saxonberg. It is as enormous and fussy as mine. And it dates from the sixteenth century like mine. I once considered donating my bed to the museum, but Mr. Untermyer gave them this one first. I was somewhat relieved when he did. Now I can enjoy my bed without feeling guilty because the museum doesn't have one. Besides, I'm not that fond of donating things.)

Claudia had always known that she was meant for such fine things. Jamie, on the other hand, thought that running away from home to sleep in just another bed was really no challenge at all. He, James, would rather sleep on the bathroom floor, after all. Claudia then pulled him around to the foot of the bed and told him to read what the card said.

Jamie read, "Please do not step on the platform."

Claudia knew that he was being difficult on purpose; therefore, she read for him, "State bed — scene of the alleged murder of Amy Robsart, first wife of Lord Robert Dudley, later Earl of . . ."

Jamie couldn't control his smile. He said, "You know, Claude, for a sister and a fussbudget, you're not too bad."

Claudia replied, "You know, Jamie, for a brother and a cheapskate, you're not too bad."

Something happened at precisely that moment. Both Claudia and Jamie tried to explain to me about it, but they couldn't quite. I know what happened, though I never told them. Having words and explanations for everything is too modern. I especially wouldn't tell Claudia. She has too many explanations already.

What happened was: they became a team, a family of two. There had been times before they ran away when they had acted like a team, but those were very different from *feeling* like a team. Becoming a team didn't mean the end of their arguments. But it did mean that the arguments became a part of the adventure, became discussions not threats. To an outsider the arguments would appear to be the same because feeling like part of a team is something that happens invisibly. You might call it *caring*. You could even call it *love*. And it is very rarely, indeed, that it happens to two people at the same time — especially a brother and a sister who had always spent more time with activities than they had with each other.

Newbery Award Acceptance

by ELAINE L. KONIGSBURG

You see before you today a grateful convert from chemistry. Grateful that I converted and grateful that you have labeled the change successful. The world of chemistry, too, is thankful; it is a neater and safer place since I left. This conversion was not so difficult as some others I have gone through. The transformation from smoker into nonsmoker was far more difficult, and the change from high-school-graduate-me into girl-chemist-me was more revolutionary. My writing is not a conversion, really, but a reversion, a reversion to type. A chemist needs symbols and equations, and a chemist needs test tubes and the exact metric measure. A chemist needs this equipment, but I do not. I can go for maybe even five whole days without thinking about gram molecular weights. But not words. I think about words a lot. I need words. I need written-down, black-on-white, printed words. Let me count the ways.

There was a long newspaper strike the first winter we moved into metropolitan New York. Saturday used to be my day off, and I used that day for taking art lessons in the morning and for exploring Manhattan in the afternoon. Our suburbs were New Jersey suburbs then, and my last piece of walking involved a cross-town journey toward the Port Authority Bus Terminal. On one of those Saturdays, as I was in the heart of the theater district, a volley of teen-age girls came larruping down the street bellowing, "The Rolling Stones! The Rolling Stones!" Up ahead, a small bunch of long-haired boys broke into a run and ducked into an alley, Shubert Alley. The girls pursued, and the Rolling Stones gathered; they pushed their collective hair out of their collective eyes and signed autographs.

I told my family about this small happening when I came home, but that was not enough. The next day I wanted to show them an account of it in the paper. But there was no Sunday paper then. It didn't get written down. I had seen it happen, and still I missed its not being written down. Even now, I miss its never having been written down. I need to see the words to make more real that which I have experienced. And that is the first way I need words. A quotation from my old world of science explains it: ontogeny recapitulates phylogeny. Each animal in its individual development passes through stages in which it resembles its remote ancestors. I spread words on paper for the same reasons that Cro-Magnon man spread pictures on the walls of caves. I need to see it put down: the Rolling Stones and the squealing girls. Thus, first of all, writing it down adds another dimension to reality and satisfies an atavistic need.

And I need words for a second reason. I need them for the reasons that Jane Austen probably did. She told about the dailiness of living. She presented a picture that only someone both involved with his times and detached from them could present. Just like me. I am involved in the everyday, corn-flakes, worn-out-sneakers way of life of my children; yet I am detached from it by several decades. And I give words to the supermarket shopping and to the laundromat just as Jane Austen gave words to afternoon visiting and worry about drafts from open windows.

Just as she stood in a corridor, sheltered by roof and walls from the larger world of her century, just as she stood there and described what was happening in the cubicles of civilization, I stand in my corridor. My corridor is my generation, a hallway away from the children that I breed and need and write about. I peek into homes sitting on quarter-acre lots and into apartments with two bedrooms and two baths. So I need words for this reason: to make record of a place, suburban America, and a time, early autumn of the twentieth century.

My phylogenetic need, adding another dimension to reality, and my class and order need, making record, are certainly the wind at my back, but a family need is the directed, strong gust that pushes me to my desk. And here I don't mean *family* in the taxonomic sense. I mean *family* that I lived in when I was growing up and *family* that I live in now.

Read *Mary Poppins*, and you get a good glimpse of upper-middle-class family life in England a quarter of a century ago, a family that had basis in fact. Besides Mary there were Cook and Robertson Ay, and Ellen to lay the table. The outside of the Banks' house needed paint. Would such a household exist in a middle-class neighborhood in a Shaker Heights, Ohio, or a Paramus, New Jersey? Hardly. There would be no cook; mother would be subscribing to *Gourmet* magazine. Robertson Ay's salary would easily buy the paint, and Mr. Banks would be cleaning the leaves out of his gutters on a Sunday afternoon. No one in the Scarsdales of this country allows the house to get run down. It is not in the order of things to purchase services instead of paint.

Read *The Secret Garden*, and you find another world that I know about only in words. Here is a family living on a large estate staffed by servants who are devoted to the two generations living there. Here is a father who has no visible source of income. He neither reaps nor sows; he doesn't even commute. He apparently never heard of permissiveness in raising children. He travels around Europe in search of himself, and no one resents his leaving his family to do it. Families of this kind had a basis in fact, but fact remote from me.

I have such faith in words that when I read about such families as a child, I thought that they were the norm and that the way I lived was subnormal, waiting for normal.

Where were the stories then about growing up in a small mill town where there was no one named Jones in your class? Where were the stories that made having a class full of Radasevitches and Gabellas and Zaharious normal? There were stories about the crowd meeting at the corner drugstore after school. Where were the stories that told about the store owner closing his place from 3:15 until 4:00 P.M. because he found that what he gained in sales of Coca-Cola he lost in stolen Hershey Bars? How come that druggist never seemed normal to me? He was supposed to be grumpy but lovable; the stories of my time all said so.

Where are the stories now about fathers who come home from work grouchy? Not mean. Not mad. Just nicely, mildly grouchy. Where are the words that tell about mothers who are just slightly hungover on the morning after New Year's Eve? Not drunkard mothers. Just headachey ones. Where are the stories that tell about the pushy ladies? Not real social climbers. Just moderately pushy. Where are all the parents who are experts on schools? They are all around me in the suburbs of New Jersey and New York, in Pennsylvania and Florida, too. Where are they in books? Some of them are in my books.

And I put them there for my kids. To excuse myself to my kids. Because I have this foolish faith in words. Because I want to show it happening. Because for some atavistic, artistic, inexplicable reason, I believe that the writing of it makes normal of it.

Some of the words come from another family part of me. From being a mother. From the part of me that urges, "Say something else, too. Describe, sure, describe what life is like in these suburbs. Tell how it is normal to be very comfortable on the outside but very uncomfortable on the inside. Tell how funny it all is. But tell a little something else, too. What can it hurt? Tell a little something else — about how you can be a nonconformist and about how you can be an outsider. And tell how you are entitled to a little privacy. But for goodness' sake, say all that very softly. Let the telling be like fudge-ripple ice cream. You keep licking vanilla, but every now and then you come to something darker and deeper and with a stronger flavor. Let the something-else words be the chocolate."

The illustrations probably come from the kindergartener who lives inside, somewhere inside me, who says, "Silly, don't you know that it is called *show and tell?* Hold up and show and then tell." I have to show how Mrs. Frankweiler looks and how Jennifer looks. Besides, I like to draw, and I like to complete things, and doing the illustrations answers these simple needs.

And that is my metamorphosis; I guess it was really that and not a conversion at all. The egg that gives form to the caterpillar and then to the chrysalis was really meant to be a butterfly in the first place. Chemistry was my larval stage, and those nine years at home doing diaper service were my cocoon. And you see standing before you today the moth I was always meant to be. (Well, I hardly qualify as a butterfly.) A moth who lives on words.

On January 13, after I had finished doing my Zorba Dance and after I had cried over the phone to Mae Durham and to Jean Karl, after I had said all the *I can't believe it's* and all the *Oh, no, not really's,* I turned to my husband and asked a typical-wife question, "Did you ever think fifteen years ago when you married a li'l ole organic chemist from Farrell, Pennsylvania, that you were marrying a future Newbery winner and runner-up?" And my husband answered in typical-David fashion, "No, but I knew it would be a nice day when it happened." And it was a nice day. It's been a whole row of wonderful days since it happened. Thank you, Jean Karl, for helping to give Jennifer and Elizabeth and Claudia and Jamie that all important extra dimension, print on paper. Thank you, Mae Durham and all the members of the committee, for deciding that my words were special. And thank you, Mr. Melcher, for the medal that stamps them special. All of you, thank you, for giving me something that allows me to go home like Claudia — different on the inside where it counts.

⁊   ⁊   ⁊

In a letter written in 1974, Elaine Konigsburg replied to this editor's question — as to what followed winning a Newbery Medal — as follows: Winning the Newbery Medal has made a difference, and it has not made a difference, too. Both — making and not — have happened in the right places.

Professionally, it has meant a happy difference. Had I not won the Newbery, I don't know if I would have had the courage to experiment, to write a historical novel about Eleanor of Aquitaine or to write (George). Receiving the award has given me the strength to go on from where I was when I got it, and I am grateful for that.

I can best explain how it has not made a difference by relating an incident. Sometime after I had won, a teacher approached my daughter, Laurie, and asked, "How does it feel to live with a famous mother?" "Famous?" Laurie replied. "My mother's just a mother. Why, I'd never argue with anyone famous, and I argue with my mother every day!"

So you see, winning couldn't send me altogether into orbit. My kids demand that my feet stay on the ground.

Elaine L. Konigsburg

by DAVID KONIGSBURG

Elaine Lobl Konigsburg was born in New York City but lived most of her precollege days in the small town of Farrell, Pennsylvania. Although she readily adapts to any environment, it is probable that the excitement of Manhattan will always appeal to her most. A keen observer, she delights in being bombarded by a multitude of stimuli. Her objectivity enables her to be a good reporter. Fortunately, her subjective responses add a unique and personal flavor to her stories.

Early in her life, there was evidence that she would be successful. But nobody would have predicted that she would achieve recognition in the field of children's literature. Elaine was valedictorian of her class in high school. Subsequently, she was an honor student at Carnegie Institute of Technology, where she majored in chemistry and was awarded the degree of Bachelor of Science. She continued her studies in chemistry in the graduate school at the University of Pittsburgh. After a few minor explosions, burned hair, and stained and torn clothes, she began to think about other occupations. Frankly, it seemed like a just end to anyone who would even contemplate writing a thesis concerning the Grignard reaction using heterocyclic compounds of a pyridine base.

Fortuitously, her husband, an industrial psychologist, made one of his many moves. The Konigsburgs left Pittsburgh and a much relieved laboratory staff to live in Jacksonville, Florida. There Elaine taught science to young girls in a private school until 1955, when Paul was born. Seventeen months later Laurie arrived, and in 1959 Ross uttered his first of many sounds of protest. It was wonderful to watch the children develop, but there was a champagne celebration when all three were out of the diaper stage.

Shortly afterwards, Elaine returned to teaching. Her initial thoughts about writing stories for children occurred during this period. Instead, however, she explored her talents as an artist. With a strong desire to excel in any endeavor, she devoted many hours to perfecting techniques. Her efforts were rewarded with prizes in local shows. On a trip to the Grand Canyon, she made friends among the Hopi Indians by sketching their little boys and girls.

In 1962 our family moved to the metropolitan New York area. Elaine took several courses at the Art Students' League. Her paintings received awards in shows held in Westchester County. As the children grew older and we became more involved with suburban living, Elaine was intrigued with the various forces exerting an influence on us.

In 1966 she began to write her first book, *Jennifer, Hecate, Macbeth, William McKinley, and Me, Elizabeth*. Laurie, Paul, and Ross were delighted to serve as models for her illustrations. The five of us danced around the room the following year when the manuscript was completed and accepted by Atheneum.

Even before she received that good news, Elaine had begun writing *From the Mixed-up Files of Mrs. Basil E. Frankweiler*. Again our children were used as the models for the illustrations. Despite a fracture in her left leg and a series of accidents which resulted in seventeen stitches in Ross's head, she persevered. Trips to the emergency room in the Port Chester hospital became almost a monthly routine.

Paul reached the age where he was involved in little league baseball, football, and basketball. We attended the games and cheered wildly for his team. If he caught the ball or made a hit, the game was a success regardless of the final score. Not satisfied with superficial knowledge, Elaine studied the official rule books. Serious discussions were held at the dinner table about the merits of a drag bunt and when it was wiser to run and hit instead of hit and run. We even got her to Shea and Yankee stadiums where she let her opinions about the managers' decisions be known. This furnished the background for her third book, *About the B'nai Bagels*, which will be published in 1969.

With fond memories, the family left Port Chester in August, 1967, and returned to Jacksonville, Florida. January 13th of the following year proved to be anything but an unlucky day. We were in the middle of moving out of an apartment into our new house when the telephone rang. Amid considerable turmoil, Elaine learned that she had received the Newbery Award. There was much hugging and kissing and shouts of joy with neighbors and friends. And we are pleased that things have not yet settled down.

To date, Elaine has performed in a superior manner as an artist and author. Her accomplishments in those areas, however, are insignificant when compared with her achievements as a mother and wife. She has an excellent sense of priorities and a value system which promotes harmony. As our youngest, who plays a competent game of poker, says, "Don't bet against her."

THE HIGH KING

written by LLOYD ALEXANDER

published by HOLT, RINEHART AND WINSTON 1968

BOOK NOTE

Taran, wanderer and Assistant Pig-Keeper of the oracular pig, Hen Wen, leads the quest for the rescue of Drnwyn, the mighty sword symbolizing the strength of the kingdom of Prydain, which has been stolen by Arawn, Lord of Annuvin, Land of the Dead. Accompanied by the Princess Eilonwy, Glew the shrunken giant, the bard Fflewddur Fflam, the faithful helpers Gurgi and Coll, and later by Gwystyl of the Fair Folk, various other Commot Folk, and Doli the Dwarf, they struggle through skirmishes and harsh winter weather to reach Caer Dathyl, seat of the High King, Math. There they discover many lords of Prydain in conflict and find that powerful King Pryderi has taken the side of Arawn. In a furious battle, Pryderi is almost defeated when the devastating column of impervious Cauldron-Born arrive from Annuvin. The High King is slain, and the black banner of Arawn flies over ruined Caer Dathyl. Yet despite the loss of old and dear friends and the problems which beset his companions, Taran keeps on with his quest until Hen Wen's prophecies most strangely do come true. With them some mysteries which arose in the four earlier Prydain books are answered, although with the help of the author's note at the beginning, this volume can be read as a complete story. All the books are set in a mythical land fully explored by the author and convincingly revealed to the reader. The characters combine traits of fantasy and heroism with human foibles, and this makes the ending of *The High King* particularly apt.

EXCERPT FROM THE BOOK

Another day's travel brought the companions across a harsh, uneven valley that lay within the shadow of Mount Dragon itself. The summit had been well named, for Taran saw its peak was in the rough shape of a monstrous, crested head with gaping jaws, and on either side the lower slopes spread like outflung wings. The great blocks and shafts of stone that rose to form its jagged bulk were dark, mottled with patches of dull red. Before this last barrier, poised as though to swoop downward and crush them, the companions fearfully halted. Achren strode to the head of the waiting column and beckoned them onward.

"There are other, easier paths," Achren said, as they entered a narrow defile that twisted between towering walls of sheer cliffs, "but they are longer and those who travel them can be seen before they reach the stronghold of Annuvin. This one is known only to Arawn and his most trusted servants. And to me, for it was I who showed him the secret ways of Mount Dragon."

Taran, however, soon began to fear Achren had deceived them, for the path rose so steeply that men and horses could barely keep their footing. Achren seemed to be leading them deep into the heart of the mountain. Mighty shelves of overhanging rocks rose like arches above the toiling band, blotting the sky from their sight. At times, the path skirted yawning chasms and more than once Taran stumbled, buffeted by a sudden chill blast that flung him against the walls. His heart pounded and his head reeled at the sight of the deep gorges opening at his feet, and terrified he clung to the sharp edges of jutting rocks. Achren, whose step did not falter, only turned and silently glanced at him, a mocking smile on her ravaged face.

The path continued to rise, though not so abruptly, for it no longer followed the slope of the mountain but seemed almost to double back on itself, and the companions gained the higher reaches of the trail only by small degrees. The huge stone jaws of the dragon's head loomed above. The trail which, for some of its course, had been hidden by grotesque formations of rocks, now lay exposed, and Taran could see most of the mountain slope dropping sharply below him. They were almost at the highest ridge of the dragon's shoulder, and it was there that Kaw, scouting ahead, returned to them and clacked his beak frantically.

"Gwydion! Gwydion!" the crow jabbered at the top of his voice. "Annuvin! Haste!"

Taran sprang past Achren and raced to the ridge, clambering upward among the rocks, straining his eyes for a glimpse of the stronghold. Had the Sons of Don already begun their attack on Annuvin? Had Gwydion's warriors themselves overtaken the Cauldron-Born? His heart pounding against his ribs, he struggled higher. Suddenly the dark towers of Arawn's fastness were below him. Beyond the high walls, beyond the massive Iron Portals, ugly and brooding, he glimpsed the spreading courtyards, the Hall of Warriors where once the Black Cauldron had stood. Arawn's Great Hall rose, glittering like black, polished marble, and above it, at the highest pinnacle, floated the Death-Lord's banner.

The sight of Annuvin sickened him with the chill of death that hung over it, his head spun and shadows seemed to blind him. He pressed higher. Struggling shapes filled the courtyard, the clash of blades and shouted battle cries struck his ears. Men were scaling the western wall; Dark Gate itself had been breached, and Taran believed he saw the flash of Melyngar's white flanks and golden mane, and the tall figures of Gwydion and Taliesin.

The Commot men had not failed! Arawn's deathless host had been held back and victory was in Gwydion's hands. But even as Taran turned to shout the joyous tidings, his heart froze. Southward he glimpsed the hastening army of Cauldron-Born. Their iron-shod boots rang and clattered as the mute warriors raced toward the heavy gates and the horns of the troop captains shrieked for vengeance.

Taran leaped from the ridge to join the companions. The

shelf of stone crumbled at his feet. He pitched forward, Eilonwy's scream rang in his ears; and the sharp rocks seemed to whirl upward against him. Desperately he clutched at them and strove to break his fall. With all his strength he clung to the sheer side of Mount Dragon, while jagged stones bit like teeth into his palms. His sword, ripped from his belt, clattered into the gorge.

He saw the horrified faces of the companions above him and knew he was beyond their reach. His muscles trembling, his lungs bursting with his efforts, he fought to climb upward to the path.

His foot slipped and he twisted about to regain his balance. It was then that he saw, plunging from the peak of Mount Dragon, the gwythaint speeding toward him.

Newbery Award Acceptance

by LLOYD ALEXANDER

Despite his faults, Taran, hero and Assistant Pig-Keeper in *The High King*, somehow manages to find enough courage and wisdom to go through the most difficult and perilous ordeals. In an equally difficult and perilous undertaking, whether his author will manage to do the same is open to serious question. For a man who has loved the English language and tried to serve it well, at this point I can only ask: Where is it when I really need it?

Exaggeration could lead to consequences as distressing as those suffered by that exuberant master of overstatement, the bard Fflewddur Fflam, whose harp strings break each time he stretches the truth: My shoelaces might snap or my necktie come suddenly undone. There's no danger of that now. Reality, in this case, surpasses Fflewddur's ability to ornament the facts. My concern is not with stretching the truth but simply with trying to measure up to it.

After Isabella Jinnette told me the Committee's decision —

and assured me it was true, and there was no danger of their changing their minds — I lapsed into a state of bedazzlement, bewilderment, and general incoherency. On top of being insufferably pleased with myself. Luckily, whenever we start feeling too insufferably pleased with ourselves, something always brings us down to earth again. In this instance, I was playing first violin in our Sunday-afternoon-rank-amateur-chamber-music society. At a glorious moment, when the first violin has a solo passage, a sublime, superb melody that soars up from the ensemble — I botched it. We collapsed in total musical disaster. The cellist put down his bow, looked at me, and shook his head.

"No doubt about it," he said, "the Newbery Medal's a wonderful thing for you. But it doesn't do anything for Johann Sebastian Bach."

I went home in disgrace, chewing over that idea. By the time I had digested it, I was able to face up to a sobering thought: Writing books or playing Bach, I still have a lot to learn and a long way to go.

Far from being a disheartening realization, it's encouraging and hopeful. Beginnings are always frightening — for a child at the first day of school, for an author at page one of a manuscript. Beginnings are signs of life and a chance for growth. The actively creative garden is plagued with its own crab grass of anxieties, doubts, and difficulties. But, as handsome as laurels may be, they are uncomfortable to rest on.

I'm speaking in terms of beginnings instead of endings for this reason: Coming to the last page of *The High King* was a sad moment for me, a feeling more akin to loss than liberation, as if something one had loved deeply for a long time had suddenly gone away. Yet, it was a loss with more than equal gain. Throughout the writing of the book, and even from the first of the five books of Prydain, I believe I had a glimpse of what it felt like to create something; of how it felt, if only for a moment, truly to be a writer. Now, perhaps, I can start being one. Certainly no work has given me greater joy in the doing; and writing for children has been the happiest discovery of all.

I have to smile, remembering myself as a very much younger man. Then, had the oracular pig, Hen Wen, foretold I would write for young people, I wouldn't have believed her. I was still looking for a way to say . . . whatever it was, if anything, I had to say. I was unsure of both form and content: a doubly discouraging combination for me — and very likely more so for my wife, Janine. The aggravations and exasperations generated by the literary temperament must be appalling, but she did put up with them. She still does. And will. I hope.

Although it didn't feel that way at the time, those years were a blessing — heavily disguised. Or, say, the kind of gift the enchantress Orddu, Orwen, and Orgoch bestow on the unwitting recipient. Perhaps we have to serve an apprenticeship to life before we can serve one to art. We can't begin doing our best for children until we ourselves begin growing up.

I still can't say precisely what unreasonable reasons brought me to write for children — beyond saying I simply wanted to. How Prydain came to be discovered is a story I've told many times over, always to my own surprise and wonder — and, I daresay, to the intense boredom of those who have heard it so often before: How the research for one book, *Time Cat*, awakened a long-sleeping love of heroic tales and legends; and how the original goal of merely retelling these ancient legends grew into something much more ambitious. Ann Durell, who had become Children's Book Editor at Holt, Rinehart and Winston, gave me the freedom to write the book as I felt it should be written. This took more courage on both our parts than might be supposed. In the very realistic realm of publishing, an imaginary realm wasn't a fast-moving item of real estate. Furthermore, at the beginning, neither one of us could quite be sure what I really had in mind.

Even though I can't analyze what led me to children's literature, I do know what I found there. For me, a true form of art that not only helped me understand something of what I wanted to say but also let me discover ideas, attitudes, and feelings I never suspected were there in the first place.

I also made a more important discovery: that everyone

seriously concerned with children's literature makes the same kind of demands on himself that a writer makes. Librarians want the best from themselves and their profession. So does any writer who hopes to be worthy of his calling. I'd call it: kinship in the pursuit of excellence.

It occurs to me I've been going on at great length about everything but the main reason why I was invited to dinner.

Accept the Newbery Medal? Yes, I do indeed, most willingly and most gladly. And the happiest thing, for me, goes beyond an individual writer's acceptance of an extraordinary honor. I should rather see it as a mutual acceptance — by readers and writers alike — of fantasy as a valid, relevant art form. Just as Frederic G. Melcher saw and as David Melcher sees even more clearly today, children's literature has gained acceptance as part of the literary mainstream — in my opinion the most life-giving current in that stream. By the same token, fantasy has gained acceptance in children's literature. Perhaps more than acceptance: affection.

At heart, the issues raised in a work of fantasy are those we face in real life. In whatever guise — our own daily nightmares of war, intolerance, inhumanity; or the struggles of an Assistant Pig-Keeper against the Lord of Death — the problems are agonizingly familiar. And an openness to compassion, love, and mercy is as essential to us here and now as it is to any inhabitant of an imaginary kingdom.

Imaginary kingdoms, however, thrive best in fertile soil. Librarians, in their striving for excellence, their deepening understanding of the imaginative experience, and their appreciation of the needs of young people, have created a climate where fantasy — and every kind of children's literature — can flourish. Through Daniel Melcher, through Isabella Jinnette and the Newbery-Caldecott Committee, I thank them on my own behalf and on behalf of every writer who tries to offer his best.

Prydain is an imaginary kingdom, but its friends are very real. To them, my real and fondest thanks. Past and present at Holt, Rinehart and Winston — Alfred Edwards, Ross Sackett

. . . Ann Durell, surely. And Beverly Bond, Mimi Kayden. . . .
That hardly even begins the roll, for the Assistant Pig-Keeper
and his companions have found friends between our own east
and west coasts and north and south borders, far beyond the
boundaries of Prydain. Many of them are here now. Many are
not — because it's past their bedtime, or should be! — yet, they
are the ones who give all of us the best reason to be here: the
children themselves.

The Committee tells me I can keep the medal now. But we
agree that where children are concerned it's not what we keep
that matters. It's what we hope to give.

*In response to the question put to all the Medal Winners, as to
how the Award might have affected them, Lloyd Alexander
wrote in 1974:* I've been racking my brain for an interesting
anecdote, all to no avail (I'll spare you accounts of late planes,
foggy or icebound airports, etc.).

I do think that anyone who accepts the Newbery must also
accept a kind of permanent responsibility to try to work at the
best of his abilities. For me, in addition, I've found myself more
and more involved in teaching and working with young people; and it seems to me that one doesn't simply write one's
books and then hole up in an ivory tower or whatever. In other
words, I feel the Newbery is an honor which is offered seriously
and should be taken seriously. It's wonderful to be the laureate
of a given year, but I think this is a kind of new starting point
in one's own growth. Except by trying to grow, and to do his
best, I don't know how else a writer could hope to return the
honor and affection given him.

Of course, I could always tell the tale of the time Philadelphia Airport was under four feet of water . . .

Who's Lloyd Alexander?

by ANN DURELL

At the cocktail party following the National Book Award presentations in New York City last March, a lady asked Meindert DeJong to autograph her copy of *Journey from Peppermint Street*, winner of the first National Book Award for children's literature. The prizewinning author looked about helplessly and then politely asked the gentleman with whom he had been conversing to lend him his back as a writing stand. The book was inscribed "To Miss Blank with best wishes written on the back of Lloyd Alexander by Meindert DeJong."

The lady checked her autograph carefully and then asked, "Who's Lloyd Alexander?"

One answer could be found in the March 1969 ALA Bulletin report on the Midwinter Meeting in Washington — "Lloyd Alexander, looking like a replica of Hans Christian Andersen. . . ."

Or in a letter to me from Robert Burch, the author of *Queenie Peavey*: "Mr. Alexander and I were on the same program at the Friday morning session on children's books (National Council of Teachers meeting in Milwaukee, November, 1968). I spoke on realistic fiction and he spoke on fantasy and both of us were pleased afterwards that our viewpoints had not clashed. I did not get to know him well, but I found him quite interesting. He looks as if he belongs in one of his stories as a character; in fact, I'm wondering if you didn't invent him for the purpose of going out to library and school gatherings! Tell the truth, is the real Lloyd Alexander locked in some back room at Holt, grinding out books, while the one I met takes the bows!"

Or in the illustrations by Evaline Ness for *The Truthful Harp* by Lloyd Alexander, in which the kingly bard (or bardic king) Fflewddur Fflam bears at least a family resemblance to — well, to Hans Christian Andersen.

Or, in Mr. Alexander's own words in *The Black Cauldron* to describe the pessimistic Gwystyl of the Fair Folk: ". . . he was extremely thin. His sparse hair was long and stringy; his nose drooped wearily above his upper lip, which in turn drooped toward his chin in a most mournful expression. Wrinkles puckered his forehead; his eyes blinked anxiously; and he seemed on the verge of bursting into tears."

Or in his description of Gwydion, Prince of Don, as first met in *The Book of Three:* "The stranger had the shaggy, gray-streaked hair of a wolf. His eyes were deep-set, flecked with green. Sun and wind had leathered his broad face, burnt it dark and grained it with fine lines. His cloak was coarse and travel-stained. A wide belt with an intricately wrought buckle circled his waist."

I have known Lloyd Alexander since 1961, when he started work on his first children's book for Holt, Rinehart and Winston, *Time Cat.* We have worked together on eight books, and since an editor gets to know an author where he lives — in his creative and creating self — I can say I am pretty familiar with this particular author at this point. And I must report that all the answers above are correct!

Lloyd is all the characters in his books, sometimes in turn, sometimes all at once. As humble as Gurgi, as brave as Gwydion, as capricious as Eilonwy, as singleminded as Achren, as questing as Taran, as greedy as Glew — the list goes on and on. Most Prydain fans, on meeting him for the first time, think he is most like Fflewddur Fflam; and indeed they are both great storytellers who cannot resist the temptation to make a good tale better even at the risk of stretching the truth to the breaking point. To me, however, if I had to choose, I would say he is most like Dallben the enchanter, custodian of *The Book of Three*, "thus called because it tells all three parts of our lives: the past, the present, and the future."

The Newbery Award **1970**

SOUNDER

written by WILLIAM H. ARMSTRONG

illustrated by JAMES BARKLEY

published by HARPER & ROW   1969

BOOK NOTE

Except for Sounder, the participants in this story are never given names. But this puts such strong focus on *the* boy, *the* father, *the* mother that their suffering and staunchness, their stubborn standing-up to the injustices which dominate their lives, take on a universal quality. Their bleak, physically exhausting life as sharecroppers, the brutality of the white sheriff and jailer, the long search by the boy for his father — who has been sentenced to a chain-gang for stealing a ham when his family was starving — are shown in a light as pitiless as the Southern summer sun. Sounder, cruelly torn by a shotgun blast when his master is captured, disappears; so for a time the boy's search is three-fold — for the dog, for his father, and for a way to educate himself. It is a simple story which is tremendously moving, because it is at once unequivocal in its emotions and eloquent in its atmosphere and understanding.

EXCERPT FROM THE BOOK

"There ain't no dog like Sounder," the boy said. But his father did not take up the conversation. The boy wished he would. His father stood silent and motionless. He was looking past the rim of half-light that came from the cabin window and pushed back the darkness in a circle that lost itself around the ends of the cabin. The man seemed to be listening. But no sounds came to the boy.

Sounder was well named. When he treed a coon or possum in a persimmon tree or on a wild-grape vine, his voice would roll across the flatlands. It wavered through the foothills, louder than any other dog's in the whole countryside.

What the boy saw in Sounder would have been totally missed by an outsider. The dog was not much to look at — a mixture of Georgia redbone hound and bulldog. His ears, nose, and color were those of a redbone. The great square jaws and head, his muscular neck and broad chest showed his bulldog blood. When a possum or coon was shaken from a tree, like a flash Sounder would clamp and set his jaw-vise just behind the animal's head. Then he would spread his front paws, lock his shoulder joints, and let the bulging neck muscles fly from left to right. And that was all. The limp body, with not a torn spot or a tooth puncture in the skin, would be laid at his master's feet. His master's calloused hand would rub the great neck, and he'd say, "Good Sounder, good Sounder." In the winter when there were no crops and no pay, fifty cents for a possum and two dollars for a coonhide bought flour and overall jackets with blanket linings.

But there was no price that could be put on Sounder's voice. It came out of the great chest cavity and broad jaws as though it had bounced off the walls of a cave. It mellowed into half echo before it touched the air. The mists of the flatlands strained out whatever coarseness was left over from his bulldog heritage, and only flutelike redbone mellowness came to the listener. But it was louder and clearer than any purebred red bone. The trail barks seemed to be spaced with the precision of a juggler. Each bark bounced from slope to slope in the foothills like a rubber ball. But it was not an ordinary bark. It filled up the night and made music as though the branches of all the trees were being pulled across silver strings.

While Sounder trailed the path the hunted had taken in search of food, the high excited voice was quiet. The warmer the trail grew, the longer the silences, for, by nature, the coon dog would try to surprise his quarry and catch him on the ground, if possible. But the great voice box of Sounder would have burst if he had tried to trail too long in silence. After a last, long-sustained stillness which allowed the great dog to close in on his quarry, the voice would burst forth so fast it overflowed itself and became a melody.

A stranger hearing Sounder's treed bark suddenly fill the night might have thought there were six dogs at the foot of one tree. But all over the countryside, neighbors, leaning against slanting porch posts or standing in open cabin doorways and listening, knew that it was Sounder.

Newbery Award Acceptance

by WILLIAM H. ARMSTRONG

In an honest effort to do a serious piece of homework for this assignment, I borrowed the latest Horn Book collection of acceptance speeches and studied them with a degree of diligence. I learned a great deal. For example, I learned about a dozen definitive definitions of that indefinable term "Literature for young readers — what it is." And I learned how some authors put books together. I am still convinced, however, that most books hang together because some patient and perceptive editor skillfully ties together a lot of loose threads. I also learned something of the lasting quality that books should contain. A most significant statement to me was "The real stamp of a book's living qualities comes with the increased pleasure from re-reading, a new discovery of hitherto unperceived riches."* Having read this statement, I wandered back in time to search out what books from my childhood measured up to these qualities.

On the big round table in a Virginia farmhouse kitchen I found a Sears, Roebuck catalogue, the *Old Farmer's Almanac*, Burpee's seed catalogue, the Bible, and *McGuffey's Third*

---

*Horovitz, Carolyn. "Only the Best," *Newbery and Caldecott Medal Books: 1956-1965*, Boston, The Horn Book, Inc., p. 162.

Reader. My mother had studied McGuffey's *Reader* in school, and kept it over the years to read to us. Especially at bedtime, she would read a prayer or two that contained the word *God.* Or a story of how good a boy felt after he had been punished for some wrong. Or perhaps a story of how proud a boy could be of work and thrift.

The Sears, Roebuck catalogue contained the quality of "increased pleasure from re-reading," for it stirred dreams that made "the haves and the have-nots" one — "if only. . . ." And although I read for sheer pleasure, and not to weigh critically, I know now that I was reading an all-time best seller. From the *Almanac* there was to read and reread: "The cultivation of the earth ought ever to be esteemed as the most useful and necessary employment in life." Or, "One or two discarded brown paper bags should provide a child sufficient material for entertainment for a rainy day." Here was brightness to dispel the ominous threat of a dark sky.

But of all the books available none carried between its pages more "increased pleasure" and "new discovery" at rereading than the seed catalogue, which usually arrived about the middle of January — when the winter was already too long. A first reading of the catalogue would change the lowering January sky and temper the cold wind that turned even the mountains on either side of the Shenandoah Valley blue. The sky would become an April sky, filled with clouds, and that April sky seemed so close that a boy could lie on his back on a hillside and reach up with a stick to punch a hole in it. And with a second reading and a third, there came a certainty that the lifeless brown and gray earth would spring to green life again. That seedtime would come, and harvest. And as one read, he might be chewing on a scabby Winesap apple from the bottom of the cellar bin, but he tasted beefsteak tomatoes, freestone Alberta peaches, and wine-red cherries from the topmost branch of the tree where the sun had ripened them first.

No one told me the Bible was not for young readers, so I found some exciting stories in it. Not until years later did I understand why I liked the Bible stories so much. It was because everything that could possibly be omitted was omitted. There was no description of David so I could be like David. Ahab and Naboth were just like some people down the road. And the first time I was allowed to visit court when my father was on jury duty, I saw Cain.

These books then, plus stories heard from a black man around that Virginia farmhouse table, formed the substance of what I remember of my own life as a young reader. Although some of the books I have mentioned were not — strictly speaking — literature, they filled a need.

And now I find myself in the precarious position of having won a prize for a book called *Sounder*, written for anyone who might like to read it.

Until I received a telephone call from Mary Elizabeth Ledlie some time in February, the word Newbery had *not* meant to me a man in England who stocked his bookshop with stories for children. But Newbery had been a word to stir the deathless joy and remembrance of a small boy's Christmas. Because if that boy were especially good from somewhere around October 27th or November 12th until Christmas, his father would take him to Newberry's five-and-dime store in town. And after he had looked at all the bows and arrows and red wagons, he could ask the jolly, red-coated Santa Claus — enthroned amid the incense of chocolate and peppermint — to leave them under the Christmas tree for him.

But Newberry's Santa never brought the bow and arrows or the red wagon. So out in the back pasture the boy would cut a maple sapling with his two-bladed barlow pocketknife that he had won for selling Cloverine Salve — guaranteed to cure shoulder-gall for horse and chapped lips for man. Then with sapling and binder twine from the hayloft, the boy would make his own bow.

But tonight it is real. The boy will not have to go home and hammer the Newbery Award out of the top of a Campbell soup can or out of a washer off the axle of his father's hay wagon.

And now, if you will, allow me one brief moment to express — as an adult — the meaning of the prize. Who gives it meaning? You, the librarians, the keepers and guardians of the memory of mankind. For that is what books are. "I gave man memory, that precious gift, along with fire," said Prometheus. As librarians, you keep watch at the gates of civilization. For when the destroyer comes, his first act is to burn the books. You, too, preside over the only true court of justice in the world. For without spiritual or temporal bias or prejudice, you allow ideas to bear witness.

And if I have added one tiny fragment to mankind's memory, it is you who will help to preserve it. For you do more than preserve it, you draw attention to it. Without you, Peggy Brennan, age ten, might never have written to me: "It [*Sounder*] made me feel very hollow inside. Because we are living comfortable while the boy's family lived uncomfortable. You made me feel like I was watching all this happening right in front of my eyes."

Some one of you gave Tina Rinaldi *Sounder* to take home. Tina, age eleven, in the fifth grade, wrote to me: "When I read your book my body felt cold but it also felt warmth."

You hear such comments all the time from many people — young and old — about many books, but these comments have come as a revelation to me, so indulge me for just two more. From Miami, Florida: "A few weeks ago, I picked up *Sounder* at our traveling library. My son and daughter are 11 and 12, and quite capable of reading themselves, but there are times when I want to read to them. And so — I did. Returning it to the library was something I regretted having to do. But it was not the end of *Sounder*. On April 18 my children gave a copy to me. It was a wonderful present — most wonderful."

And one last note from Sharon, age eleven, whose librarian had read the book one Saturday morning: "Our librarian was the first to discover this terrific book. It was sad and a few of us cried silently. At first, I closed my ears to the book, but then I realized that I should listen."

I should like to end by saying that as long as you remain, and your audience of Sharons remains, we are not lost. Rather, we are found, renewed, and sustained.

William H. Armstrong

by CHRISTOPHER, DAVID, and MARY ARMSTRONG

William H. Armstrong was born on a farm in the Shenandoah Valley near Lexington, Virginia, on September 14, 1914. Here in a stern, but warm Scotch-Presbyterian atmosphere, he learned respect for discipline, work, thrift, and his Creator.

His lifelong love of history took root at a very early age. He rode the same hills over which Robert E. Lee had ridden his famous horse Traveller after the Civil War, when Lee came to Lexington to be the president of Washington College. The self-discipline of the mighty "Stonewall" Jackson also left its impression on the boy, who was reminded often by this or that Sunday School teacher that Stonewall had once taught Sunday School "in this very same church." And besides the soldier-heroes, there were those who had sprung from the soil of Rockbridge County and gone on to fame: Archibald Alexander, Cyrus McCormick, and Sam Houston.

William spent the last three years of his preparation for college at Augusta Military Academy, forty miles up the valley from Lexington, at Fort Defiance, Virginia. Here his interest in history found further stimulation. The school had been founded by Colonel Charles Roller after his return from the Civil War. The Old Stone Church at the edge of the campus had been built with stones carried on horseback from Middle River six miles away by the women of the community.

In Captain Joseph Ernest's English composition class the young cadet presented his first literary effort. The assignment was to write an original story. Cadet Armstrong wrote a story of what went on inside the mind of a crippled boy who sat helplessly at his window, looking out at the apple orchard where he would never be able to run and jump. At the climax of the story the boy's pet cat climbed one of the trees and destroyed a nest of baby birds. Helplessly the boy watched the parent birds flutter in anguish and finally fly away.

Then other members of the class read their stories. There was the usual collection of compositions about winning football games, trips in summer, and visits to grandmothers. When the class ended, Cadet Armstrong was asked to stay behind. Captain Ernest wanted to know from what source he had copied his story.

An ordeal that took the young man first to Major Alexander Dean, head of the English Department, and next to Colonel C. S. Roller, Jr., headmaster of the school — both of whom also doubted that the work was original — prompted the decision on the part of young Armstrong to write English themes from that day forth exactly like those that everybody else wrote. He ended his creative writing career at that school as he left the headmaster's office. He still, however, held on to his story "Not Even with Wings" — now practically worn to shreds from its many skeptical readings.

Seven years later when he was editor-in-chief of his college's literary magazine, the magazine won the Southern Collegiate Press Association's first prize for excellence. Congratulations came from three people at his old school — Captain Joseph Ernest, Major Alexander Dean, and Headmaster C. S. Roller, Jr.

As a freshman at Hampden-Sydney College, he submitted "Not Even with Wings" to the literary magazine, and it was published. Before he graduated cum laude from college in 1936, he had edited the literary magazine in his junior year, been managing editor and columnist of the college newspaper his senior year, and had been made a member of the national literary fraternity, Sigma Upsilon. At graduation, he won the school's literary awards for both poetry and prose. In the meantime he had convinced the editor of his hometown paper *The Lexington Gazette* that he could write a column entitled "As the World Moves." This he did weekly from his sophomore year until graduation.

At graduation he chose teaching rather than a job with *The Washington Post*. This, he says, "was perhaps the wisest decision I ever made." Along with his teaching he pursued graduate study at the University of Virginia.

Ever since 1945 he has been teaching history at the Kent School in Connecticut. He bought a rocky hillside, cleared the land, and built his house with his own hands. Here his three children were born — Christopher, David, and Mary. Here his wife Martha died suddenly in 1953 when Christopher was eight, David, six and a half, and Mary, not yet five.

"Without even the aid of a housekeeper, we managed," is the way William Armstrong sums it up. And they managed well. Today Christopher, graduate of Washington and Lee University, with a master's degree in Criminology from the University of Pennsylvania, pursues his doctorate there. David, graduate of Bucknell, is a teaching fellow and graduate student at the University of Indiana. He is an artist of note, and his work hangs in the Hammer Galleries in New York. Mary, graduate of Northfield School, spent a year abroad at Down House School in England and is in her junior year in art at Boston University.

During these busy years as teacher and farmer, William Armstrong has found time to write several books: *Study Is Hard Work*, 1956; *Through Troubled Waters*, 1957 (published in Germany as *Durch Wasser der Trübsal*, 1958); *Peoples of the Ancient World*, 1959, in collaboration with Henry Ward Swain;

Eighty-Seven Ways to Help Your Child in School, 1961; *Tools of Thinking,* 1968; *Sounder,* 1969. In 1963 he was recipient of the National School Bell Award "For distinguished interpretatation in the field of education."

On his rocky hillside above the Housatonic River in Connecticut he raises Corriedale sheep, teaches "his boys" at the Kent School, and guards his privacy. Up and down the river William Armstrong is known by his neighbors as "the last pioneer."

The Newbery Award **1971**

THE SUMMER OF THE SWANS

written by BETSY BYARS

illustrated by TED COCONIS

published by THE VIKING PRESS 1970

BOOK NOTE

In a quietly stated but intense build-up of suspense, this seems
to be a simple and direct story of a fourteen-year-old girl's
concern during twenty-four hours for the safety and recovery
of her mentally retarded brother, who runs away in the night
to see the swans once more and becomes lost in the forest. But
Sara Godfrey's feelings about herself, her attractive older sister
Wanda, her abrupt but kind Aunt Willie who runs the house
and tries to run her three charges, and most of all, Sara's empathy and patience with slow, mute, suffering Charlie have as
many subtle tones as the layers of dye on her tennis sneakers.
All the characters have reality and depth, remarkably developed in such a concentrated story, which steers clear of any
sentimentality but is unafraid of emotion.

EXCERPT FROM THE BOOK

Charlie turned, motioned that he wanted another roll for the
swans, and she gave him the last one. He threw it into the
water in four large pieces and put out his hand for another.

"No more. That's all." She showed him her empty hands.

One of the swans dived under the water and rose to shake its
feathers. Then it moved across the water. Slowly the other
swans followed, dipping their long necks far into the water
to catch any remaining pieces of bread.

Sara leaned forward and put her hands on Charlie's shoulders. His body felt soft, as if the muscles had never been used. "The swans are exactly alike," she said. "Exactly. No one can tell them apart."

She began to rub Charlie's back slowly, carefully. Then she stopped abruptly and clapped him on the shoulders. "Well, let's go home."

He sat without moving, still looking at the swans on the other side of the lake.

"Come on, Charlie." She knew he had heard her, yet he still did not move. "Come *on*." She got to her feet and stood looking down at him. She held out her hand to help him up, but he did not even glance at her. He continued to watch the swans.

"Come on, Charlie. Mary may come up later and help me dye my shoes." She looked at him, then snatched a leaf from the limb overhead and threw it at the water. She waited, stuck her hands in her back pockets, and said tiredly, "Come on, Charlie."

He began to shake his head slowly back and forth without looking at her.

"Mary's coming up to help me dye my shoes and if you don't come on we won't have time to do them and I'll end up wearing these same awful Donald Duck shoes all year. Come *on*."

He continued to shake his head back and forth.

"This is why I never want to bring you anywhere, because you won't go home when I'm ready."

With his fingers he began to hold the long grass on either side of him as if this would help him if she tried to pull him to his feet.

"You are really irritating, you know that?" He did not look at her and she sighed and said, "All right, if I stay five more minutes, will you go?" She bent down and showed him on his watch. "That's to right there. When the big hand gets *there*, we go home, all right?"

He nodded.

"Promise?"

He nodded again.

"All right." There was a tree that hung over the water and she went and leaned against it. "All right, Charlie, four more minutes now," she called.

Already he had started shaking his head again, all the while watching the swans gliding across the dark water.

Squinting up at the sky, Sara began to kick her foot back and forth in the deep grass. "In just a month, Charlie, the summer will be over," she said without looking at him, "and I will be so glad."

Up until this year, it seemed, her life had flowed along with rhythmic evenness. The first fourteen years of her life all seemed the same. She had loved her sister without envy, her aunt without finding her coarse, her brother without pity. Now all that was changed. She was filled with a discontent, an anger about herself, her life, her family, that made her think she would never be content again.

She turned and looked at the swans. The sudden, unexpected tears in her eyes blurred the images of the swans into white circles, and she blinked. Then she said aloud, "Three minutes, Charlie."

Newbery Award Acceptance

by BETSY BYARS

During the past few years I have on occasion found myself in front of a classroom or in a library trying to talk to children about writing books. I have never been a success at this. For one thing, I have learned that questions come in twos. If one child asks, "When did you start writing?" then the next question is going to be, "Wow, how old are you?"

Or there will be no questions. Not one child can think of anything to ask, and I know that the important thing to children is not what *I* say, but what *they* say. The afternoon is a success if the child can walk out of the room saying to a friend, "Hey, did you hear what I asked?" Finally, on a slow afternoon, one child thinks of a question. "How long did it take you to write *The Summer of the Swans?*" Even before I give my answer another hand goes up. "How long did it take you to write *The Midnight Fox?*" Now a bolt of electricity goes through the room. Everyone has a question. The children are all but leaping into the air to be called on, because they are aware that there are twenty-eight children left and only six books. In moments like this I always feel that any writer worth his salt would at least have written enough books to go around.

But, as of January, these difficulties are over. If the questions get personal or the afternoon is dull, I can say, "And now I'm going to tell you what it was like to win the Newbery Medal."

I get instant silence, rapt attention. I have already learned that no detail is too small or insignificant to be included. I can tell where I was standing when the phone began to ring that Tuesday morning. I can tell what I had on, what I thought when I picked up the phone. Even my first word in that fateful telephone call — "Hello" — seems strange and prophetic.

In fact, I have learned that there is no way to make a bad story of it. I admit to you, for example, that my part of the telephone conversation that morning was frankly disappointing for a person who had just won an award for words. I could not think of anything to say.

And I admit that when I hung up the phone that morning and turned around, absolutely bursting with this tremendous news, it would have been more dramatic if there had been someone there to share it with, other than two dogs and two cats. Still, you would be amazed at how pleased dogs and cats look when you turn to them and say, "Listen, I just won the Newbery Medal."

I would like to be able to tell you exactly how *The Summer of the Swans* was written, because I myself like nothing better than to hear writers tell how they happened to write their books. Often this is the best part. And long after I have forgotten details of character and plot, I can remember that a specific book was written in the shade of an olive tree by a wheat field in Umbria with a number-two pencil.

But I am like Jerome K. Jerome. He was asked how he wrote one of his books, and he said that actually he could not remember writing the book at all. He was not even sure he had written it. All he could remember was that he had felt very happy and pleased with himself that summer and that the view of London from his window at night had been beautiful.

I am like that. I know I wrote *The Summer of the Swans*, because two of my daughters claim it is the size of their feet that plays an important role in the story, and also I have a three-inch-high stack of rewrites that could not be explained in any other way. But all I really remember about that winter is that I felt enormously fine, that none of the children had the flu, and that the West Virginia hills had looked beautiful when they were covered with snow.

Since I cannot tell you exactly how *The Summer of the Swans* was written, I will tell you how I write in general, and perhaps you can imagine the rest.

I write in four stages. In the first stage I mainly sit around and stare at a spot on the wall or at my thumbnail. This is a difficult stage for a writer who has children. Anytime my children see me sitting there staring at my thumbnail, they come running over with skirts that need hemming and blouses that need ironing and baskets of dirty clothes.

I can protest for hours that I am working, that I am writing a book in my head, but they will not believe me. And the situation will end in bad feelings when one of the children says, "You just don't *want* to wash these clothes!" And, of course, there is no denying that.

The second stage is the best. At some point in this "head writing" I become gripped with enthusiasm. There is nothing like my enthusiasm when I first begin writing. People who have seen me in this stage would never ask, "How do you find time to write?" because it is obvious there is no time for anything else. I can hardly wait to get to the typewriter in the morning. I have even awakened in the middle of the night, glanced at my desk, and wondered if it would disturb my husband if I got up and typed quietly in the dark.

The third stage comes so gradually that I almost do not notice it, but soon the words which have been flying out of my typewriter in paragraphs, now start coming out in sentences. Then they start coming out in phrases, then one by one, and finally they do not come out at all.

I look on this as a desperate situation, requiring great personal discipline. This is what works for me. I say to myself, "All right, today you are either going to have to write two pages or you are going to have to defrost the refrigerator." Sometimes I do decide that the refrigerator is the lesser of the two evils. Sometimes I clean closets and wash cars, because writing at its worst is bad indeed. Sooner or later, however, I will find something that *is* worse. After all, there is always the attic.

The last stage is the longest and the most trying. It involves reading what I have written and trying to make something of it. I have never read a manuscript in this stage without becoming aware again of the enormity of the gap which exists between the brain and a sheet of paper. I just do not know how it is possible to have something in your mind which is so hilarious you are all but chuckling as you write, and then when you read it over, it is completely flat.

Or, there is a scene in your mind which is so sad, so touching, you can barely see the typewriter keys through your tears. And when you read it back, you find it is as touching and as moving as a recipe for corn bread.

I do not know how this happens, but I do feel that the gap between the brain and a sheet of paper is at least as formidable as the generation gap. And whenever I read statistics on the number of books published in a month or a year, I never think of all those books. I think, "That many authors conquered the gap this year!" And I am impressed.

In this last stage I always ask my children to read my manuscript, even though they are my severest critics. They are not in the least tactful about what they do not like, either. If they find, for example, their interest is lagging, they draw a small arrow in the margin of the manuscript, pointing downward. A small, down-pointing arrow in the margin of a manuscript can be starkly eloquent. It can say more than a thousand words. In my most terrible and haunting nightmares, I open a magazine or a newspaper to read a review of one of my books and find that the review consists of a great blank space, no words at all, and in the center of the space is a small arrow — pointing down. The possibility is enough to make one tremble.

Five years ago on the night before my son's eighth birthday he was enormously excited because he was getting a bicycle. Sleep was impossible and he kept coming in my room where I was working at my desk to tell me how much trouble he was having falling asleep.

Finally in desperation he said, "You know, maybe it would help me get to sleep if I read some of your failures."

I asked after a moment if there was any particular failure that would induce sleep better than the others, and he named one. I opened my failure drawer — I had never thought of it as being that before, but in an instant that was what it had become — and handed it to him. He read for about three minutes, yawned, went into his room and fell fast asleep. It was a humbling moment.

And I tell you about it because perhaps if you know I have failures that can anesthetize a child in three minutes, then you will know how very much I mean it when I say, "Thank you."

✓   ✓   ✓

Thinking back about the news of the award, and then the Newbery-Caldecott dinner, Betsy Byars wrote in 1974: When I first learned that I had won the Newbery Award, I became instantly overwhelmed with the thought, "Now I'm going to be read!" I envisioned librarians all over the country pressing my book into readers' hands.

The first letter that I got from a child, however, said:

Dear Mrs. Byars,

I'm dying to read your book that won the Newbery Medal, but our librarian has made a display of it and won't let anybody check it out.

It was something of a come-down, but since up until that time I had never even been a display, I really couldn't complain.

One of the most interesting things that happened as a result of winning the award was the mail that I received. I got tapes from classes which I was supposed to retape and send back; I got letters; I got questionnaires.

I recall a questionnaire in which one of the questions was, "What do your children think of having a Newbery Award winning mother?" My husband was reading the questions at the table, and as he got to that one he turned to our fourteen year old daughter and said, "Well, what do you think of having a Newbery Award winning mother?" And she gave that shrug that only fourteen year olds can give and said, "Well, it's no big deal."

The Newbery Award ceremony remains something of a blur to me (I was very nervous about giving my speech), but I do recall two things clearly.

The banquet was held in Dallas and the room was huge and elegant. Eighteen hundred people were there, and the people who were to sit at the head table formed a sort of procession through the tables. Leading us were two teenaged boys in kind of King Arthur page boy suits and they were bearing large banners. The boy preceding me had a banner on which there was a swan made of real swan feathers (hand sewn, one by one) and it was gorgeous. I almost felt I was back in medieval times. Then just before we were to enter the boy turned to me and said, "I could just kill my mom for making me do this." Instantly I was back in the twentieth century.

My second and most poignant memory is the blueberry cheesecake. That is my favorite food in the world, and all during the banquet — and the food looked great — I was not able to take a bite. Indeed I considered myself fortunate to be able to get down a few glasses of wine. Then came the blueberry cheesecake and I could have wept because there was no way I could have even swallowed one berry.

I got up to give my speech, fearful that a throat nervous

enough not to accept cheesecake, might also be too nervous to form intelligible speech, but I got started all right. Toward the end, I began actually to relax a little, and at that moment a terrible hunger came over me. All I could think of was that cheesecake. I could see it in my mind waiting there for me. Later my husband told me that the only thing wrong with the way I gave my speech was that I talked too fast at the end.

As soon as I delivered my last line, I was ravenous. I rushed back to my seat, ready to grab my fork, and the blueberry cheesecake was gone.

Now, I have had many pieces of blueberry cheesecake in the intervening years, but I tell you I have never had one that would have been as good as the one I would have had if I could have delivered my whole speech at the same rapid pace that I delivered the last few lines.

Betsy Byars

by EDWARD F. BYARS

I have been asked to give some insight into the personality of Betsy Byars. I know only enough about this woman to realize that I do not know her very well; but since I am doubtless better qualified than anybody else, I guess I must give it a go. My qualifications result only by virtue of my having lived with her for twenty-odd years. With such limited exposure I should know better than to try to "explain" a woman or her personality, especially such a complex one, but not knowing how to decline gracefully, realizing I'm damned if I do and damned if I don't — with trembling pen, here goes.

In most outward ways, Betsy is a normal woman — a typical American housewife with four normal healthy kids, a reasonably respectable husband, and a suburban home complete with mortgage and all that sort of thing. Physically very attractive, she is personally rather shy, certainly not extroversive or pretentious in the least. You have to be around her awhile before you realize there is a difference. This difference sneaks up on you, as I discovered many years ago, and I have had this confirmed by many others. She tries not to let it show, but it becomes apparent with exposure. She is smart! I mean she has real brains, the kind that are disgusting at the times when they outperform yours.

Perhaps readers would like to know her likes, dislikes, and peculiarities. I could never get away with a list but perhaps a few "for instances" can be cited.

Normal likes, such as spending money, are in evidence: "Money should be enjoyed, not saved." Normal dislikes, such as housework and cooking, are as expected. A trait seemingly abnormal to me, seemingly normal to her, is a desire (or rather insistence) that a manuscript not be seen or a writing idea not even be discussed before final completion and submission. The children usually get a look but nobody else that I know of. It took me a few years to learn not to try to be helpful. On occasion I have peeped at a manuscript left carelessly lying about and usually have thought it great and would have liked to say so but did not dare.

When Betsy gets really interested in a project she sometimes gets consumed by it and becomes tenacious. For example, just after the Newbery Award was announced, I kidded her by saying that she now had it made, and since she would never again have to look a rejection slip in the face and could even get her PTA minutes published, I should chain her to the typewriter and retire.

Instead she got so interested and involved in another project that I was worried for a while that she might never write another book. She was taking a graduate Special Education course at the University and was tutoring a class of mentally retarded junior-high pupils. She and an energetic music teacher decided to write, produce, and direct an operetta for these children. By her own admission she wrote the whole thing nonstop in one sitting. After I was finally allowed a look, I honestly thought it showed more brilliance than *The Summer of the Swans* and *The Midnight Fox* together. Neither the fact that no one outside the community would ever see it nor the fact that it would never make a penny ever occurred to her (only to me).

The patient work Betsy and her friend did with these special children was astonishing. In the years I have known her I have never seen her work harder on any project — writing or otherwise — or worry about the success of a project so much. I worried a lot too during this time; my worry was that she had abandoned the typewriter. Remember, this was just after the Newbery announcement. Needless to say, the operetta was a smash hit and I will admit that even my untrained eyes were amazed.

Now that the operetta and the Special Ed courses are over for the year, I expect to hear the typewriter or see evidence of its use. Other things worry me now. Betsy has a serious heretofore unmentioned weakness which has been accentuated by the Newbery Award. She cannot say no. The only thing that is helping her overcome this weakness is her strong dislike for speech-making. Also, she admits that it is harder now that she is an award winner because, as she says, "The audience looks more expectant; they're waiting for the great wise word."

I, too, am trying to overcome my nervousness at Betsy's indulging in nonproductive activities. I am, in fact, in a quandary just now. In the past, we have spent a large and important part of our summers engaging in the very serious sport of soaring (you heard right — it is high-class gliding; you know, flying in airplanes with no motors). While I fly the contest tasks, Betsy serves as my crew chief. This means helping assemble by lifting wings and holding a fifty-pound wing tip over her head for long periods, polishing the wings, taping the joints, driving the car with a thirty-foot glider-trailer attached, while working the radio, settling arguments among the children, and doing various other sundry tasks. Also, she has to find me when the day is done, oftentimes in a remote field.

One day when I was soaring in southwest Texas, Betsy and I were plagued by radio difficulties, and when I landed late in the day (after an eight-hour flight) in a remote and deserted field behind a mesa, I knew she would never find me. There was no telephone within miles, and one lone farmer appeared through the dust to tell me not to worry because another glider pilot had once landed there and his crew had found him within ten minutes, I went on to explain to the farmer the difficulties of my situation, but he remained confident. Suddenly he glanced up and said, "See, what'd I tell you. There she comes."

To this day Betsy has never explained exactly how she did it, and it remains a great mystery since a pilot who landed in the same field a day later spent the night there while his crew drove round and round and round. It is after days like this that I become convinced that such a relaxing, diversionary activity is just what a creative writer needs. Who knows — maybe a great children's book on soaring will be forthcoming one of these years.

MRS. FRISBY AND THE RATS OF NIMH

written by ROBERT C. O'BRIEN

illustrated by ZENA BERNSTEIN

published by ATHENEUM PUBLISHERS 1971

BOOK NOTE

Mrs. Frisby, mother of Teresa, Martin, Cynthia and Timothy, has made a cozy winter mouse-home in a cement block in Farmer Fitzgibbon's garden. When Timothy falls ill, Mrs. Frisby seeks help from another mouse, Mr. Ages, and on the same journey rescues a crow, Jeremy, from the Fitzgibbons' cat, Dragon. When she realizes Timothy is not going to recover in time for their necessary Spring Moving Day, Mrs. Frisby is flown by Jeremy to consult an old owl, who tells her to go to the rats, whose entrance hole is under the rosebush in the farmyard. There Mrs. Frisby meets Justin, Nicodemus, and Brutus, and sees the underground complex built to house themselves and their offspring by the twenty educated rats who escaped from NIMH. When they learn she is the widow of Jonathan Frisby, they tell her their amazing history, which includes her husband's heroic death, and of their Plan for the future: for rats to be self-sufficient and never steal again from men. When Mrs. Frisby offers to slip a sleeping powder into Dragon's food, so the rats can move her home to safety, she is caught in the farmer's house and learns that all the rats are in immediate danger of extermination. There is a dramatic ending, baffling to Farmer Fitzgibbon, disappointing to the doctors from NIMH, but satisfying to the Frisbys, most of the rats, and The Plan. The human thought and intellectual ideals given to these clever animals, the sensitive observance of their natural world of farmyard and forest, and the scientific purpose of the NIMH laboratories seem incongruous elements. But the author's skill in blending them creates an unusual, convincing, and totally intriguing story.

EXCERPT FROM THE BOOK

And now there were rats. Rats by dozens — rats standing and talking in groups of twos and threes and fours, rats walking slowly, rats hurrying, rats carrying papers. As Mrs. Frisby stepped from the elevator, it became obvious that strangers were a rarity down there, for the hubbub of a dozen conversations stopped abruptly, and all heads turned to look at her. They did not look hostile, nor were they alarmed — since her two companions were familiar to them — but merely curious. Then, as quickly as it had died out, the sound of talking began again, as if the rats were too polite to stand and stare. But one of them, a lean rat with a scarred face, left his group and walked toward them.

"Justin. Mr. Ages. And I see we have a guest." He spoke graciously, with an air of quiet dignity, and Mrs. Frisby noticed two more things about him. First, the scar on his face ran across his left eye, and over this eye he wore a black patch, fastened by a cord around his head. Second, he carried a satchel — rather like a handbag — by a strap over his shoulders.

"A guest whose name you will recognize," said Justin. "She is Mrs. Jonathan Frisby. Mrs. Frisby, this is Nicodemus."

"A name I recognize indeed," said the rat called Nicodemus. "Mrs. Frisby — are you perhaps aware of this? — your late husband was one of our greatest friends. You are welcome here."

"Thank you," said Mrs. Frisby, but she was more puzzled than ever. "In fact, I did not know that you knew my husband. But I'm glad to hear it, because I've come to ask your help."

"Mrs. Frisby has a problem," said Mr. Ages. "An urgent one.

"If we can help you, we will," said Nicodemus. He asked Mr.

Ages: "Can it wait until after the meeting? An hour? We were just ready to begin again."

Mr. Ages considered. "An hour will make no difference, I think."

Nicodemus said: "Justin, show Mrs. Frisby to the library, where she can be comfortable until the meeting is over."

By this time the last of the other assembled rats had made their way into a large meeting hall, where they sat facing the raised platform. Nicodemus followed them, pulling some papers and a small reading glass from the satchel at his side as he walked to the front of the room.

Justin led Mrs. Frisby in another direction, down a corridor to their left, and again she had the impression of a faint, cool breeze against her face. She realized that the corridor she had walked in up above was merely a long entranceway, and that the halls around her were the rats' real living quarters. The one down which Justin led her was lined with doors, one of which he opened.

"In here," he said.

The room they entered was big, square, well lit, and had a faint musty smell. "It's reasonably comfortable, and if you like to read . . ." he gestured at the walls. They were lined with shelves from floor to ceiling, and on the shelves stood — Mrs. Frisby dredged in her memory. "Books," she said. "They're books."

"Yes," said Justin. "Do you read much?"

"Only a little," said Mrs. Frisby. "My husband taught me. And the children . . ." She started to tell him how. Laboriously scratching letters in the earth with a stick — it seemed so long ago. But Justin was leaving.

"Excuse me — I've got to go to the meeting. I hate meetings, but this one's important. We're finishing up the schedule for the Plan." He pronounced it with a capital P.

"The Plan?"

But he was out the door, closing it gently behind him.

Mrs. Frisby looked around her. The room — the library, Nicodemus had called it — had, in addition to its shelves of books, several tables with benches beside them, and on these were stacked more books, some of them open.

Books. Her husband, Jonathan, had told her about them. He had taught her and the children to read (the children had mastered it quickly, but she herself could barely manage the simplest words; she had thought perhaps it was because she was older). He had also told her about electricity. He had known these things — and so, it emerged, did the rats. It had never occurred to her until now to wonder *how* he knew them. He had always known so many things, and she had accepted that as a matter of course. But who had taught him to read? Strangely, it also emerged that he had known the rats. Had they taught him? What had been his connection with them? She remembered his long visits with Mr. Ages. And Mr. Ages knew the rats, too.

She sighed. Perhaps when the meeting was over and she had had a chance to talk to Nicodemus — and had told him about Timothy and Moving Day — perhaps when that was settled, he could explain all this to her.

She noticed at the far end of the room a section of wall where there were no bookshelves. There was, instead, a blackboard, covered with words and numbers written in white chalk. There were pieces of chalk and an eraser in a rack at the bottom of it. The blackboard stood near the end of the longest of the tables. Was the library also used as a classroom? When she looked at the blackboard and, rather laboriously, read what was written on it, she saw that it was not. It was, rather, a conference room.

At the top of the board, in large letters, were printed the words:

THE PLAN OF THE RATS OF NIMH

Newbery Award Acceptance

by ROBERT C. O'BRIEN

I am sorry that my doctor will not let me deliver this speech myself, and I am grateful to Jean Karl for agreeing to read it for me, leaving me free to lead the applause at the end.

I am grateful also to the American Library Association for the very great honor its members have given to me and to *Mrs. Frisby and the Rats of NIMH.*

I am grateful that there *is* a Newbery Medal, and not just because I won it. After Anne Izard telephoned me to tell me my book had been chosen (as I told her, that was the best phone call I ever got), I went out and found a list of all the Newbery titles over the years. I was familiar with quite a few of them, but my youngest daughter knew them all and had read most of them. Obviously the Newbery Medal works. It gets the books to the children and the children to the books.

Ever since I wrote *Mrs. Frisby and the Rats of NIMH,* I have been asked two kinds of questions, one quite sensible, the other quite incredulous. The sensible one is: Why do you write books for children? The incredulous one is: Why, with all the world to choose from, did you have to write about *rats*?

One of the first critics to review *Mrs. Frisby* wrote as follows: "When I first got the book, the title bothered me. Who wants to read about rats? They're filthy, thieving, ravenous and cruel. But once beyond that mental block. . . ." Well, once beyond that mental block the critic went on to write one of the most enthusiastic reviews I have ever read. But the question was valid, and I still hear it. If you choose rats as heroes, you're going to turn some people off. So why do it?

Of course, rats are not without precedent in children's books. There is a fine character named Rat in *The Wind in the Willows.* There is a friendly rat named Melchisedec in *A Little Princess.* There have been others I could mention. Still, it set me thinking. Why *did* I choose rats as subjects for a children's story?

I regret to say that if there was ever a precise answer to that question, it is lost. I have searched my memory and my files to try to find out how and when the idea first came to me. My files show that I began writing the book in November, 1967, and that by March, 1968, I had finished only two chapters and was debating whether or not to continue. (I was, at the time, also working on another book.) But I have no recollection at all of Mrs. Frisby's initial appearance in my thoughts. I think that may be true of many works of fiction. They are rather like plants. You put a seed under ground. You come back a few days later and find a small green stalk growing. But how often do you actually see the stalk emerge?

I do know some of the thinking and reading I had done before I wrote about Mrs. Frisby, and I know that these must have been connected with her sudden appearance. I had been, and still am, concerned over the seeming tendency of the human race to exterminate itself — as who is not? I have wondered: If we should vanish from the earth, who might survive us? What kind of civilization might follow ours? I had read in a scientific journal that scorpions were good candidates for survival, since they are resistant to radioactivity. I read the same about cockroaches. But I was unable to imagine a cockroach or a scorpion civilization. (I expect Jean Karl is glad to hear that.)

By coincidence, I had been reading a book by Loren Eiseley called *The Immense Journey*. There was in it a chapter about prairie dogs. It discussed the evidence paleontologists have found that the prairie dogs' ancestors drove our ancestors, the ancestors of the simian primates, out of the prairies and into the woods. In short, the prairie dogs were, millions of years ago, ahead of us in the race toward dominance. While we were still in the trees, they were building little villages. And prairie dogs, as we know, are not dogs at all, but rodents.

Dr. Eiseley's essay reminded me in turn of another essay — one by Clarence Day called "This Simian World." It was required reading when I was in college. That was a long time ago; but, as I recall, it begins by pointing out that many of the things people do — for example, talking a lot and gathering in large groups — are traceable to their simian ancestry. (Monkeys do these things, too.) Then the essay goes on to speculate on what the world would be like if people were descended not from monkeys but from, say, dogs or cats. I remember that Clarence Day thought a cat civilization would be much less gregarious than ours: Cats walk by themselves. Also, a cat culture would be more musical than ours, with a lot of singing.

Still thinking about survival, I began to speculate: Rats are tough, highly adaptable to a changing environment, and enormously prolific. Maybe, if people should eliminate one another by means of war or pollution, rats would be the survivors. Or if not the only survivors perhaps the most intelligent.

What, then, would a rat civilization be like? This, of course, is not precisely what *Mrs. Frisby* is about. In the book there is no war, and the human race has not been exterminated. But it was this *kind* of speculation that led to the birth of *Mrs. Frisby and the Rats of NIMH.*

I suppose it's a rather grim idea to serve as background for a children's book. But once I got it started, the rats took charge, and they turned out to be much saner and pleasanter than we are.

To the much more general question — Why do I write books for children? — the honest answer is not very enlightening. I write them because a story idea pops up in my mind; and that really is the way it feels, to me at least. And since I am in the writing business, when I get a story idea I write it down before I forget it. It isn't always for children, of course, but those are the stories I most like to write, because children like a straightforward, honest plot — the way God meant plots to be — with a beginning, a middle, and an end: a problem, an attempt to solve it, and at the end a success or a failure.

I would prefer to rephrase the question. Why is it *good* to write books for children? The answer to that is easy: because it is good for children to read books.

I have a friend, a scientist, who has a collection of seeds. He has arranged them as a display, and they fill a box the size of a suitcase. They range from seeds as small as a pea to seeds as big as a coconut. They are in various shapes — round, flat, pod-like; some are streamlined like boats; some have appendages for catching winds or currents. All have two things in common: They are waterproof, and they float. My friend's hobby is the study of the spread of plants by water — across the oceans from island to island and from continent to continent.

Now I am going to skirt a very hot argument that has been going on recently between two scholars in Cambridge, Massachusetts, about what the human mind is, and what its relationship is to the brain. And as I skirt it, you may think that I am going to suggest that minds, like tiny submicroscopic seeds, come floating in from far-off space and take root in our brains — that they are more than human. Well, I've thought about that, and I don't think I believe it. But I do believe that the analogy is usable anyway.

A seed washes up on the barren shore of the new island of Surtsey. It germinates, takes root, and grows into a tree, a flower, or a weed; and the island is never the same again. The plant is made of the same carbon, oxygen, hydrogen, and other elements that existed there before, but it is more than these. And so the mind is more than the brain, more than the cerebral cortex, nerve tissue, synapses, and electrical impulses. It has a life of its own, and like the plant it needs certain stimuli to make it grow.

In college I took a very elementary course in psychology. The professor who taught it was a behaviorist, and one of the ways he explained consciousness, intelligence, awareness — that is, the using of the mind — went something like this. You approach a door, turn the knob; the door opens; and you walk through. You do this a hundred times, it always works, and your mind remains dormant. It is an unconscious act. But the hundred-and-first time something goes wrong — the door sticks, or is locked, or the knob comes off. At this point, consciousness flickers on; the mind comes to work; intelligence awakens, studies the problem, directs the eye and hand to turn the key; and the door opens. The mind may stay active a few seconds longer — wondering who locked it; then it glimmers and goes out. In other words, the mind comes to life when something doesn't work, or when something new comes up. Consciousness, this psychologist said, is merely the pause, the delay between the attempt and the success.

At this point I disagree with the psychologist — if indeed I understood him correctly. I think the mind is more than a pause, more than a flurry of activity in the brain cells. I think that there is a true dualism here and that the mind continues to exist when it is not being used. I don't know exactly what my mind is, but I am sure that it is more "me" than my brain is, or my hand, or my endocrine system.

I also believe that it is improved and strengthened by being used. Putting it the other way around, it seems obvious that the mind would disappear if it were perpetually unused — rather like a vestigial tail. If all of our needs and desires were easily and instantly met all of the time, we would become mindless. It might take a few generations, but it would happen — precisely because the mind *is* a real, living entity and not just a momentary manifestation of brain mechanics. It can starve to death — or fly back into space and look for a better planet.

Thus we may be happy that our society is not yet perfect. Still, we must not strive for imperfection; it is contrary to our nature. We cannot go around taking the knobs off doors so they won't open, merely because it would keep our minds alert.

Or can we? Of course we can. That's what books are all about — books of fiction, at least. We make a world, and put people in it, and make things go wrong, all without doing any damage at all to the real world. Then we activate our characters, and they set to work solving the problems we have given them. Readable fiction has to do this. Could Jim Hawkins get along without Long John Silver? Or Tom Sawyer without the murderous Injun Joe, or Frodo without Gollum? Who would want to read about Sara Crewe if her father had not died, if she had just led a happy and protected life as Miss Minchin's star boarder?

Furthermore, the problems in a book can be much more

horrendous than any we would willingly face in real life, and the solutions can be more ingenious. In fact, the characters are quite capable now and then of coming up with solutions better than those the author had planned; unfortunately, they can also develop unexpected new problems of their own. These they toss to the writer to work out.

When a child (or an adult) reads a book, I think his mind is getting pretty much the same kind of exercise it gets when it deals with real-life problems, though perhaps less intensely. It is certainly not turned off or lulled. If you watch a child reading — or better, recall your own reading as a child — how often did you put the book down for a minute and wonder: How is the hero going to get out of *this* mess? And try to figure out ways, hoping he would turn right at the next corner, because that's the way the bad guys went.

As the mind-seed wonders, it grows. Having put down roots, it opens its leaves and looks around. It learns about love, hate, fear, sadness, courage, kindness. All these things are in the world around it. But all of them come to life in books in a way that is peculiarly suitable for examination, for contemplation, and for evaluation.

Did I mention bad guys? Did I say Long John Silver? Long John is a liar; he is unctuous, greedy, tricky; he is a thief. Then why do we like him better than anybody else in the book? The mind learns that it is not easy to separate good from bad; they become deviously intertwined. From books it learns that not all doors are simply open or shut, and that even rats can become heroes.

And the lovely thing about a book is that when you finish wondering about these things and pick the book up again, the story is still there, right where you left it. You can't do that with movies or television.

Not that I am against movies or television when the programs are reasonably good. There are thousands of children who would never read a book anyway — there always were, long before electronics — and a television program can let them know who Romeo and Juliet were, or at least what it's like to go to the moon. And I don't think the medium weans many real readers away from books.

My own children, who are omnivorous and voracious readers, tend to watch television in spurts which may last an afternoon or two. Then they get tired of it, and I see them back with a book again. They got the reading habit early, and now I think they are hooked for life.

Which, of course, is why it is good to write books for children.

✻ ✻ ✻

Editor's Note: Robert C. O'Brien was a pen name for Robert Leslie Conly, who died of a heart attack on March 5, 1973. Besides his Newbery Medal winner, his books under this name include *The Silver Crown* (Atheneum, 1968) written for children; *Report from Group 17* (Atheneum, 1973) for adults; and a book for young adults, *Z for Zachariah* (Atheneum, 1975). This last book had been almost completed at the time of his death, and was finished, from his notes, by his wife and one of his daughters.

A thorough professional in his writing, he apparently preferred to have his own work published pseudonymously, since he had already made the name of Robert L. Conly well-known in a slightly different field: for twenty-two years he was an editor in Washington, D. C., for *National Geographic Magazine*.

Robert C. O'Brien

by SALLY M. O'BRIEN

There is a sign much in evidence these days which proclaims, "If you aren't nervous, you just don't understand the situation." My impression of Robert C. O'Brien is that he has, since early childhood, "understood the situation" — i.e., he was and is a nervous being. On the other hand, he has — also since childhood — had a formidable set of skills or talents for dealing with that nervousness. First, and probably most important, was a talent for music. He could sing before he could talk; his favorite amusement was the family windup Victrola; and he has had a lifelong preoccupation with music both as a listener and as a performer. If he is not playing the piano himself (or if one of his children is not playing it), he turns on the phonograph or radio. In his house there is always the sound of music — it has been his greatest refuge.

He loved reading and showed an early facility with words, writing rhymed poetry and even a novel about the adventures and exploits of a young boy who traveled around the world.

He had a propensity and talent for dreaming. He could and did regularly create splendid imaginary worlds, with himself in dazzling, heroic roles. While all children do this to some extent,

Robert O'Brien's fantasy world was so vivid that he still remembers the place and hour when he (by then a student in high school) made a solemn decision to give it up and to concentrate on living in the real world.

Another great strength was his self-discipline. In late adolescence he regularly arose at four o'clock in the morning to study, to practice the piano, to walk on the beach while the rest of his family was still asleep. Along with this discipline went a determination and a refusal to compromise almost akin to perversity.

These were not characteristics to make him an endearing, easygoing child. Born a middle child into a literate, sharp-witted, sharp-tongued Irish family, he had an extraordinarily bad case of "middle-itis." His younger sister, now his good friend, says frankly, "We hated him." His mother, harassed beyond endurance, once threatened to drown him. He was sick a great deal. He despised and feared school and some mornings was literally dragged screaming into the classroom. He was, for a year, a college dropout when such action was cause for disgrace. Still he was not ever drifting. In a hard, uncomfortable-for-those-around-him style he was shaping up; but he was doing it, as he always would, in his own way. His respect for language, his talent for dreaming, and his self-discipline were combining to make him a writer. Writing has been his only profession: Since 1943 he has earned his living writing news stories, articles, poetry, and, finally, fiction.

His first book, *The Silver Crown*, was written for children and published in 1968; his second, *Mrs. Frisby and the Rats of NIMH*, won the current Newbery Award; his first adult novel, *Report from Group 17*, was published in March of this year. He is now at work on a second adult novel.

In middle age Robert O'Brien is a cultured, fastidious, rather solitary man who likes order and quiet, and works by schedule in spite of a busy household. His most long-lasting hobbies, aside from music, have been furniture making (he turns out exquisitely fitted and finished pieces) and growing luxuriant flowers in neatly arranged, weed-free beds.

He has been married for twenty-nine years to the same wife; and his children have neither turned on nor dropped out, but have gone cheerfully off to highbrow schools where they developed the expensive habit of staying until they graduated.

In his fiction, though, there is some evidence that Robert C. O'Brien has not entirely outgrown influences of his childhood. One finds in his books a fascination with valleys, with hidden worlds, with new societies; he writes with particular sympathy for and perception of children and children's feelings. And children respond. They write him so many letters — smudged, misspelled, tremendously moving documents. A surprising number begin, "Dear Mr. O'Brien, I too am writing a book." These letters he considers extra sacred. They are, he knows, from the special children, from the dreamers. They are from our future writers.

JULIE OF THE WOLVES

written by JEAN CRAIGHEAD GEORGE

illustrated by JOHN SCHOENHERR

published by HARPER & ROW   1972

BOOK NOTE

The thirteen-year-old girl who learns how to become part of
a wolf-pack in order to survive on the Arctic tundra has two
names, each important to her story's conflicting elements. She
is brought up as Miyax by her father, Kapugen, a famous Upick
Eskimo hunter at his seal-hunting camp. He is her hero, both
for his extensive knowledge of animals and birds and for his
adherence to Eskimo wisdom, which holds the riches of life to
be intelligence, fearlessness, and love. But at nine, Miyax must
live in a town and attend school, where she is called Julie
Edwards. Her father soon disappears on a seal-hunt and is
presumed dead. Julie acquires a pen pal in San Francisco, and
through Amy learns of an entirely different world she longs to
visit. Instead at thirteen she is sent north to Pt. Barrow to
marry Daniel, son of an old friend of her father's, in an arrange-
ment made long ago. A wedding is performed, but Julie learns
she is really needed to help make Eskimo clothes for tourists.
When dim-witted Daniel takes his role as husband seriously
enough to horrify her, she runs away, intending to cross the
North Slope to Pt. Hope and take a boat to San Francisco. Lost
on the tundra, she turns to her old self, Miyax, and her father's
teachings. Finding a pack led by a handsome wolf she calls
Amaroq, she studies their signals of submission and loyalty
until she is accepted as one of them. They save her life. But as

she nears Pt. Hope, Amaroq is killed, shot from a plane by hunters for sport. Miyax then hesitates to return to civilization, until she hears that a famous hunter named Kapugen lives nearby. She visits him, only to find he has changed and now makes his living flying the sporting hunters. The identity crisis of Julie/Miyax is acute, and while its resolution probably could not be otherwise, her final decision is sad for her and her people. The story is complex; but most of the telling of it dwells on her survival on the tundra with the wolves. It is convincingly and compellingly told by an experienced naturalist who observes and relates details with accuracy and yet conveys the profound beauty and awesomeness of the spacious Arctic.

EXCERPT FROM THE BOOK

Miyax pushed back the hood of her sealskin parka and looked at the Arctic sun. It was a yellow disc in a lime-green sky, the colors of six o'clock in the evening and the time when the wolves awoke. Quietly she put down her cooking pot and crept to the top of a dome-shaped frost heave, one of the many earth buckles that rise and fall in the crackling cold of the Arctic winter. Lying on her stomach, she looked across a vast lawn of grass and moss and focused her attention on the wolves she had come upon two sleeps ago. They were wagging their tails as they awoke and saw each other.

Her hands trembled and her heartbeat quickened, for she was frightened, not so much of the wolves, who were shy and many harpoon-shots away, but because of her desperate predicament. Miyax was lost. She had been lost without food for many sleeps on the North Slope of Alaska. The barren slope stretches for three hundred miles from the Brooks Range to the Arctic Ocean, and for more than eight hundred miles from the Chukchi to the Beaufort Sea. No roads cross it; ponds and lakes freckle its immensity. Winds scream across it, and the view in every direction is exactly the same. Somewhere in this cosmos was Miyax; and the very life in her body, its spark and warmth, depended upon these wolves for survival. And she was not sure they would help.

Miyax stared hard at the regal black wolf, hoping to catch his eye. She must somehow tell him that she was starving and ask him for food. This could be done she knew, for her father, an Eskimo hunter, had done so. One year he had camped near a wolf den while on a hunt. When a month had passed and her father had seen no game, he told the leader of the wolves that he was hungry and needed food. The next night the wolf called him from far away and her father went to him and found a freshly killed caribou. Unfortunately, Miyax's father never explained to her how he had told the wolf of his needs. And not long afterward he paddled his kayak into the Bering Sea to hunt for seal, and he never returned.

She had been watching the wolves for two days, trying to discern which of their sounds and movements expressed good-will and friendship. Most animals had such signals. The little Arctic ground squirrels flicked their tails sideways to notify others of their kind that they were friendly. By imitating this signal with her forefinger, Miyax had lured many a squirrel to her hand. If she could discover such a gesture for the wolves she would be able to make friends with them and share their food, like a bird or a fox.

Propped on her elbows with her chin in her fists, she stared at the black wolf, trying to catch his eye. She had chosen him because he was much larger than the others, and because he walked like her father, Kapugen, with his head high and his chest out. The black wolf also possessed wisdom, she had observed. The pack looked to him when the wind carried strange scents or the birds cried nervously. If he was alarmed, they were alarmed. If he was calm, they were calm.

Long minutes passed, and the black wolf did not look at her. He had ignored her since she first came upon them, two sleeps ago. True, she moved slowly and quietly, so as not to alarm him; yet she did wish he would see the kindness in her eyes. Many animals could tell the difference between hostile hunters and friendly people by merely looking at them. But the big black wolf would not even glance her way.

A bird stretched in the grass. The wolf looked at it. A flower twisted in the wind. He glanced at that. Then the breeze rippled the wolverine ruff on Miyax's parka and it glistened in the light. He did not look at that. She waited. Patience with the ways of nature had been instilled in her by her father. And so she knew better than to move or shout. Yet she must get food or die. Her hands shook slightly and she swallowed hard to keep calm.

Newbery Award Acceptance

by JEAN CRAIGHEAD GEORGE

Last January the 30th my telephone rang about eight o'clock in the evening, and I picked it up in the kitchen. Luke, my sixteen-year-old son, and I had just learned that it is a felony to overdraw a bank account in the state of Utah, where his older brother Craig was a sophomore in college. We were wondering how Craig, who thinks about mountains and backpacks rather than budgets, would fare with his allowance in a Utah bank. This was in the front of my mind when I answered the ring.

"It's long distance," I called to Luke, who was leaning over his homework at the dining room table. "Oh, oh," he said, as I braced myself for the sound of clanking chains. The telephone clicked, and in bright contrast to my dark fears, I heard Priscilla Moulton's pleasant voice:

"The Children's Services Division of the American Library Association," she said, "has selected you to be the recipient of the 1973 John Newbery Medal for the most distinguished contribution to American Literature for Children. The award proclaims your outstanding achievement in the creation of *Julie of the Wolves*."

"Oh, no," I said, just like that, which apparently confirmed Luke's worries. His eyes widened; his jaw dropped. As quickly as I could, I called to him: "I've won the Newbery Medal!" Luke grinned, blew a sigh of relief, and then gave me a twinkling smile; for he knew well what the Newbery Medal means.

Not many years ago his sixth-grade teacher had said at the end of a long discouraging day: "Look, kids, if you'll just read all the Newbery books, you'll get a terrific education, and it'll be a lot more pleasant for both of us." Luke had taken her advice, and now he cheered me.

As for my own reaction, I was electrified and then unbelievably calm. I serenely opened a can of dog food and handed it to a guest who dropped in, put the book I had been reading in the refrigerator, and washed a batch of clean clothes.

As I boarded the plane for Washington, D. C., where the 1973 winners of the Newbery and Caldecott Awards were announced, a most beautiful feeling sparkled through me. It persists today; for there is no author of children's books who does not work with greater inspiration and a more vivid direction because Fredric Melcher created the medal that recognizes a children's book as art. To win that medal is wholly gratifying.

It was fitting that Luke was home the night Priscilla called, for it was he who stepped off the plane with me in July of 1970 and looked out upon the Arctic Ocean at Barrow, Alaska. The severity of the Arctic biome hushed our voices as we walked to the small wooden terminal that looked like a house trailer by a road. The sky vaulted above us, clouds of birds wheeled overhead, and not far away on the beach, we could see a wall of ice that stretched a thousand miles to the North Pole. As we waited for our luggage, Luke pointed to a small fur-clad child who was walking into the wilderness over which we had just flown.

"She's awfully little to be going that way alone," he said, shoving his hands deep into his pockets and stepping closer to me. The little girl walked with determination, her straight back expressing confidence and inner strength. Months later, she, of course, was to become Julie.

At that moment, a children's book was the farthest thing from my mind. Luke and I were in Alaska because of several scientific investigations. One was *The Wolves of Mount McKinley* (1944) by Adolph Murie; another, *The Social Relationships in a Group of Captive Wolves* (1967) by G. B. Rabb, J. H.

Woolpy, and B. E. Ginsburg of Chicago's Brookfield Zoo. Mr. Murie's book is the ecological study that first pointed out that wolves have baby-sitters, rituals, and spring and summer dens. He also noted that the wolves keep the population of big-game animals in balance and that they harvest the sick and infirm. The Brookfield study, on the other hand, was a breakthrough in canine behavior. Facial expressions, movements, and positions of tails, ears, and heads were seen as "a language." Not long after the publication of this work, scientists began to speak freely about "the language of animals": the squirrel flashing his tail in a semaphore, the song-call of the humpback whale. Now, it is known that when a wolf mouths another wolf on top of the muzzle, he is saying: "I am leader of the pack." The wolf who rolls on his back and shows his light belly waves the "white flag of surrender," and the aggressor ceases his attack. No blood is shed. After discussing this provocative material with the editors of The Reader's Digest, I was dispatched straightaway to the Arctic Research Laboratory at Barrow, Alaska, where scientists were studying captive packs.

As Luke and I deplaned, we sensed that the adventure was going to include more than wolves. The world in which we stood was as unique as a coral reef, a desert, or a tidal pool — the other so-called biomes. The first uniqueness we noted was the weather. The winter ski clothes we wore were inadequate. The temperature rarely reaches 50 degrees Fahrenheit in Barrow, and the wind brings the chill factor down to about zero. We shivered as we walked to the hotel along treeless streets where the cold crops the plant life down to low grasses and lichens. Front yards were strewn with oil cans, old cars, parts of boats, refrigerators, and airplanes — the midden of the U. S. Navy and Air Force. The strangeness absorbed us, and we walked in silence past one-room Eskimo homes, stores where manufactured goods were sold, past a restaurant and a large Quonset hut that was an Eskimo community house. Even as we walked, we felt the push and pull of two cultures — a feeling which became a reality when we saw our hotel. This wooden structure had the simplicity of Eskimo art and a name right out of a television commercial — Top-of-the-World Hotel. Inside was a small sitting room lined with parkas, and a narrow corridor flanked by tiny rooms.

Almost immediately, Luke discovered that there was no running water in this hotel and that the ice in the drinking water cooler had been chipped off an iceberg. (The salt settles out of these oceanic glaciers and leaves them as fresh as a frozen spring.)

That night when we dined at an Eskimo restaurant, I ordered whale, and Luke ordered reindeer soup. Both were so rich and greasy that we could barely swallow them. Three days later, however, we were to discover that the body has its own intelligence. The cold had so changed our physiological needs that the whale, reindeer soup, even blubber, tasted like filet mignon. We were burning fats as I burn wood in my fireplace in winter — morning, noon, and night.

The element of the Arctic to which we never quite adjusted was the midnight sun. To Luke and me, the light seemed to say it was constantly four o'clock in the afternoon, no matter what the clocks said. After a few sleepless nights and after conquering the feeling that it was always time to quit work, we observed that the Eskimos and birds handled this situation by disappearing around noon and midnight for two sleeps instead of one. Unfortunately, we never got an opportunity to join the birds and Eskimos in their rhythmic naps during the endless day, for the gussaks had clocks and kept hours. *Gussaks,* by the way, is an Eskimo corruption of *Cossacks,* the first white men in Alaska. Eventually, we learned to solve our sleeping problem by pretending we were taking an afternoon nap. Exhaustion took care of the next eight hours.

Five miles down the gravel road from Barrow is the Arctic Research Laboratory. To this we bumped each day in the town taxi, a jeep, whose driver was skilled at dodging snowmobiles. Eskimos so admire these mechanical dog teams that they run them over the gravelly land in summer. Unfortunately, snowmobiles cannot really replace the dog team, of which there were but two left in all of Barrow for the tourists to see; for when snowmobiles break down far out on the tundra, they are not warm and life-sustaining. Human casualties are high.

The Arctic Research Laboratory is composed of Quonset homes for the staff, and a modern building of glass and pilings. The complex is maintained by the U. S. Navy and administered by the University of Alaska. About thirteen families live on the grounds the year round, keeping such fascinating pets as wolverines and seals. Gussak children are bused to the Eskimo school in Barrow. Off and on during the year, approximately 160 scientists from all over the world come to the lab to study the Eskimo, circadian rhythms, ice flow, the effects of oil spill on the tundra, wildlife, physics, oceanography, and weather. The library is a gold mine of information on the Arctic biome.

One of the first scientists that Luke and I looked up was an old acquaintance, Dr. Edgar Folk, Jr., who was studying the effects of leadership on the heart rate of the alpha male wolf, the leader of the pack. When we came upon Dr. Folk, he was watching an alpha through a closed-circuit TV. A small radio was attached to the wolf, and it beeped to a cardiograph in the lab the rate of the animal's heart as he trotted around an enclosure with the omega wolf, the low wolf on the totem pole of wolf status. The alpha's heart rate was low and steady; the omega's was rapid and frantic. Dr. Folk then returned the alpha to his pack. His heartbeat instantly went up and stayed there.

When I heard this, my image of a wolf began to change. Here was an animal who assumed responsibility with such conscious effort and concern that it affected his heart rate. This, I said to myself, is a trait heretofore attributed only to man.

Working with Dr. Folk was Dr. Michael Fox, author of the *Behaviour of Wolves, Dogs and Related Canids,* as well as of two children's books. A professor at Washington University, St. Louis, Missouri, Dr. Fox was running experiments on litters of pups to determine the characteristics of the alpha. He concluded that a wolf leader is fearless, initiates activities, and sticks to jobs longer than other wolves. He makes all the decisions for the pack and communicates with them by voice, gesture, and pose.

Luke and I began to study this language so we could "talk" to the wolves. In time we became rather good at the submissive grin and could recognize the signal of appeasement — ears drawn back, mouth slightly open. We could grunt-whine to solicit attention in a friendly manner and would greet the wolves with their own posture for "hello" — an open-mouthed smile. The most significant man-wolf talk, however, was between Dr. Fox and a wild alpha male wolf. One morning the scientist opened the door of this wolf's pen and stepped inside. Gently Dr. Fox bit him on the top of his nose. The alpha sat down before his "leader," and the two conversed in soft whimpers.

That was the genesis of *Julie* for me. For Luke it was a different challenge. He wanted the wolves to talk back to him, too. One day he walked up to a litter of prancing pups, opened his arms, and picked one up. The puppy kissed him with a lick and tucked his head submissively under Luke's chin. Luke kissed his nose, and the game manager smiled. "Take him home," he said. "You are his alpha now." I was sorely tempted until I recalled the problems that a friend had had with his pet wolf in Arizona. The wolf would trot off in the late afternoon and bring home groceries that had been delivered to neighbors' back porches. He also gathered up boots, chair cushions, garden equipment, and all manner of presents. Eventually, my friend had to pen the wolf to inhibit his need to provide for the pack.

After supper in the sunny night, Luke and I would walk out on the tundra to try to understand this unique biome with its permanent frozen ground called permafrost, its tough, durable plants, and clouds of birds. In time, we came to a deeper understanding of the complex tundra and the relationship between the owl, weasel, lemming, grass, caribou, bear, bird, fox, and Eskimo. The ecology of the Arctic is like a Chinese wooden puzzle; each piece locks into the others, and if one is not right, the whole thing falls apart.

Of this complex ecology, Charles Edwardson, Jr., an Eskimo leader of the Arctic Slope Natives Association, said to me: "To survive in the Arctic you have to be innocent and respect nature. The white man rushes the North and hence destroys it." He pointed to the beach in front of the Arctic Research Lab. A truck was dumping black stone upon it. "The gussaks are putting back the beach," he said. "They used it for fill; the ocean adjusted and began to snatch the whole shore. It threatened to demolish the laboratory." The gussaks were paying for their lack of respect for nature.

Toward the end of our stay in Barrow, Luke and I met Julia Sevegan, an Eskimo mother of three sons, an employee of the hospital, and wife of a hunter. Julia and her family gave Luke and me insight into the Eskimo in Barrow, Alaska, in the year 1970. Despite sewing machines and radios, gas stoves and electricity, Julia was part of the past. She had seen a ten-legged bear, a sighting that made her a sort of shaman, or a woman of great importance. Because Julia's husband had heard that I bore good credentials from the lower forty-eight states, he invited me to his home to meet Julia.

While she sat on the floor sewing warm mittens, I learned of bears and moons and family love. Snowmobiles screamed by the doors; jets roared overhead. In the kitchen Julia's sons chatted, and occasionally harsh English gave way to the beautiful bell-like language of the Eskimo. As I sat among plastics and machines, I lamented the passing of the Eskimo culture that had sustained these remarkable people under the most adverse conditions in the world. Yet, Julia was more comfortable because of her warm gas stove and her radio that filled the room with music. She could not, nor would anyone want her to, go back to severity. But something beautiful has been lost.

As I left Julia's house, I realized we have given the Eskimo everything but meaningful values; because of this, some are violent, some are drunk — they are deprived. Many others, however, like Julia and Charlie Edwardson, are finding a new direction in ten-legged bears and in a respect for nature.

Just before we departed from Barrow, word came via the scientific grapevine that Gordon C. Haber, a Ph.D. candidate from the University of British Columbia, was observing a pack of wild wolves in McKinley National Park. We hopped aboard a bush plane, swept out over the vast North Slope, then winged down the Anaktuvuk Pass, through which the Trans-Alaska Pipeline is plotted. I thought of Charlie Edwardson as I looked down on the Hickel Highway, a road that is supposed to parallel the pipeline. Three huge road graders had scraped back the grasses and mosses from the tundra and let the sunlight strike the ice crystals. The ice crystals had melted zipper-fashion — one after the next — and turned the soil to a mush that avalanched the huge machines down the mountainside into the river. I could hear Charlie's firm voice: "You can't rush the North."

In Mount McKinley National Park we found Gordon Haber cutting wood beside his cabin at Sanctuary River. Jays sang around him, and ground squirrels watched him, for Gordon was part of the ecology. He had spent three summers with the wolves and was preparing for his second winter. When I explained that I was in Alaska to write about wolves, he took Luke and me to watch a pack at their summer den.

For ten days we lay on our bellies, peering through a spotting scope and binoculars at these remarkable beasts. We saw the black alpha awaken, saw his pack nuzzle him under the chin ceremoniously, heard him open the hunt song with a solo. When all were alert, he would swing through the willows, his huntsmen at his heels, to test their crop of moose and caribou for harvesting. We never witnessed a kill, but we saw the ravens hover over kills and the hunters return home as fat as barrels to regurgitate food for their pups. We watched the puppies play bone ball, tug o'war, "jump on the baby-sitter"; and we became wholly involved in wolves. Luke, who had come to Alaska to fish, never strung up his rod again.

One dawn we joined Haber on a trip to the deserted nursery den of his pack. We hiked through bog, sphagnum moss, and over the tundra to a remote valley. Pushing our way through tangled willows, we climbed to a bluff high above the river. There in a layer of white sand was the birthing den, a generous tunnel dug into the earth. It was topped with flowers and set beneath a small garden of twisted spruce. The entire home expressed family love. A play yard was worn in front of the den. Around it were the large saucer-like beds of adults. I could envision them watching the tumbling pups, grins on their faces.

Most heartwarming, however, was a shaft that led straight down to the nursery chamber. It was a sort of telephone. During the first few weeks after birthing when the female remains in the den with the pups, the other adults stand over this hole and listen to the sounds from the den below: whimpers, sucking sounds, the contented grunts of happy puppies. When an adult wags his tail, he says, "all is well"; and the other wolves wag their tails, too.

Just before leaving the den site, I sat down beside the entrance and scanned the wide valley. I wanted to see the rocks and mountains as the wolf sees them. I looked down, and my blood turned to ice. There below was an enormous grizzly, head down, fur swinging as he came down our trail. Instinct warned me to stand still, but reason told Gordon to act. He wanted us ahead of the bear so that we would not meet him face to face when he turned around to go home. "Run!" Haber said. Luke shot off like a prong-horn antelope; Gordon like a deer. I ran as if I were weighted with lead, but I must have been zooming. As I leaped down a frost heave, I passed a jay in flight.

When we were safely ahead of the bear, we heard a wild sound as if an orchestra were tuning up. I looked back. On the top of the hill stood the female wolf and her nine fat puppies, who bounced forward to greet us. One yip from their mother, and all the pups vanished. If there was any doubt in my mind that wolves speak to each other, it was banished in that moment.

Within the next few days, I was also to learn that wolves control their birth rate. This is done by the alpha male. When the land is rich and there are many moose and caribou, the alpha will permit two or even three females to mate with their lifelong mates and have puppies. If, on the other hand, the crop is poor, the alpha will prevent their mating. He achieves this by approaching a pair in January-February when the females come into estrus. Because he is the leader, they must grovel before him or at least sit down on their haunches. This effectively stops breeding. Eventually, the alpha need only glance at a pair to keep them apart. None argue back. In some years, the alpha does not breed, possibly to vary and strengthen the genetics of the pack.

The wolves that Luke and I were watching had mysteriously solved another problem. The pack had but one female; the number of the adults was low and the land was rich. As if to rectify all three problems at once, the female gave birth to nine puppies. A large litter is six.

I was now convinced that wolves and men have much in common. Both have leaders, population problems, are hunters, and live together all year round. Both have language. So the difference, I said to myself, is that man shares and cares about his fellow man. Then I heard this: When the beta of the Toklat pack was injured by a moose, he limped off to a deserted patrol cabin, seemingly to die. Gordon Haber saw him collapse on the floor. The next evening, as Haber snowshoed home, he saw the alpha — with a large piece of meat in his mouth — slip into the cabin and drop it before the beta. The alpha returned every night to feed his friend until he was well. Upon hearing that story, I felt that the line that separates man from beast had faded forever. For me it was replaced by a sense of continuity. Even brotherly love, I said to myself, has evolved from the animals.

To realize this was at first disconcerting, then very exciting. Perhaps we are, after all, traveling a beautiful road. Perhaps we are evolving toward a mutual aid and not toward killing and destruction. Perhaps the growing attitude — that we must share the earth wisely with plant, beast, and man — is much more deeply rooted than we suspect.

When I returned home from Alaska, I was unable to publish my article on the wolf for *The Reader's Digest*. The editors used a piece by a scientist, L. David Mech, author of that remarkable work *The Wolves of Isle Royale*. His was a beautiful story, and yet I was frustrated. I had notebooks of material from generous scientists, and I had lived with and talked to wolves.

One afternoon an old friend, Pat Allen of Harper and Row, called, and I poured out my problems. "Let's talk," she said. The following afternoon I was telling Pat about wolves and about my idea. By now, I understood why Romulus and Remus, the legendary founders of Rome, were suckled by a wolf. If there is an animal who might raise a human child, it is the puppy-loving, communicative wolf, who is sophisticated enough to share. To me the ancient statue of Romulus and Remus is a symbol of the continuity between the lower forms of life and civilized man.

"I want to write a story," I blurted to Pat, "about a girl who lives with a pack of wolves and learns about mankind." A year and a half and three rewrites later, I turned in a battered manuscript to Harper and Row.

That this book won the Newbery Medal intrigues me, because so many people have shared so much with me in its creation: Dr. Fox, Dr. Folk, Gordon Haber, and a lifetime of brilliant editors — Elizabeth Riley formerly of Thomas Y. Crowell, Andrew Jones of *The Reader's Digest*, Ellen Rudin of Harper and Row. Josephine Rogers, my agent, gave me encouragement through sunshine and blizzard. And John Schoenherr, the gifted illustrator, has made Julie and her wolves walk off the pages into life.

My parents, Frank and Carolyn Craighead, are also part of this book. They have bestowed upon me, my three wonderful children, my brothers, nieces, and nephews — our whole pack — a love of nature and a deep respect for the earth and its precious cargo of life.

Thank you, librarians, for this great honor. For you are the ultimate sharers; you give your love of books to our children.

I have one last bouquet to toss, the bouquet of inspiration, and by now you must have guessed where I am going to throw it — right out across the vanishing wilderness, across the wild rivers, and tundras, over the delicate wildflowers and grasses, past the nose of the ten-legged bear, right into the midst of the vanishing species. I throw this bouquet to the loving wolves.

ᕃ   ᕃ   ᕃ

At the end of 1973, Jean Craighead George wrote that it had been a "provocative and wonderful year" but she would like to make the following comments: Last winter at the annual meeting of the California School Librarians in San Francisco, a member asked with deep concern if I would comment on "that page" in *Julie* (page 102, I presume). She went on to say that she would like to read the book aloud and recommend it to her children, but felt that if she did so, she would be encouraging boys and girls "to do *that* too." I was distressed, but not surprised, for there has been criticism of the incident that motivated Julie to be and find herself. I would like therefore to try and answer the librarian from San Francisco.

To me the "violence" (I do not call Daniel's actions "rape" because their physical relationship had been sanctioned by marriage) is the end of Julie's childhood. With that incident, which is to me the artistic zenith of the book, Julie accepts responsibility for herself.

The transition from childhood to adulthood is a painful and dangerous period for all the higher species of life. The bird flutters and falls from the nest; the bear cub is run up a tree and deserted; the fox pup is attacked. Children also "suffer" in the transition; but in our complex industrial society the break with the dream-world is not as clear cut as in less confusing societies. In the Eskimo culture of forty years ago, the transition to maturity was more clearly defined and therefore more helpful to children. Child-marriages often ended in separations. Since the relationships were unreal — the partners were children not adults — they usually terminated in violence: a shock that forced the boy or girl to see the other, not as a mother or father, but as a man or woman. Each would move on to establish a more mature relationship. Julie was idealistic and saw Daniel as a "brother" which was not the situation. His awkward attempt to make love opened her eyes and Julie walked off to grow up. Our children go through such a transition when they learn there is no Santa Claus or that their parents cannot do their homework or buy their way out of trouble.

When the break is made, the human child is able to mature and go on to attain the highest wonders of all the animals on Earth — creative work and the accumulation of knowledge. Julie's maturity is confirmed when at the end of her trials she sees her father not as a God, nor even a benevolent alpha male wolf, but as a human being with faults — and accepts him.

I do not think any child would spend two minutes on the explanation I have just written; but I believe they understand every movement Julie makes.

A society is all right when one is free to write honestly for children or adults. I applaud the Children's Services Division of the American Library Association, the publishing industry, and the teaching profession for creating a tolerant intellectual climate out of which only better children's books can come.

Elizabeth Winthrop

Jean Craighead George

by HELEN MELVIN

It was the first day of school, September 1957. I led my son
Tom across our road to wait for his first ride on the big yellow
bus. We both felt a bit apprehensive. Jean George and her son
Craig were there. They had just moved to our neighborhood
in Chappaqua, New York, and it was Craig's first day of school,
too. We introduced ourselves and stood there talking, relieved
that each of our sons would now have a friend on the bus. As
we talked, I kept noticing a large black bird on the fence next
to us; it seemed eerie to me. Finally I said to Jean, "Say, look
behind you. There's a bird watching us!" She laughed and
said, "Oh, that's New York, our pet crow."

This was the beginning for Jean and me — for Craig and
Tom, for New York and a long line of other wildlife pets of the
George family and our family — of friendship, solid and loyal,
warm and rare. After our sons climbed on the bus, Jean came
over to my house for a cup of coffee, the first of thousands
we have consumed together. For although Jean has a full-time
writing career, it is difficult for me to remember when she has
ever said no to a coffee break, an invitation to lunch, an SOS

to come care for an injured bird, a request to speak to a school-ful of children, or just about anything anyone asked of her. To this day I haven't figured out when she has had the time to write thirty-five books, and over fifty articles for *The Reader's Digest* and other publications, but I suspect she is up with her friends, the birds.

During our first meeting I learned that Jean was a naturalist and an author and illustrator of children's books. She was then working on *My Side of the Mountain*, one of the many books that she has illustrated herself. Awards and recognition were just beginning to come her way. It has been fun celebrating each occasion with her; for, happily, these successes have never changed her from being friendly, open, and democratic.

Jean received the Aurianne Award for Literature with *Dipper of Copper Creek*, which she coauthored with her former husband, Dr. John L. George. *My Side of the Mountain* was a Newbery Honor Book and also appeared on the Hans Christian Andersen International Honor List; incidentally, it was made into a movie by Robert Radnitz and Paramount Pictures. Two other books, *Hold Zero* and *Spring Comes to the Ocean*, were included on the Notable Children's Books list of the American Library Association. *All Upon a Stone* won the Book World Children's Spring Book Festival Award for the Best Picture Book of 1971. Jean has recently been named a Roving Editor for *The Reader's Digest*.

Her newest book, *All Upon a Sidewalk*, is now at press and will come out in the spring of 1974. Other recent books include: The Thirteen Moons, a series of ecological tales that relate the effect of each month of the lunar year upon an animal character; *Who Really Killed Cock Robin?*, an ecological mystery; *Julie of the Wolves*, the Newbery Medal winner this year; and *Beastly Inventions*, her only book for adults.

Jean Craighead George grew up in Washington, D.C., and spent her summers on a family farm in Pennsylvania. Her father, Dr. Frank C. Craighead, now eighty-three, is still at work in Florida in his field of entomology. Her twin brothers, Dr. John J. and Dr. Frank C. Craighead, are both ecologists, living on the banks of the Snake River in Moose, Wyoming. All four attended Penn State University. Upon graduating from college, Jean was voted by her classmates as Most Versatile Senior Woman. I think they should congratulate themselves for their accurate prediction. In 1968 the university named her Penn State Woman of the Year. After graduating from college, she was awarded a modern dance scholarship at Louisiana State University. With the outbreak of World War II, she dropped plans for a career in dance and went to Washington, D.C., to work as a reporter for the International News Service and *The Washington Post.*

Jean has three children: Twig, a senior at Bennington College; Craig, a sophomore at Utah State; and Luke, a high school junior in Chappaqua. Through the years, her family and mine have become very close. Whereas most of our friends have dinner parties for adults only, Jean's invitations always say, "Bring the kids." This caused some rather hectic evenings when our children were younger, but I believe it is one clue to her success as a children's author. Children have always been included in her circle of friends. And now that these children are older, they are often found in her home, sharing a meal, or just for an evening of talk. I have never known a woman who so successfully defies the generation gap.

The Georges live in an old-fashioned brown shingle house. It's big and unstylish. The inside reflects Jean's personality and wide range of interests. The walls and tables are covered with paintings, drawings, collages, and sculptures — many, her creations; and others, the work of her family and friends. An indoor pond with a bubbling fountain surrounded by plants is stocked with fish supplied by the junior fishermen of the neighborhood. Except at the peak of summer, you can bet on a fire in the fireplace, often at the breakfast hour. Last year, in a two-day burst of creative energy, Jean and her daughter Twig made macramé curtains for their living room. Luke and his friends recently put up an authentic tepee in their yard. The home has a casual, joyous, eclectic atmosphere, which uniquely reflects Jean George.

Being ecologically aware is relatively new for most people

today, but ecological awareness has been Jean's specialty for years. We used to belittle the location of our house, since it is surrounded by wetlands. She taught us to love our marsh long before it became prized and fashionable.

For the past three years she has demonstrated her commitment to our community by conducting Sunday morning walks as part of our continuing education program. These walks are the most popular course in the curriculum, although they require the participants to be up at 5:30 A.M. in all kinds of weather. These nature tours prompted her to write *Walking Wild Westchester*, a small booklet with maps, which has opened the eyes of many to the wonders of nature, the unspoiled places, right in our own county.

The Newbery Award **1974**

THE SLAVE DANCER

written by PAULA FOX

illustrated by EROS KEITH

published by BRADBURY PRESS   1973

BOOK NOTE

Jessie Bollier, a thirteen-year-old boy who plays his fife for pennies on New Orleans streets, is kidnapped and forced on board *The Moonlight*. He soon learns the ship is headed for Africa, where she will take on a cargo already illegal in 1840 — slaves. His job will be to pipe for the slaves to dance, so exercise will keep them fit. On the outward voyage he sees the cruelty of the corrupt Captain, Cawthorne; glimpses the underlying evil in Benjamin Stout, whose mild kindness disguises his real self; and discovers to his bewilderment that Purvis, the rough crewman who kidnapped him, is a less evil and a more honest man. After the slaves are taken on board, he is caught up not only in the revolting details of their survival under inhuman conditions, but of his own emotional survival; for despite his sympathy for the slaves, he comes to hate them for the pain they cause his imprisoned conscience. Weather, disease, and brutality kill some slaves and crewmen, but the final tragedy comes when the ship is pursued during a storm off Cuba, and there are only two survivors, Jessie and one black boy. The horror and cruelty which are the stuff of this story are not thrown in for the sake of sensational violence; but are the means by which Jessie learns that life and death are such close partners that one cannot be experienced without the other. Because there is a lyric quality in the writing, there are moments of surprising beauty to lighten it; and as the story makes clear that human compassion can be present in great tragedy, one puts the book down with faith and hope, rather than revulsion.

EXCERPT FROM THE BOOK

With a small smile, Stout said, "Get ready to play your music, lad," then reached out his hand to pat my shoulder. I moved back quickly as though a cottonmouth had struck in my direction. I saw, as clearly as I could see the cat-o'-nine-tails in his other hand, those fleshy fingers gripped around the ankle of the dead little girl.

I went below and got my fife, but stood unmoving in the dark until I heard them shouting for me.

The slaves from one of the holds were being hoisted one by one to the deck. Only the women and the youngest children were unshackled.

In just a few days, they had become so battered, so bowed by the fears that must have tormented them, that they could barely stand up. They blinked in the bright white light of the growing day. Then they sank to the deck, the women clutching weakly at the children, their shoulders bent over as though to receive the blows of death.

All hands were present; even Ned was ordered to leave his workbench and stand to attention.

The slaves were given their water rations and fed rice with a sauce of pepper and oil. When they saw the food and water, sighs rose from them like small puffs of wind, one following so close on the other that in the end, it seemed one great exhalation of air.

"Some of them think we eat them," whispered Purvis to me. "They think that first meal was only to fool them. When they see we intend to keep on feeding them, they grow quite cheerful."

I saw no cheer. The adults ate mournfully, the food dribbling from their lips as though their spirits were too low to keep their jaws firm. The children spoke among themselves. Sometimes a woman held a child's head as though she feared its voice might draw down punishment upon it, and rice from the child's mouth would spill across her arm.

When they had finished their meal, the Captain said to Stout. "Tell them to stand up. And tell them we have a musician for them and that they are to dance for me."

"I can't tell them all that, Sir," Stout replied. "I don't know their words for dancing or for music."

"Then tell them *something* to get them to their feet!" cried the Captain angrily as he flourished his pistol.

Stout began to speak to the slaves. They did not look at him. Some stared up at the tarpaulin as though there were a picture painted on it; others looked down at their feet.

We had formed a circle around them, dressed, shod, most of us armed. Many of them were naked; a few had ragged bits of cloth around their waists. I glanced at the sailors. Ned's eyes were turned upward toward heaven. I suppose he was reporting to God on the folly of everyone else but himself. But the rest were staring fixedly at the slaves. I felt fevered and agitated. I sensed, I saw, how beyond the advantage we had of weapons, their nakedness made them helpless. Even if we had not been armed, our clothes and boots alone would have given us power.

There was something else that held the attention of the men — and my own. It was the unguarded difference between the bodies of the men and women.

I had told no living soul that on some of my late walks through the old quarter at home, I had dared the chance of hell fire by glancing through the windows of certain houses where I had seen women undressing, and undressed. I can only say that I didn't *linger* at those windows. Sometimes, after my peeking, I had been ashamed. Other times, I had rolled on the ground with laughter. Why I was chagrined in one instance and hilarious in another, I don't know.

But what I felt now, now that I could gaze without restraint at the helpless and revealed forms of these slaves, was a mortification beyond any I had ever imagined.

At the increasingly harsh shouts of Ben Stout, some of the black men had risen, swaying to their feet. Then others stood. But several remained squatting. Stout began to lay about him with the cat-o'-nine, slapping the deck, flicking its fangs toward the feet of those who had not responded to his cries with even a twitch. At last, he whipped them to their feet. The women had risen at the first word, clutching the small children to their breasts.

"Bollweevil!" called the Captain.

Ned suddenly lit up his pipe.

I blew. A broken squeak came out of my fife.

"Tie him to the topmost crosstrees!" screamed Cawthorne. Stout, smiling, started toward me. I blew again. This time I managed a thin note, then some semblance of a tune.

The cat-o'-nine slapped the deck. Spark clapped his hands without a trace of rhythm. The Captain waved his arms about as though he'd been attacked by a horde of flies. A black man dropped toward the deck until Spark brought his heel down on his thin bare foot.

I played on against the wind, the movement of the ship and my own self-disgust, and finally the slaves began to lift their feet, the chains attached to the shackles around their ankles forming an iron dirge, below the trills of my tune. The women, being unshackled, moved more freely, but they continued to hold the children close. From no more than a barely audible moan or two, their voices began to gain strength until the song they were singing, or the words they were chanting, or the story they were telling overwhelmed the small sound of my playing.

Newbery Award Acceptance

by PAULA FOX

Nearly all the work of writing is silent. A writer does it alone. And the original intention — that first sudden stirring of one's imagination — is made up of many small, almost always humble, things. Because a major effort of writing is reflection, which is silent and solitary, I place thought under the heading of the experiences I had while I was writing *The Slave Dancer.*

By thought, I do not mean the marshalling of one's intellectual forces to refute an argument or to bring about a temporary victory over what agitates and bewilders us. All such victories are, I believe, transient. By thought, I mean that preoccupation with what we feel and why we feel it, and the enormous effort we must make to educe from a tangle of impressions and fleeting images the nature of those feelings. In this sense, thought is the effort to recognize.

It is an effort carried about against formidable enemies: habit; inertia; the fear of change and what it will entail; the wish to preserve our idiot corners of safety, of being "right"; and self-righteousness — the most dangerous enemy of all, full of a terrible energy that would turn us away from pondering the mystery of existence towards its own barren pleasures.

This effort to recognize is an effort to connect ourselves with the reality of our own lives. It is painful; but if we are to become human, we cannot abandon it. Once set on that path of recognition, we cannot forswear our integral connections with other people. We must make our way towards them as best we can, try to find what is similar, try to understand what is dissimilar, try to particularize what is universal.

Once we accept the responsibility of our connection with others, we must accept that we are like them even in our differences; and if in one instance, we are not a victim, we can be in another. And if in one instance we do not persecute, in another we will. And if we have not experienced the ultimate shame and anguish of captivity, of utter helplessness, we have experienced — at some time in our lives — something approximate to it, something from which we can construe a sense of what it is like to be other than ourselves.

Thought and feeling and recognition are the fruits of effort, and some of them are bitter. Once, years ago, I had a fleeting notion while I was reading a news story about a man pursued by a mob which intended to hang him. I thought: I could have been the victim, and I could have been one of the mob. Victim and mob are composed of my kind. We need not forgive what is vile in ourselves, but we must try to understand what is vile. If we cannot concede that we are born into this world with a capacity for cruelty, we cannot act against it.

The cat may not die from curiosity; but without it, the cat will likely perish. This curiosity, this puzzlement about our own existence and the lives of other people, is not an idle thing. It awakens the imagination, and the imagination makes it possible for us to realize that our own experience of life is both special to ourselves and generic to our kind. When we understand the continuity, the indivisibility, of human experience, we can begin — timidly perhaps, and with many a backward glance to the illusory snugness of those idiot corners — to consider the fact of our union with all others. Against the habitual indolence of the imagination, curiosity pushes itself, asks its shocking questions, and shoves us up against the folly of our wish to remain singular — and unmoved.

Writing is immodest although the experience of it is full of chagrin, even of mortification. A writer dares to claim that he or she will tell you a story about people and circumstances you know the writer could not have known. Because writers have sovereignty over their own inventions, they appear to make an outrageous claim. They will tell you everything about the characters in their stories. This is a world, they say; and every stick of its furnishings — every gesture and grimace of the people who live among these furnishings — is true and revealed. But this is not what happens in life. In real life, we stammer, we dissimulate, we hide. In stories, we are privy to the secrets, the evasions, the visions of characters in a fashion which real life only permits us during periods of extraordinary sensibility, before habit has made us forget that the cries behind the locked doors are our own.

The effort of writing is to approximate being, but our books can only have a degree of success. As we all know, when we put away the book we have been reading and return to the consciousness of the moment, art is not life. Our own individual lives are not finished inventions, but questions we can only partly answer.

No writer can truly answer the question, "Why did you write that book about those people?" Because, though the story between the book's covers is finished, the impulse that generated the story has been a question all along. I write to find out. I write to discover, over and over again, my connections with myself, with others. Each book deepens the question. It does not answer it.

The ultimate experience of abandonment is to be abandoned; the ultimate experience of injustice is to feel its outrage in every part of one's life; of hunger, to be hungry; of violation, to be violated. And so the immodesty and claims of a novelist are appalling. Yet, lying just behind that immodesty is a nearly overpowering sense of how little one knows, of how one must labor with the stuff of one's own life and struggle against the narrowness of one's own experience of life. It *is* an appalling claim. Without that claim and without those stations along the way that fall far short of ultimate experiences but from which one can sense what it might be like to go the whole journey, no book can be written.

The story of human slavery is a terrible story. Yet how one's heart clenches at the knowledge that there are those who wish it forgotten, even denied. The Spanish playwright Calderón said, "To seek to persuade a man that the misfortunes which he suffers are not misfortunes, does not console him for them, but is another misfortune in addition."

Last year, I saw on the television news an elderly woman standing in front of a half-completed housing unit in Newark, New Jersey. She was a picket among a group who were determined that such a housing unit for black people was not going to be built. Clutching her pocketbook close to herself, her face as shut as any vault door, she explained her action this way: "Why should *they* get special housing?" she cried. "Their people decided to come to this country on ships just like mine did."

They decided! Is it conceivable that this woman could actually have believed that the black people who were forcibly packed into slave ships, who perished by the millions, had decided upon such a fate? The belief of that woman is not "thought." It is the brute self, rising up to obliterate all other claims to a just life for fear its own claim is threatened. And it is that brute self which is the enemy of all justice. Surely that woman must have read, even in those textbooks of her own youth with their indecently hurried references to slavery, something of what really happened.

Yet even she, at the furthest outpost of denial, poses a question. Her stance in front of the television camera was one of alerted stupidity, which did not entirely conceal her fear and confusion. If I were to write a story about her, I would wonder what she had in that pocketbook, why she clutched it so fiercely, what she thought she was protecting, what she thought *special* meant, and why, during the middle years of her only life, she was walking in a picket line that sought to prevent other people from their rightful acquisition of shelter.

There are those who feel that slavery debased the enslaved. It is not so. Slavery engulfed whole peoples, swallowed up their lives, committed such offenses that in considering them, the heart falters, the mind recoils. Slavery debased the enslavers, and self-imposed ignorance of slavery keeps the mind closed and the heart beating too faintly to do other than insult and wound with such phrases as *special housing*.

There are others who feel that black people can be only humiliated by being reminded that once they were brought to this country as slaves. But it is not the victim who is shamed. It is the persecutor, who has refused the shame of what he has done and, as the last turn of the screw, would burden the victim with the ultimate responsibility of the crime itself.

When I read the records of the past, I sometimes wanted to turn away from what I was learning — to sleep. But as I read on and heard the words of the captive people themselves, as I began to feel the power of their endurance, I perceived that the people who had spoken so long ago of every conceivable human loss were not only survivors, but pioneers of the human condition in inhuman circumstances. They not only maintained life, they had nurtured it, and what they knew springs toward us, out of ashes, out of a holocaust.

To battle one's way into the past and to attempt to bring back what Lionel Trilling has called "the hum of the past" is to discover that history is a kind of fiction. We know that such a man was born and died, that such a battle was fought and lost, that such a charter was signed. Through personal records, drawings, artifacts of one sort or another, we can say to ourselves the past existed, *was*; that is how people dressed, this is what they ate, how they were buried. But that "hum" is another matter. We must invent.

And so what we write must, as E. M. Forster says, "go beyond the evidence." What we have for that task is our knowledge of ourselves in our own time. I lived for three months in New Orleans, near Rampart Street, where the line between black and white dwellings was then a stretch of pavement; and on the banks of the Mississippi, I used to eat my lunch — a "poor boy" sandwich, which, as a consequence of the inflationary tendencies of modern life, has come to be called a "hero." I spent years in Cuba when I was a child, living on a sugar plantation where no stick remained of the stocks in which slaves had once been punished only a few decades earlier. In ships' logs, I discovered weather, winds I would never feel, the names of currents I had not known existed, seas which I had not crossed. But once I was on a ship in a nearly disastrous storm at sea.

I wrote *The Slave Dancer* as a never-quite-to-be-freed captive of a white childhood in a dark condition. When I read a footnote in a book, the title of which I can't now recall, that said that slaver crews often kidnapped youthful street musicians and signed them on ships as slave dancers — for such were they called — something consonant with, or peculiar to, my own sense of myself set me on the course of writing my book.

Writing *The Slave Dancer* was the closest I could get to events of spirit and flesh which cannot help but elude in their reality all who did not experience them. Still, the effort to draw nearer is part of the effort of writing. It is not so different from the effort to understand our own infancies which become fictions because we cannot consciously recall them. Yet a few powerful images maintain their grip on our imaginations for all of our lives. If we are able to invoke even fragments of those images, we can, sometimes, despite formidable differences in circumstance, rouse them up in others. Little though we may feel we have in common, there is enough for us to take on the truest obligation we have — recognition of the existence of that which is other than ourselves.

Once I read a fairy tale of a poor fisherman who cast his net into the river and caught a genie in a bottle. Having released the genie, the fisherman and his wife wished for all the strange things we are supposed to wish for — worldly power and possessions, and a staggering number of castles. But this couple grew sated and wanted an end to wishing. Then they discovered the price of all that beneficence — the genie would not return to his bottle until they had guessed his true name.

In *The Slave Dancer*, I have made an effort to call the genie by his name. But the genie is not back in the bottle. Other efforts have been made and will be made. Each time, perhaps, we get a little closer to the fires of that holocaust which have burned for so many centuries, and so begin to put them out.

I am profoundly grateful to all of you for your recognition of my effort.

Jill Krementz

Paula Fox

by AUGUSTA BAKER

The Slave Dancer is Paula Fox's first historical novel, though she has written fourteen books, eleven for children and three for adults. The novel is set in 1840, but its vividness reaches beyond the past — beyond the horror, the cruelty, and the ugliness of the slave trade — to touch us today. "I don't think there's anything in the book that older children couldn't face," Paula Fox has said. "It was a true terror as opposed to the made-up horrors of the movies. Human history is partly a history of suffering. Children know more of pain than one thinks, and they don't need artificially happy endings."

Paula Fox knew her share of pain as a child. A New Yorker by birth, half Spanish, half Irish-English, she was sent at the age of eight to live with her grandmother in Cuba. She soon became fluent in Spanish, which she learned from the village children; they were her friends, and before long she was a player on the baseball team — the only girl. She remembers the heat of the midday sun, the noise of the animals — guinea fowl and monkeys; and she made these memories live for me as we sat together in her home in Brooklyn. The children she knew as a child and those she has known as an adult are the ones she writes about in her books, whether they are the abandoned boys in *How Many Miles to Babylon?*, or the privileged but isolated child in *Portrait of Ivan*.

When Batista came to power in Cuba in 1934, Paula returned to New York City. She describes herself as "a traveling child," who seldom lived any place longer than a year or two, and seldom saw either of her parents. (However, her father was a writer, and she feels that her writing has been a "hook-up" with him.) "I attended nine schools before I was twelve, by which time I had discovered that freedom, solace, and truth were public libraries." She had the feeling of being a transient, of not knowing what was going to happen the next day. People beyond her family offered her what permanence she knew.

Paula began working at seventeen. But for years "writing was at the edges" of her life. She got a job with a newspaper, and another as a machinist for Bethlehem Steel. In San Francisco, she and three young Mexican-Americans worked to help six hundred Mexican families who were left stranded after their jobs on the railroad were terminated. She found that they had to protect the children of these families from exploitation by the community itself — police, courts, social workers. In London, Paula worked as a reader for a movie company as well as for a British publisher. In 1946 she got a job with an English news service and was assigned to Paris and Warsaw. Upon returning to New York, she married; had two sons, Adam and Gabriel; but then was divorced. As for writing, she says, "I had to wait until I could type without dogs or kids in my lap."

She studied at Columbia University; then worked at a special school for emotionally disturbed children in Dobbs Ferry, New York. She taught English to Spanish-speaking children, and for several years taught fifth grade at the Ethical Culture Schools in New York City. She often read to her students — from Dickens, Joyce, Tolstoy, Orwell, Stevenson. "There was no tension of accomplishment or grades connected with the reading," she says. "It simply *was*, as literature should be." Recently, during her semester's appointment at a branch of New York State University, Paula discovered that young adults liked being read to for the same reasons the fifth graders did.

In 1962 Paula married Martin Greenberg, one-time *Commentary* editor and now Professor of English at C. W. Post College. She wrote a TV script and, to her surprise, sold it; then two short stories were published by *Negro Digest*. A Guggenheim Fellowship of her husband's took the family to Greece for six months: "a golden time," as Paula describes it. Adam, then twelve, worked for a carpenter; Gabe, ten, for a cobbler. And Paula began to write without interruption — which she has continued to do since the family returned to the United States.

Since the publication of *Maurice's Room*, Paula Fox has given us many children in her books. One feels in her warmth, compassion, and sense of connection with young people that she has known them all somewhere in her life and that she sees herself in them.

The Newbery Award **1975**

M.C. HIGGINS, THE GREAT

written by Virginia Hamilton

published by Macmillan Publishing Company   1974

BOOK NOTE

M.C. Higgins lives on Sarah's Mountain, where he spends his
days watching over his younger brothers, Lennie Pool and
Harper, and his sister, Macie Pearl. His mother, Banina, walks
every day to town to work in other people's houses. IIis father,
Jones, works in a steel mill when there is a job for him. Sometimes M.C. does his watching from the top of a gleaming forty-
foot steel pole, which his father gave him as a prize for swimming the Ohio River. On his pole, he is Mayo Cornelius
Higgins, the Great, observer of everything moving on Sarah's
Mountain: the strip-mining machines at the top; the growing
heap of spoil which could slide and crush his house; the
changing weather; his great-grandmother Sarah's ghost; the
arrival of a dude to record Banina's voice; and the explorings
of an intruder, a young girl, Lurhetta Outlaw. He meets his
friend Ben Killburn when no one can see them together, because the Killburns are witchy people. On one level the story
conveys realities: M.C.'s yearning that the dude's recording of
Banina's remarkable voice will mean they can move away
from the threatening spoil; his relationship with his emotionally strong mother and his physically strong father; and his
testing of himself with Lurhetta. But on another level the
story purveys pure imagination: in the intensely felt atmosphere of the mountains and the lake; in the unusual Killburn
community; in the pole; and in M.C. Higgins himself. It is
an extraordinary and unforgettable story.

EXCERPT FROM THE BOOK

M.C. turned back to the gully again and walked a third of the way into it. To his right was Sarah's Mountain, a great swell of earth rising to outline the sky. Her growth of trees was washed light green by morning sun and mist. Halfway up was the ledge of rock, the outcropping, on which M.C. lived with the rest of his family. The whole outcropping was partially hidden by trees. Only one who knew where to look would see a house at all.

Near the house, something was shining. M.C. caught a blinding gleam right in the eye. He smiled, clambering over the lip of the gully and onto a path that rose steeply up the face of the mountain. Holding onto tree trunks and branches when he had to, he picked and sometimes nearly clawed his way. There was an easier path beginning farther along the lip of the gully, but M.C. was in too much of a hurry to take it. He panted and grunted with the effort of his climb. He paused to look up and was rewarded by a sharp flash of light.

"I got a ticket to ride," he gasped. "I . . . got-a-ticket-to . . . ri-i-ide."

The path veered closer to the outcropping where there was undergrowth of sweetbrier. It cut through the tangled, prickly mass of the brier and brought M.C. out onto the outcropping. The ledge he stood on was like a huge half-circle of rock sticking out of the mountain. Behind it, the mountain rose another three hundred feet to the summit. Up there, just below the summit, was a gash like a road all the way across. It had a seventy-foot vertical wall made by bulldozers hauling out tons of soil to get at the coal seam. And up there was something like an enormous black boil of uprooted trees and earth plastered together by rain, by all kinds of weather. Some internal balance kept the thing hanging suspended on the mountainside, far above the outcropping, in a half-congealed spoil heap bigger than M.C.'s house.

At home, finally, he saw that the house was shut tight. His mother, his father, both gone to work. The kids, on their way to swim. One side of the house to the rear was smack up against the mountain where the ledge curved around it. On the other side of the house was a grape arbor, the expanse of yard and M.C.'s prize like no other.

It was always his shining beacon.

Pretty thing, you.

He had won it, practicing on the Ohio River, testing his strength against strong currents every day for weeks. He had known when he was ready.

I wasn't scared. I did it and I never want to do it again. I won't ever have to.

Jones said, name what you want, real quick. And I saw it just as clear. All over town in Harenton. Front of the post office. The police station.

His prize was a pole. It was forty feet of glistening, cold steel, the best kind of ride.

M.C. gazed up at its sparkling height. There was a bicycle seat fixed at the top. He had put it there himself and had attached pedals and two tricycle wheels below it on either side.

He didn't know how his father had got the pole without money. Jones had let him deep-foot the pole in the midst of the piles of junk in their yard. There were automobile tires, fenders, car bodies, that Jones had dragged up the mountain over the years. But Jones had long since forgotten about putting together a working car.

Wonder why he won't ever throw away that junk, M.C. thought. How'd he get the pole? Probably the same way he got the junk. Maybe he just took it.

Maybe it had been abandoned, like the cars, or perhaps it had been given to Jones out of the rolling mill in the steelyard at Harenton. Ten feet too tall, it could have a flaw somewhere, a weak structure from uneven firing.

Looks just fine from here, M.C. thought. He stood there studying his pole, admiring its black and blue tint in the sun. It was the one thing that could make him feel peaceful inside every time he saw it.

Gingerly, M.C. climbed up on the car junk. He leaned over and gripped the pole.

"Let's go for a ride."

He dried his sweating palms on his shirt. Then he jumped off the pile. And twisting his legs around, he climbed the slippery, smooth steel the way only he knew how.

Newbery Award Acceptance

by VIRGINIA HAMILTON

It is my great pleasure to accept the Newbery Medal. I am so very grateful to the American Library Association, whose Newbery-Caldecott Committee selected *M.C. Higgins, The Great* as the "most distinguished contribution to American literature for children" in 1974.

In my home town, which is a small, relatively obscure Midwestern community, my family has been, if not well-known and well-heeled, at least talked about from one generation to the next. My mother's large, extended and complex Perry clan literally plummets individual Perrys into the spotlight. For example, it was an uncle of mine who single-handedly cornered the culprits who robbed a nearby bank. Rather than be taken in by a madman — wearing nothing more than a flannel nightshirt and with Jack Daniel's on his breath — who shot at them with two gold-plated pocket pistols, they jumped down an empty well, breaking first arms and ankles and then legs and wrists, when Uncle staggered too near the edge and plummeted down the well on top of them.

It was another uncle of mine who in 1937 had the finest, sleekest black touring car in the county. And in the same year, on the clearest, sunniest summer day on record, he met his maker when he spotted an elk in the trees at the side of the road; grabbing his shotgun at the ready, he took careful aim and with deadly accuracy shot it while he and the touring car sailed serenely over a cliff at twenty miles per hour. If that isn't plummeting, I don't know what is.

It was my favorite, immensely superstitious aunt who was the first among the Perrys to come in at the middle of Orson

Welles' alarmingly realistic radio version of H. G. Wells' *War of the Worlds*. On that scary night of mists back in 1938, Aunt Leah terrified and aroused Perrys in three counties to limited action against invading Martians. Apparently my own immediate family of Hamiltons knew enough about Perrys to spend the next six hours sensibly in Grandpa Perry's root cellar, while all of the male relatives and Aunt Leah searched the skies and shotgunned anything that moved.

Don't blame me if tomorrow you discover that the three tales I've related are exaggerations. For they were told to me by other Perrys, and none of us is known to tell a story the same way twice. What I meant to imply by the above confession is that folks in my community have been primed for three-quarters of a century to expect some action from my end of town. I'm sure little or nothing is known of the exploits of Perrys in the last quarter of the last century because they were too busy, I suspect, acquiring land and seed and wives and generally keeping their hands on the plow so that subsequent Perrys might raise hell and tell tales on one another in the relative security of mounds of millet and manure.

So when it was announced in the local papers that one of the Perry clan was the recipient of this Medal, older members in particular of my community were more or less conditioned to respond.

"I wasn't a bit surprised," an octogenarian of my acquaintance told me at the reception given me by the Greene County Library, Yellow Springs Branch. Although my elderly friend did seem a bit disappointed that the Medal had not been given to me for something slightly more outrageous than writing the best children's book of the year. Still, she soon seemed happy enough and pumped and patted my hand long and hard.

I'll never forget the gentleman who, after regarding me from a distance for a time, quietly came forward, his face still wet and glasses foggy from the rain. It rained a total of thirty-eight hours before, during, and after my reception; the land flooded, but still hundreds from my county and from miles around came out to visit with me. This gentleman, red-necked and suspendered, solemnly spoke: "You may not recollect me," he said, "though I do recall you from a child. I am the elder Standhill, and I knew your dad, and I must say Kenny Hamilton would have been good and proud of you upon this day."

Something inside me went dead quiet at the sound of the man's stark Midwestern voice, sweet to my ears and so like my own late father's stirring accent. I caught the essence of it and filed it away in that place where writers keep extraordinary human sounds, while struggling with my memory and the gentleman's not unfamiliar face.

"I think I remember you," I said.

"Surely," he answered. "Your brother, Buster, went to school with my boy, Don." When I looked on blankly, he was quick to say never mind. "What I wanted to tell you," he said, "was that we are all so proud of you. And I want you to know — we are aware of the significance of this award in the *lit'ry world*."

I was speechless and near tears when the gentleman, whom I still couldn't place, grinned and patted my hand.

"I wasn't going to tell you this," he said, "but I was the one, against my wife's will, who let you charge your potato chips and those of a slew of your friends on your dad's account each lunch-noon. You remember me now? When you were in fifth grade? And I had the grocery?"

I nodded, a flood of memories of wooden shelves reaching to the ceiling and glass counters of candy coming to me, clear as water.

"I knew you'd remember," he said, "and I'd like to think that through that small indulgence, I was one who helped you get your way in life."

I am certain he was one, as were many others; and I told him as much.

Experiences such as this are some of the small wonders of receiving the Newbery Award. And through all of the kindness shown me in relation to it, nothing has so moved me as that reception in my home town. All of my mother's Perrys turned out, looking, as usual, absolutely different from other people, black or white. For Perrys you can single out of any crowd by that mysterious combination of furious intelligence and shrewd humor seen in their eyes. I hope I resemble them, if only slightly. But they are stand-offish from all others, at the best and worst of times. So they were at my party, never quite overcoming their Midwestern shyness. That look they have says to me that Perrys are here today because through thick and thin we knew how to survive — that there would always be at least one of us to remember those who had gone before. And when my own mother, Etta Belle Perry Hamilton, told me after having read *M.C. Higgins, The Great* that young M.C. atop his outlandish pole was no less than a Perry in disguise, I knew she had to be right. For M.C., too, knew well how to survive.

No book of mine was ever in more danger of being a failed labor of love than was *M.C. Higgins, The Great*. None was to bring me more pleasure and pain in the writing. I had conceived the idea for it sometime after writing *The House of Dies Drear* in 1968. I had worked through one chapter of *M.C.*, another, and another — when abruptly nothing more of it would come. So I put the manuscript aside, trusting my instinct which warned me I wasn't yet ready to write this one. What is instinct but a natural, primordial aptitude for foreknowledge and forewarning? Call it Muse or "in the mood," if you like, but I trust it equally with reason and understanding. I know that the one will not work without the others. Instinct, then, is that sudden capacity for limited precognition, that half-conscious idea that inexplicably causes a writer to be absolutely certain there is a perfect story waiting just up ahead.

So over the years, M.C. was never far back in my mind, although other books intervened. Then imagine the day in New York in early 1972 when I burst in on my editor and shouted the news that I had this wild, barefoot youth atop a forty-foot steel pole on the side of a mountain called Sarah's. And if this weren't enough of a really swell story idea, at the summit of Sarah's Mountain was a spoil heap left from strip-mining the land, and this heap was moving relentlessly an inch at a time toward the kid atop the pole. Moreover, to cap the whole thing off, I had this incredible red-headed family of six-fingered vegetarians who were capable of healing mountains.

Picture if you will Susan Hirschman: My editor's capable smile seemed to thin on hearing the news. Her cautious-kind reply was, "I can't *wait* to read it, Virginia."

However, Hirschman has nerves of steel. Wait she did, over the next few months until the second of our consultations in her office in New York. I anguished and protested to her that this time the book defied solution or completion. How do I write, I worried, when all of my subjects upon creation immediately suggest intangible objects? And I said to Susan, "How do I keep mountains, rivers, and, yes, black people from turning into myths or emblems of themselves? They are somehow born on the page too large," I said, "and no sooner do I put them there all together than the river becomes The-One-That-Has-To-Be-Crossed; the mountain is The-One-That's-Got-To-Be-Climbed; and my people? A mere symbol of human STRUG-GLE, in capital letters, *Against Adversity*, in italics. And that would be playing them cheap," I said.

Having said that, I slumped back, glumly eyeing Hirschman, the smell of defeat as unsavory as wild onion in my nostrils.

She stared back rather unsympathetically, I thought at the time, and totally uninterested in my fading confidence.

"What about the pole?" she asked.

"What about it?"

"What's *it* a symbol of?"

"It's . . . just what the kid sits on?" I asked, tentatively.

"But why doesn't he 'just' sit on the mountain or on the porch; why a forty-foot pole on the side of a mountain?"

"Well, it's not his mountain," I said, feeling unaccountably annoyed, "it's Sarah's . . . but the pole belongs to him, and that's why he sits on it."

"But where did he get it," she persisted, "and what for, and . . ."

I cut her off. "It's his!" I said, nearly shouting. "He won

it . . ." I was getting this really fantastic scene in my head.

"What did he win it for?" Hirschman asked, carefully removing sharp objects from her desk top.

"Swimming!" I shouted with glee. "For swimming!"

"Remarkable," she said. "I hadn't known he was a swimmer."

"Not just any swimmer," I said, "but a great swimmer. And once he swam the Ohio River . . . and there's a lake in the mountains . . . and there's a tunnel!"

"A train tunnel?" she said.

"No, no . . ." By then I was out of my chair, grabbing my suitcase and, in my mind, already on the plane home.

"Don't forget to write," Hirschman called softly as I reached the door.

"Yeah, sure," I said, by way of farewell.

That was it. There would be no more of those talks between us for quite a spell.

Actually, I've oversimplified quite an interesting method between editor and writer of defining story area and limits. It is never as simple as I've described it, nor does it happen as quickly. However, when symbols begin to build at the outset, they must be made to yield at once to the things they stand for. In other words, before one can see the mountain, one must know its heat, its flies, its wind, and its place against a total breadth of sky. Writing such fascinating detail keeps me going — over long months of plotting; but it is with character that I must always begin.

I began with M.C. atop a forty-foot pole, lofty, serene. Too serene, perhaps, too above it all, and so I conceived Ben Killburn, created out of darkness at the foot of the pole. Earthbound, Ben is dependable in a way M.C. is not. Ben, in turn, is constricted by Jones Higgins, M.C.'s father, a man of strength and integrity, yet superstitious and unyielding. So, too, is Jones illuminated by the Dude from out of nowhere, who clarifies for M.C. his father's inability to face the reality of the endangered mountain.

As though in a spiral from the top of the pole, each character bears light to the next until they all form a circle revolving at the base of the pole. The Dude in his turn is made less imposing in the presence of M.C.'s mother, Banina, and by the simple magnificence of her voice. Finally, how easily random chance in the slim shape of a whimsical teenage girl might have brought tragedy to Banina's beloved family.

Thus, the circle of characters moves about the pole, their lives as intertwined and fragile as the thin, flashing ribbons of a May dance. There they reel precariously on the side of Sarah's Mountain under a black cloud — the spoil hovering above. The Higgins' mountain has within it the element of its own destruction in the form of coal; yet it also contains the building materials of rock and dirt which become the means for M.C.'s affirmative action. At the last, M.C. builds a wall in order to stop a spoil heap. Correction: He begins to build a wall. Whether it would really stop the force of tons of falling debris is open to question. But in terms of story and fiction, it is necessary that we see him move to save himself.

We do know the truth, however. Appalachian hills are flattened; the Belmont counties of Ohio are decimated by the GEMs (Giant Earth Movers) of Hanna Coal Company. Acids released by mining destroy wells, crops, livestock, and land. Because of them, people starve and people die.

But no one dies in *M.C. Higgins, The Great* or in any of my books. I have never written demonstrable and classifiable truths; nor have my fictional black people become human sacrifices in the name of social accuracy. For young people reading *M.C.*, particularly the poor and the blacks, have got to realize that his effort with his bare hands to stay alive and save his way of life must be their effort as well. For too long, too many have suffered and died without cause. I prefer to write about those who survive — such as old Sarah McHiggon of the mountain, Banina Higgins, and the Killburns, who have good cause for living.

A letter I received from a young female student in Toronto is typical of letters I receive from young people of various racial groups. She said, "Miss Hamilton, I am white, but I just as well could be black. Either kind, I'd be okay. Your books taught me to say that."

Most young people who write me tell that my books teach them things — ways to live, how to survive. Having set out to be nothing more than a teller of tales, I have come to feel responsible — that what I have to say is more worthwhile than I had first thought.

I would like to thank everyone who helped make *M.C. Higgins, The Great* the book it is. To my family, Arnold, Leigh, and Jaime — thank you for bearing with me. To Phyllis Larkin and Elizabeth Shub, I appreciate all you have done. To Janet Schulman, who unstintingly saw *M.C.* through — you are here with us in spirit, and we thank you. And last and most, to Susan Hirschman. The past is prelude, and you are the best there is.

One final note: This event here this evening is, in part, an historic occasion. I am the first black woman and black writer to have received this award. May the American Library Association ever proceed.

Virginia Hamilton

by PAUL HEINS

Virginia Hamilton recently told me, "There are three things I can remember always wanting: to go to New York, to go to Spain, and to be a writer. It feels nice to have done all three. I haven't had to want anything for some time." What is most remarkable about these statements is not the somewhat in-genuous remark that "It feels nice to have done all three," but the fact that she hasn't "had to want anything for some time." For her concluding remark is disarmingly simple and reflects her uniqueness as a writer and as a person. I think we can ignore the accomplishment of her desire to go to Spain. But her need to go to New York and her need to become a writer were in part prophetic, and in their fulfillment are to be found essential portions of the substance of her life. For she "grew up yearning for the unusual, seeking something unique in myself," and in her maturity she has continued both to accept and to explore the meaning of her individual percep-tions and experiences.

Her experiences have deep roots, for she lives in the Miami Valley in southern Ohio, the land of her immediate ancestors. Her maternal grandfather, Levi Perry, who had been born a slave in 1855, ran away from the Kentucky-Tennessee area with his mother and settled in Jamestown, Ohio. He later married into the Adams family living nine miles away in Yellow Springs, and Virginia grew up among Adamses and Perrys, who had increased and multiplied and become farmers and landowners on the periphery of the village. She tells how, as a child, she had the run of neighboring farms which belonged to the Perrys and how her cousins, aunts, and uncles were always glad to see her. Moreover, she stresses the power of kinship: "The relationship of my relatives to past and present is something I learned as a child, and the learning is still going on. I know how people interact. I know what an exceptional spiritual experience is the extended family."

Her father, Kenneth Hamilton, was born in Alton, Illinois, and although he was a graduate of the Iowa State Business College, he could not find a job to make use of his training. He wandered through North America and at one time ran gambling halls in mining towns in the Dakotas. From him Virginia learned about Dr. W. E. B. Du Bois, Paul Robeson, and many other noteworthy black personalities; and at an early age she became acquainted with her father's books — especially with the works of Poe and Kafka. For she was encouraged to read, and when she began to write at the age of nine or ten, her literary activities were taken for granted.

By the time she finished high school and received a full scholarship to Antioch College in Yellow Springs, she had absorbed the traditional lore and the storytelling inclinations of the Perry clan, undergone the stimulating influence of the African Methodist Episcopal Church, and become aware of her personal ambition to be a writer. She spent three years at Antioch, where she did well in her writing and literature courses.

But for the next fifteen years or so, she engaged in a flirtation with New York — intermittently paying visits to the city, working, singing in obscure nightclubs, studying at the New School, and becoming acquainted with musicians, artists, and other writers. During this period, there was an interlude of two years at Ohio State University; then she capitulated and remained in New York. Her reason for ultimately leaving New York discloses the way in which she comes to grips with her experiences: "I loved the City until the moment I could no longer stand it, which happened one day between four and five in the afternoon. I think what happened was that I had always found it too stimulating. No time to think, only time to recoil or react. I felt no control over my life. I could not initiate or change anything. I had no *effect*."

Before she left New York, Virginia had met and married Arnold Adoff, an attractive, intelligent, and witty teacher from the Bronx; in the course of searching for suitable materials for his classes in Harlem, he found himself launched on his career as a well-known anthologist of black poetry. With their children, Leigh and Jaime, Virginia and Arnold turned towards Ohio. Virginia was returning to the large family community from which she had sprung; and purchasing some land from her mother, she and Arnold built in Yellow Springs a contemporary house — which she calls her castle.

It is massive, made of redwood and glass, and has no windows, only sliding glass doors and clerestory lights. Virginia originally saw the design in *Better Homes and Gardens* and convinced Arnold that they should use it as a model. Much of the time they live and work at home, surrounded by their two-acre park; and Virginia feels both fortunate and happy to be located in the town of her origin. "People here are so supportive, and yet they know how to leave us alone. I know generations of people here. It is a comfort to see families regenerate themselves."

Her knowledge of these generations has given her a sense of the continuity of her people. As a writer, she has absorbed the experiences of black history, both from her early personal background and from her later studies, and has transformed them into literature. Hovering in the background of *Zeely* is Africa; hidden at the very center of *The House of Dies Drear* lies the ambiguous relationship between the runaway slave and his white neighbors. *The Planet of Junior Brown* lets us glimpse New York through the eyes of black characters; Sarah's escape from bondage is the very pivot of *M.C. Higgins, The Great.*

Although there is plenty of realistic detail in her writing, Virginia Hamilton is not sure whether she is a realist; actually, she often feels that she is a symbolist. One might call her an inventor. She accepts her subject matter as she accepts herself or her experiences and then molds her material in accordance with a pattern suggested by her intuition, an intuition both aesthetic and human. She admires Faulkner: "Perhaps Dostoevsky is greater than Faulkner, but Faulkner is more deeply human. More appalled and obsessed by flawed, weak humanity. . . . I think Henry James and Thomas Mann are miraculous, but I love Faulkner"; and it is illuminating to discover that she prefers to read novelists who are storytellers: "I am impatient with self-centered, confessional writing." What she herself reaches out for in her writing is always some exterior manifestation — historical or personal — that she has examined in the light of her feelings and her intelligence.

Virginia Hamilton's calm and beautiful presence is aglow with knowledge and intuition. She knows that the lands between Yellow Springs and Xenia, Ohio, were the ancestral home of the Shawnee nation, and that her grandmother was said to be half Cherokee. She treasures her father's mandolin — "of a rare scroll design, very old with inlaid ivory"; and she can intone a melody brought by her ancestors from Africa. She has even dared to characterize her own children: "They have great presence and often seem to listen with their eyes. My son is verbal-witty, while Leigh is mainly quiet and inward. They are loners, poor things, but are well-liked." In commenting on her writing, Virginia Hamilton says, "I am learning to go backward and forward in time with the feeling of simultaneousness." It is remarkable that this accomplishment applies to her personal life as well as to her art.

A Decade of Newbery Books in Perspective

by JOHN ROWE TOWNSEND

There is always argument about book awards. It is to be expected, and it is healthy. Literary judgments can never be absolute. They are affected by changing tastes and attitudes, subjective preferences, and the differing experience of individuals. It would be astonishing if all Newbery choices met with universal approval, and even more astonishing if there were universal approval for the choices of bygone years. The consensus reached by twenty-three informed people who meet to discuss the carefully sifted output of a year is clearly valuable, but it is not definitive. The most authoritative of all critics is Time, and no committee can tell what picture will emerge in the longer perspective. In most years it would be a rash person who would assert that one book could be established permanently and beyond all doubt as "the best."

The important questions to ask about a decade of Newbery books are not whether these are, in a competitive sense, the rightful winners — an issue on which discussion could be endless and would certainly be inconclusive — but whether they are in fact books of high excellence; whether they offer a fair representation of "quality" publishing for children over the past ten years and, if so, whether they indicate that standards are rising or falling. A calm look at the books themselves is obviously required. It is not possible in one short essay to set each book into its context and offer a sustained critical appraisal. My judgments are personal and will necessarily be somewhat abbreviated. I do not claim that everybody ought to agree with them. I should like most of all to think that readers of this essay would turn to, or return to, the books themselves and make up their own minds.

Members of the Newbery-Caldecott Committee are not themselves bound to observe a prescribed set of criteria, and I think this is right. There are some assumptions, however, that it seems safe to draw from experience and from the consideration of past choices. I assume that the general standard is one of literary merit, and that in looking for a good book for children the committee is looking for a good book, period. I assume that popularity is not a key test; that one aims to find a good book and make it popular, rather than to find a popular book and proclaim it good. I assume, moreover, that a children's book should be accessible to children in the sense of not demanding from them a greater experience of life and literature than can reasonably be expected. Finally, I assume that educational or "developmental" values, or the achievement of a social aim, are not in themselves criteria — although, of course, by enriching a child's imagination and deepening his or her perceptions, books may well work indirectly toward other good ends.

✓   ✓   ✓

One cannot expect ten Newbery books to form a readily discernible pattern, since each has been chosen separately in isolation from the rest. Actually the range of genres in the decade under review has been wide. Without going into too many classificatory niceties, it could be said that the winners include one straight historical novel (*I, Juan de Pareja*); one historical adventure-story (*The Slave Dancer*); one example of "high fantasy and heroic romance" (*The High King*); one humanized-animal fantasy with science-fictional overtones (*Mrs. Frisby and the Rats of NIMH*); two stories of real life which are set back to different degrees into the past but within present or recent memory (*Sounder* and *Up a Road Slowly*); three novels of contemporary life (*From the Mixed-Up Files of Mrs. Basil E. Frankweiler, Summer of the Swans,* and *M.C. Higgins, The Great*); and one hard-to-classify contemporary story of animals and people in relation to their environment (*Julie of the Wolves*).

Anyone who cares to arrange the ten books under different headings is welcome to do so; I have only classified them in order to indicate the breadth of the spread. It could also be noted that four of the books are concerned in varying ways with the black experience. And it must be recorded that, as she herself remarks without undue emphasis at the end of her acceptance speech, Virginia Hamilton is "the first black woman and black writer to have received this award."

Looking at the books in their order of publication, one could say that *I, Juan de Pareja*, 1966*, and *Up a Road Slowly*, 1967, are respectable, worthy books of a traditional award-winning kind: a survival, it might seem, from the previous decade. Juan de Pareja is the slave, son of a black woman and an unknown Spaniard, who finds himself in the service of the painter Velázquez, and who rises through his own loyalty and talent to be Velázquez's friend and fellow-artist. It is a reassuring story of virtue rewarded. Pareja is shown in words as Velázquez showed him in paint: a serious, dignified personage, a true Spaniard in spite of his origin. One might suspect that the book reflects in part a well-meant, but no longer acceptable, view of a black man as being a white man under the skin; for whom the brightest prospect is that of raising himself into acceptance by his former superiors. The main characters — Pareja, Velázquez, King Philip IV — all have a formal, oil-painting kind of dignity; one does not doubt the accuracy of the portraits, but they do not seem to move.

Up a Road Slowly is not so much a story as a progress — as indeed, in a different way, is the same author's *Across Five Aprils*. It traces the development of a girl called Julie from child to young woman. The book begins promisingly; Irene Hunt has a good ear, writes elegant prose, and creates some attractive characters, notably handsome Uncle Haskell, whose golf bag is full of bottles bearing "the English translation of *Le Vieux Corbeau*." And there is a sharply perceptive realism in the treatment of poor Aggie Kilpin, the child who smells and whom the other children loathe. Yet as the book goes

---

* The dates given are for the year of the award, not the year of publication.

on it is pervaded by a sweetness that eventually cloys. Stern Aunt Cordelia's heart of gold shines ever more brightly; Uncle Haskell redeems himself by starting Julie on a writing career; and in the end we have a girl who has grown up under wise and kind guidance into charming young ladyhood. Though not without faults, Julie seems at last just a little too good to be true, and so does the adult world in which she has won her place. That it is not *our* world is evident, and is not a just cause for complaint; but was the world ever quite like that?

To turn from *Up a Road Slowly* to *From the Mixed-Up Files of Mrs. Basil E. Frankweiler*, 1968, is to leap a generation gap. Here is the tone of voice of our own time; here, in Claudia, is a girl of cool idiosyncrasy who is never going to be slotted into an approved pattern. Claudia, considering that her family needs to be taught a lesson in Claudia-appreciation, runs away from home — not, as any child might, on a sudden wild impulse, but after careful planning. She takes with her as financial adviser her younger brother Jamie, who is suspiciously successful when playing cards with his contemporaries. Their refuge is not a cave nor tree-house nor beaten-up shack, but the Metropolitan Museum of Art in New York, no less. This is an elegantly paradoxical choice which gives great scope for the author's humor and inventiveness.

But there is more to it than that. Claudia is a child of advanced urban civilization, for whom the call of the wild holds no appeal. Yet she desperately needs to be different; to come back changed by her experiences. This need involves her in an attempt to discover whether a figure of an angel in the museum was actually carved by Michelangelo. It also brings her into contact with a rich, elderly collector, Mrs. Frankweiler, and Mrs. Frankweiler can see that

"Claudia doesn't want adventure. She likes baths and feeling comfortable too much for that kind of thing. Secrets are the kind of adventure she needs. Secrets are safe, and they do much to make you different. On the inside where it counts."

So Mrs. Frankweiler lets Claudia into a most satisfying secret about the statue. Clearly Claudia's adventures when she grows up are going to be late-twentieth-century adventures: adventures of the mind and sensibility. That is how she is different.

Mrs. Frankweiler plays a vital part, and has an important affinity with Claudia; it is quite likely that she herself is a Claudia grown elderly. She understands Claudia, and helps the reader to understand her. Yet the fact that Mrs. Frankweiler narrates the whole story, which she herself does not enter until near the end, seems to me to be a major structural flaw. Events are seen through Claudia's eyes, and information is given about Claudia's thoughts and feelings which Mrs. Frankweiler, however great her understanding, could hardly have had. In this case the first-person narration is a clumsy device that does not really work. And something must be said about the book's title, which I personally find too long and trendy to be tolerable.

Lloyd Alexander's *The High King*, 1969, must be considered as a single book to which the award was made; but it nevertheless is linked to the previous four books of Prydain. It presents the climax and conclusion of the long struggle between the Light and the Dark, represented by the Sons of Don and by the forces of Arawn, Lord of Annuvin. The hero, Taran, from humble beginnings as an Assistant Pig Keeper has become a companion in arms to Gwydion, war leader of the Sons of Don. In this last book, the Dark Lord Arawn is finally defeated in his own stronghold; Taran becomes High King of Prydain, and the Princess Eilonwy, for whom his love has grown throughout the five books, relinquishes a heritage of enchantment to be his queen. Taran has among his companions the bard Fflewddur Fflam, whose harpstrings break when (too frequently) he strays from the truth; the well-meaning but ineffectual Prince Rhun, who becomes King of Mona and who dies in this last book; and the faithful, hairy creature Gurgi, forever cherishing his poor tender head.

Lloyd Alexander has remarked that writers of heroic romance, "who work directly in the tradition and within the conventions of an earlier body of literature and legend, draw from a common source: the 'Pot of Soup,' as Tolkien calls it, the 'Cauldron of Story' which has been simmering away since time immemorial."* The story of Prydain is based largely on Wales and its legends. I have said elsewhere** that I cannot believe Lloyd Alexander has caught the true spirit of either. This unfortunately I still think to be the case. It is possible that I have not allowed sufficiently for the American-ness, the humor and satire of the Prydain books, and that their "true spirit" should not be expected to be that of ancient Wales. Prydain should be seen as Lloyd Alexander's own invented country rather than any that ever existed. He himself has observed that the personae of myth and fairy tale, "though gorgeously costumed and caparisoned, are faceless. The writer must fill in their expressions. Colorful figures in a pantomime, the writer must give them a voice."*** If this passage defines, in part, his aims, then perhaps it can be forgiven him that Prydain so often suggests a backdrop rather than a real three-dimensional landscape. Yet when every allowance has been made, one faces, reluctantly, the fact that the Prydain saga, with its constant anachronism, its slack repetitive action, its cast of two-dimensional figures and failure to compel serious belief, is not a satisfying epic; not, I believe, a front-rank work. *The High King*, however, is probably the best of the five books.

William H. Armstrong attributes the story of *Sounder*, 1970, to the gray-haired black man who taught him to read more than fifty years ago. Sounder is a great-coon dog belonging to a poor Negro sharecropper who steals food for his hungry children during a hard winter. The man is arrested, and Sounder is shot and dreadfully injured by the deputy sheriff; but although a mere wreck of a dog he holds on to life until his master's return, when, old and broken, both die. The story is told from the viewpoint of the eldest child, a boy, who, with his mother, keeps life going; the boy, through looking for his father, finds the beginnings of an education.

---

* Alexander, Lloyd, "High Fantasy and Heroic Romance," *The Horn Book Magazine*, December 1971, pp. 577-584.
** Townsend, John Rowe. *Written for Children*, Philadelphia and New York, Lippincott, 1975, p. 251.
*** Alexander, *op cit.*

The Bible is known to these people and is quoted several times; there is no other support available to them in their hardship. That they are poor, illiterate, without friends or advisers, is as significant as that they are black. They do not know what is happening; they are imprisoned by ignorance. The story itself has a Biblical simplicity and dignity. It is without malice; and the casual brutishness of the sheriff, his men and the jailer is more telling, more fearful too, than positive villainy would have been. It is not suggested that Sounder's master did not steal. That he did steal, in these circumstances, wins more sympathy and makes a deeper impression than a false accusation would have done. It is a painful story, but more inspiring than depressing, because people and dog are faithful to each other and undefeated by their oppressors. They endure. It is a kind of victory.

The author of *Sounder* has been accused of "white fundamentalism," stereotyping, and emasculation of the black. In an essay in *Interracial Books for Children*, Albert V. Schwartz referred to the fact that the members of the sharecropper's family are identified as the father, the mother, the boy, rather than by name.

"This [Professor Schwartz said] would be an acceptable device in the hands of a Black author. For a white author to resort to it immediately raises the issue of white supremacy. Within the white world, deep-seated prejudice has long denied human individualization to the Black person. . . . In *Sounder*, did the Black storyteller really narrate the story without names? Or was the unconscious racism of the white transcriber of the tale actively at work?"*

This comment seems to me, as I said in my book *Written for Children*,** to be obviously misguided. It must have been the author's intention that his characters should appear universal, not tied down to a local habitation and a name. His leaving them bleakly anonymous is in keeping with the elemental nature of his story.

---

* Schwartz, Albert V. "*Sounder*: a Black or White Tale?", *Interracial Books for Children*, Vol. III, No. 1, 1970. Reprinted in MacCann and Woodard, *The Black American in Books for Children*, New York, Scarecrow Press, 1972, pp. 89-93.

** Townsend, *op. cit.*

The Summer of the Swans, 1971, by Betsy Byars, is a contemporary story about fourteen-year-old ugly duckling Sara who takes "an enormous step up" from the shadows of her dissatisfied adolescence on the day when she helps to find her missing younger brother Charlie — a small boy who is retarded and a nuisance to her, but whom she loves more dearly than she had realized. The people in *The Summer of the Swans* are credible, tones of voice are accurately caught, and there is a frequent wry humor in the dialogue; but the book seems to me to be a slight one. True, the subject of mental retardation is serious and difficult; but I feel that *The Summer of the Swans* does little more than touch upon it — lightly, delicately, convincingly, but not substantially. Betsy Byar's beautiful and funny *The Midnight Fox* is, in my view, a more satisfying book.

Robert C. O'Brien's *Mrs. Frisby and the Rats of NIMH*, 1972, is based on the notion that laboratory rats might be raised to human levels of intelligence and given a vastly extended life-span. Obviously, if that happened they would not wish to remain in cages. How would they escape, how organize themselves, how cope with an environment planned by and for much larger creatures? Might their intellectual development be matched by a moral advance that would make them want to abandon the ways of rats and work for a living?

The author has some fascinating speculative material here. I am not sure that he makes the best use of it by telling the story, largely in retrospect, in the person of one of the rats involved; and by grafting it onto a more ordinary talking-animal story about a fieldmouse and her family whose home is threatened by the plow. The rats save Mrs. Frisby, the mouse, and she in turn serves and saves them. It seems to me that the fact that all the animals talk and behave intelligently from the beginning of the story detracts from the spectacular development of the laboratory rats; and I find that after three readings I do not remember any of the rats as characters (though I remember Mrs. Frisby and the aptly named cat Dragon, indeed a dragon as far as rats and mice are concerned). *Mrs.*

Frisby and the Rats of NIMH is a pleasing book, but I find it mildly frustrating; it might have been something more than it is.

Mr. O'Brien was concerned, while planning Mrs. Frisby, with "the seeming tendency of the human race to exterminate itself." A concern with pollution, self-destruction, the perils of upsetting the balance of nature was becoming widespread by this time; and in a different form was part of the theme of Jean Craighead George's *Julie of the Wolves*, 1973. This story, based on personal knowledge acquired in the Arctic on the ways of wolves, does not only pinpoint the threat to a much-maligned species; it looks at the possibilities of communication between people and animals, and shows a girl poised awkwardly between the oil-drum-and-snowmobile civilization of today's Alaska and the way of life of her Eskimo forebears:

"The old Eskimos were scientists too. By using the plants, animals, and temperature, they had changed the harsh Arctic into a home, a feat as incredible as sending rockets to the moon. . . . They had adjusted to nature instead of to man-made gadgets."

One is reminded of the animal stories of Ernest Thompson Seton and Charles G. D. Roberts; also to some extent of Scott O'Dell's *Island of the Blue Dolphins* and Mrs. George's own *My Side of the Mountain*. Julie (in Eskimo she is Miyax) learns through long months of Arctic survival, alone except for her friends of the wolf pack, that she is emotionally committed to the Eskimo way; yet at the end she is singing sadly, in her best English, that "the hour of the wolf and the Eskimo is over." The details of the girl's relationship with the wolves are totally absorbing, but as a story the book seems to me to be slightly deficient. Julie/Miyax is supposed to be running away toward San Francisco where her pen-friend lives; but I for one cannot quite believe in the pen-friend, who seems rather obviously a literary device to enhance the Julie-Miyax contrast and to get the girl out into the tundra on her own. One ceases at an early stage in the story to suppose that Julie will ever get anywhere near San Francisco.

The narrative is restrained almost to the point of bleakness. So far as human beings are concerned, *Julie of the Wolves* is essentially a one-character story; the people in it, other than Julie, are peripheral and glimpsed only briefly. This is not in itself a fault, but it presents an author with obvious difficulties which in the present book have not, I think, been surmounted. Julie remains curiously remote; it is hard to feel for and with her, to enter through her into the middle of things and live the story.

The last two books of this decade of Newbery winners are both remarkable. Both are concerned with aspects of black experience, but both are concerned with much more than that, and it is important to keep them in perspective. Paula Fox's *The Slave Dancer*, 1974, is a first-person narration by a boy called Jessie Bollier, who lives in New Orleans and plays the fife. He is pressed aboard a slave ship, on its way to pick up black cargo in exchange for rum. His job is to "dance" the slaves and thereby keep them in good physical condition to fetch a high price in the market. The horror of having human beings treated as expendable lumps of flesh is refracted through Jessie himself, seeing everything for the first time, and also through the hardened, casually-brutal crew. Miss Fox can see with a fearful perceptiveness how this decent boy will be driven to feel when his conscience cannot bear its burden any more:

"I hated the slaves! I hated their shuffling, their howling, their very suffering! I hated the way they spat out their food upon the deck, the overflowing buckets, the emptying of which tried all my strength. I hated the foul stench that came up from the holds no matter which way the wind blew, as though the ship itself were soaked with human excrement."

So does vileness on such a scale overwhelm even those who oppose it.

The *Moonlight* is wrecked — as indeed a slave ship of that name was wrecked in the Gulf of Mexico in 1840. Jessie and a black boy named Ras are the only survivors. Jessie makes his way home and lives out his life; but there is one memory that does not soften with time.

"I was unable to listen to music. . . . For at the first note of a tune or of a song, I would see once again as though they'd never ceased their dancing in my mind, black men and women and children lifting their tormented limbs in time to a reedy martial air, the dust rising from their joyless thumping, the sound of the fife finally drowned beneath the clanging of their chains."

In its superficial aspect, *The Slave Dancer* is a sea-adventure story; yet the true adventure of Jessie Bollier is a spiritual adventure into the most terrible depths of human nature.

Virginia Hamilton's *M.C. Higgins, The Great*, 1975, achieved the extraordinary triple-feat of winning the *Boston Globe-Horn Book* Award, the Newbery Medal, and the National Book Award. It is a difficult book if one tries to measure it with the traditional tools of rational analysis; easier if one takes it on its own terms, lets it go its own way, and tries to be receptive to its highly individual vibrations. Virginia Hamilton has said:

"In my own writing, I attempt to recognize the unquenchable spirit which I know exists in my race and in other races in order to re-discover a universality within myself. My assumption, of course, is that non-white, although different, is as essential as white — that non-white literature, defined through its diversity, is as American as white. The experience of a people does not exist for me merely in present time, nor in past or future, but in a time I appropriate from all of these . . . the experience of a people must come to mean the experience of humankind."*

M.C. Higgins, great-grandson of a slave, spends much of his time sitting on top of a forty-foot pole, halfway up a mountainside which is overhung by a dangerous spoil heap. M.C. Higgins is rough, rural, rooted — and yes, he is great; he will always take risks to ride high. To summarize in detail the action of the story — involving M.C.'s family, his friend Ben, Ben's family, a straying dude, a straying girl, an unlikely belief that M.C.'s mother will become a singing star — would be difficult, and would be pointless when done. The novel follows not a plot line, but what the British writer Jill Paton Walsh has called a trajectory — the emotionally-loaded path through the material.

---

* Hamilton, Virginia, "High John Is Risen Again," *The Horn Book Magazine*, April 1975, pp. 113-121.

At the end of the book, M.C. is staying put on the mountain-side and building a wall that may or may not hold back the spoil heap. What has happened in the story is partly a matter of relationships — people reacting upon each other; partly a matter of self-realization; partly a mystery which can be returned to at will. If one could unravel every strand of it, one wouldn't want or need to. As of this writing, *M.C. Higgins, The Great* is too large and still too close to be seen whole; the perspective of time is needed to discern its shape and its standing; but I should not be surprised if it emerged as being the nearest thing to a masterpiece to appear on the children's lists in its decade.

✦   ✦   ✦

The question whether the decade's Newbery awards offer a fair representation of "quality" publishing for children must, I think, be answered, "On the whole, yes." No sensible commentator would expect to find a list that fitted his own prescription exactly; everyone would agree that, with benefit of hindsight, it would be pleasant (though clearly impracticable) to reshape the list, remove the weaker titles, and bring in books that now seem to have been mistakenly passed over. No two people would agree on what books should be discarded or introduced.

For myself, I am sorry that Russell Hoban's *The Mouse and His Child*, Vera and Bill Cleaver's *Where the Lilies Bloom*, Ursula Le Guin's *A Wizard of Earthsea* and *The Tombs of Atuan* are not Newbery Medal-winners; and I would have preferred that Irene Hunt should be honored for *Across Five Aprils* and Betsy Byars for *The Midnight Fox*, rather than for the books which actually received the award. But we can all make complaints of this kind; we can all, and I dare say many of us do, form a private one-person Newbery-Caldecott Committee in our own heads.

It would not be a welcome development if the committee were suddenly to go overboard and start coming up with wild, way-out choices. But it can and should be expected to move with the times and not remain stuck in traditional grooves; and, encouragingly, there does seem to be a distinct movement away from the deserving but dull books that have sometimes been associated with literary awards; a growing readiness to look at books that are doing something new and different.

What inferences can be drawn about the state of American children's fiction? Here one has to move with great caution. It is noteworthy that the two Newbery winners, which, to me, have the most faded look are those which came at the beginning of the period, while the two best ones have come at the end. *The Slave Dancer* and *M.C. Higgins, The Great* are books of real distinction; and most of their recent predecessors, if not totally successful, have at least shown qualities of originality and of willingness to present interesting ideas and tackle difficult themes. A period of ten years is brief, and the processes by which books are generated are chancy and unorganized; it would be dangerous to suggest on such slight evidence that there is a clear improvement, or, if so, that it is likely to be permanent. But at least there are hopeful signs.

One lack is very evident in children's books generally (and, indeed, in the adult novel). That is the absence of fine, sustained comic writing. There is also a shortage of books that grip the reader and carry him or her along with the sheer impetus of the story. The power and importance of story ought never to be underrated. On the credit side, it is good to see fantasy of quality being produced and recognized in the United States, which for a long time has led the way in the realistic mode of children's writing, but has tended to lag behind in this field. *The Mouse and His Child*, *Mrs. Frisby and the Rats of NIMH*, and *A Wizard of Earthsea* are all well known and much admired on the other side of the Atlantic. Perhaps the most exciting book of all to find is the one like *M.C. Higgins, The Great* (and its predecessor, *The Planet of Junior Brown*) which, without being fantasy, transcends realism and, splendidly, makes its own rules.

The Caldecott Awards

1966-1975

Illustration by NONNY HOGROGIAN

From *Always Room for One More*

by SORCHE NIC LEODHAS
Published in 1965 by *Holt, Rinehart and Winston*
Awarded the 1966 Caldecott Medal

And then the whole lot of them stood at the door,
And merrily shouted, "There's room galore!
Now there will always be room for one more,
Always room for one more!"

Twenty-six percent reduction

SIZE: 7⅛" x 8¼", oblong, 32 pp. (unfolioed)

ARTIST'S MEDIUM: Three-color preseparated art,
line and halftone, using pen for black line;
chalk and wash for color

PRINTING PROCESS: Offset lithography

ILLUSTRATIONS: Colored endleaves; title page
and ten doublespreads in three colors

TYPE: Van Dyke

Illustration by EVALINE NESS

From *Sam, Bangs & Moonshine*

by EVALINE NESS

Published in 1966 by *Holt, Rinehart and Winston*

Awarded the 1967 Caldecott Medal

On a small island, near a large harbor, there once lived a fisherman's little daughter (named Samantha, but always called Sam), who had the reckless habit of lying.

Not even the sailors home from the sea could tell stranger stories than Sam. Not even the ships in the harbor, with curious cargoes from giraffes to gerbils, claimed more wonders than Sam did.

Forty-one percent reduction

SIZE: 7¾″ x 10″, vertical, 48 pp. (unfolioed)

ARTIST'S MEDIUM: Line and wash halftone

PRINTING PROCESS: Offset lithography

ILLUSTRATIONS: Printed endleaves; double-spread title page, fourteen doublespreads and four full pages in three colors

TYPE: Monophoto Bembo

Illustration by ED EMBERLEY

From *Drummer Hoff*

Adapted by BARBARA EMBERLEY
Published in 1967 by *Prentice-Hall*
Awarded the 1968 Caldecott Medal

Twenty-nine percent reduction

SIZE: 10 3/16″ x 7⅝″, oblong, 32 pp. (unfolioed)

ARTIST'S MEDIUM: Woodcuts

PRINTING PROCESS: Offset lithography, four-color process

ILLUSTRATIONS: Colored endleaves; 32 pages, including front matter, in color

TYPE: Caslon

The Fool of the World put on the fine clothes and stood there as handsome a young man as a princess could wish for a husband. He presented himself before the Czar, fell in love with the Princess and she with him, married her the

Illustration by URI SHULEVITZ

From *The Fool of the World and the Flying Ship*

A Russian Tale retold by ARTHUR RANSOME

Published in 1968 by *Farrar, Straus and Giroux*

Awarded the 1969 Caldecott Medal

same day, received with her a rich dowry, and became so
clever that all the court repeated everything he said. The
Czar and the Czaritza liked him very much, and as for the
Princess, she loved him to distraction.

Forty percent reduction

SIZE: 10⅜″ x 9″, oblong, 48 pp. (unfolioed)

ARTIST'S MEDIUM: Pen and brush with black
and colored inks

PRINTING PROCESS: Offset lithography, camera
separated in four colors

ILLUSTRATIONS: Printed endleaves; doublespread
title page, and doublespreads in full color
throughout

TYPE: Palatino; Palatino display

Illustration by WILLIAM STEIG

From *Sylvester and the Magic Pebble*

by WILLIAM STEIG

Published in 1969 by *Windmill / Simon and Schuster*

Awarded the 1970 Caldecott Medal

SIZE: 9″ x 12″, vertical, 32 pp. (unfolioed)

ARTIST'S MEDIUM: watercolor

PRINTING PROCESS: Offset lithography, four-
color process

ILLUSTRATION: Colored endleaves; title and 30
pages in color

TYPE: Caledonia

You can imagine the scene that followed — the em-
braces, the kisses, the questions, the answers, the loving
looks, and the fond exclamations!

Illustration by GAIL E. HALEY

From *A Story, A Story*

An African Tale retold by GAIL E. HALEY

Published in 1970 by *Atheneum*

Awarded the 1971 Caldecott Medal

He set the little doll at the
foot of a flamboyant tree where
fairies like to dance. Ananse
tied one end of a vine round
the doll's head and, holding
the other end in his hand,
he hid behind a bush.

In a little while, Mmoatia the
fairy-whom-no-man-sees came
dancing, dancing, dancing, to the
foot of the flamboyant tree.
There she saw the doll holding
the bowl of yams.

Thirty-seven percent reduction

SIZE: 10″ x 10″, square, 36 pp. (unfolioed)

ARTIST'S MEDIUM: Woodcuts

PRINTING PROCESS: Offset lithography, four-
color process

ILLUSTRATIONS: Colored endleaves; front matter
and fifteen doublespreads, one full page, in
color

TYPE: Century Expanded

Illustration by NONNY HOGROGIAN

From *One Fine Day*

by NONNY HOGROGIAN

Published in 1971 by *The Macmillan Company*

Awarded the 1972 Caldecott Medal

He saw a pail of milk that an old woman had set down
while she gathered wood for her fire. Before she noticed the fox,
he had lapped up most of the milk.

Thirty seven percent reduction

SIZE: 10″ x 8″, oblong, 32 pp. (unfolioed) plus
    endleaves

ARTIST'S MEDIUM: Oil paintings

PRINTING PROCESS: Offset lithography, four-
    color process

ILLUSTRATIONS: Printed endleaves; front matter
    and thirteen doublespreads and one full page
    in color

TYPE: Optima; Foundry Optima display

Illustration by BLAIR LENT

From *The Funny Little Woman*

Retold by ARLENE MOSEL

Published in 1972 by *E. P. Dutton*

Awarded the 1973 Caldecott Medal

"Hurt her! I should say not," said the wicked *oni*.
"I'm going to take her home and have her cook for
all of us."

"Tee-he-he-he," laughed the little woman, as the
wicked *oni* took her down the road to a wide river.
He put her into a boat and took her across the river
to a strange house.

Thirty-three percent reduction

SIZE: 9½" x 9", oblong, 40 pp. (unfolioed)

ARTIST'S MEDIUM: Pen and ink line drawings
combined with full color acrylic paintings

PRINTING PROCESS: Offset lithography, four-
color process

ILLUSTRATIONS: Front matter and twenty-nine
pages in color

TYPE: Palatino; Palatino Semi-Bold display

Illustration by MARGOT ZEMACH

From *Duffy and the Devil*

A Cornish Tale retold by HARVE ZEMACH

Published in 1973 by *Farrar, Straus and Giroux*

Awarded the 1974 Caldecott Medal

The one that looked like Jone gave the creature with the tail a swig of beer from time to time. Between times she scratched a tune on a fiddle, and the creature and the witches danced round the fire, faster and faster, swirling like the wind.

The squire watched it all gawk-eyed, until at last a feeling came over him of wanting to get in on the frolic. So he swung up his hat and his hunting staff, and let out a whoop: "Go to it, old devil, and witches all!"

Forty-seven percent reduction

SIZE: 8½″ x 10⅜″, vertical, 40 pp. (unfolioed)

ARTIST'S MEDIUM: Pen and ink drawings with watercolor

PRINTING PROCESS: Offset lithography, camera separated in four colors

ILLUSTRATIONS: Colored endleaves; front matter and illustrations in full color throughout

TYPE: Bembo; Chisel display

Illustration by GERALD McDERMOTT

From *Arrow to the Sun*

A Pueblo Indian Tale adapted by GERALD McDERMOTT

Published in 1974 by *The Viking Press*

Awarded the 1975 Caldecott Medal

Forty-two percent reduction

SIZE: 10⅝″ x 9½″, oblong, 40 pp. (unfolioed)

ARTIST'S MEDIUM: Gouache and ink, black line
preseparated

PRINTING PROCESS: Offset lithography, four-
color process

ILLUSTRATIONS: Printed endleaves; doublespread
title page, front matter, and eighteen doublespreads in full color

TYPE: Clarendon Semi-Bold

ALWAYS ROOM FOR ONE MORE

illustrated by NONNY HOGROGIAN

adapted by SORCHE NIC LEODHAS *from an old Scottish folk song*

published by HOLT, RINEHART AND WINSTON   1965

BOOK NOTE

The expansiveness of Lachie MacLachlan who invites all passers-by during stormy weather into his wee house in the heather, even though it is already crammed full with his wife and ten bairns, is also caught in the exuberance of Nonny Hogrogian's black-line figures. The tinker, the tailor, the sailor, the fisher lass, the shepherd, the merry wife and the four peat-cutters all crowd in and forget the weather as the piper pipes till they dance the house down. But after they've done with their blether over such a catastrophe, they shout, "For Lachie MacLachlan, his wife and bairns, we'll raise up a bonny new house." Since the house they raise up is bigger and better, "the whole lot of them stood at the door, and merrily shouted, 'There's room galore. Now there will always be room for one more!'" The original inspiration for this version of Lachie's story was an old Scottish song; the music for which is included in the book.

The frolic of the rhythmic verse is emphasized by the artist's use of movement and space in each doublespread. A tonal background of heathery purple and green against a murky sky holds the lively figures onto the page. The figures were done in pen-and-ink line and a cross-hatch technique. The gray wash for the sky was dabbed on with paper napkins, and the purple heather and green fields were done with pastels.

Caldecott Award Acceptance

by NONNY HOGROGIAN

When I told my sister the news of the Caldecott Award she dropped the telephone. My mother was speechless for at least two minutes, and various friends reacted with similar surprise. Their surprise was nothing compared with my state of shock following my telephone call from Mrs. Crossley.

The shock was soon replaced with glee, and for a long time after there was always room for another celebration or interview or speech, and my work habits "dinged down" like the house in the heather.

The sobering moment came with the arrival of a package of copies of *Always Room for One More* that I had ordered for friends. I spent a time examining the book to try to understand why it has received such enthusiastic approval, and after re-reading it, I realized that I could not miss with such a beautiful manuscript.

From my first encounter with her work, I have been a fan of Sorche Nic Leodhas, and I have enjoyed illustrating her books enormously, especially since recovering from my first brief failure with *Gaelic Ghosts*. I take great pride in doing careful research, and when Miss Nic Leodhas informed me that the bone structure of my first Scotsman was more like that of a Roumanian than that of a Scot, I was crushed. Taking a new look at my art work, I realized that he was perhaps a touch more Armenian than either Scot or Roumanian, and I promised myself that I would never make a mistake like that again. I began to study photographs of Scottish people with great care, and spent a while staring at the bone structure of a friend who hails from the Highlands. I hope he was not too uncomfortable. The result was a beautiful working relationship with my author, an author without whom I would not be standing here today.

After the publication of *Always Room for One More*, I received a lovely letter from her, in which she said that I "seemed to sense her very mood." How could I not sense it when she conveyed it so beautifully? She caught the essence of sharing and turned it into poetry. And I, joyfully, was able to add it to my own dimensions for a child's world. As soon as I began to read about the lovely people who filled that "wee house in the heather," my head danced with images and I could hardly wait to get to my drawing table. There was some preliminary work, all of it enjoyable: time spent in the library finding pictures of the clothes that Lachie and his friends might wear (I found costumes for all but two, the fishing lass and the gallowglass, and the author graciously supplied descriptions of them); an evening with my Scottish friend poring over slides of the cottages on the isle of South Uist to find one with a but and a ben; and an afternoon at Korvette's buying a couple of Ewan MacColl records that would help transport me to the Scotland that I have known only through words and music.

The next step was to capture the spirit of the song. Woodcuts, long my favorite medium, were too strong for the gentle folk in the heather. So I pulled out my water colors and chalks, some ink and a pen, and before long, in an almost effortless way, the drawings seemed to flow. Miss Nic Leodhas had set the mood. The rest was easy.

It is doubly nice to receive the Caldecott Medal for a book which in itself was so gratifying that it hardly seemed like work at all.

I would like to thank Mr. Melcher, Mrs. Crossley, and the Newbery-Caledcott committee for this great honor.

I thank my family and friends for their encouragement, Elizabeth Riley for the first push, all of the many people at Holt who were responsible for turning our work into a lovely book, Scribners for bearing with me through the last few months, and all of you for giving me and sharing with me my happiest of days.

Nonny Hogrogian

by JOHN PAUL ITTA

Nonny isn't short for anything. Nonny is Nonny.

She is of average height and average weight, and that is where her averageness ends. Her face, her hands, her movements, as she walks and even as she sits silently working, be it on a woodcut, drawing, or painting, are quite distinctive. Or, to put it another, more meaningful way, if you met her once, you would be likely to remember her for a long time. At least that was my experience.

I met Nonny years ago when I was a student at Columbia. I have only a vague memory of the circumstances of the meeting. It seems to me it was fall, or some other time of year when the sky above takes on the same color as the soot-soaked limestone around Morningside Heights and little patches of green make you especially self-conscious about the campus, or lack of it, when visitors come. Nonny and two friends of mine were walking from Lowe Memorial to Butler Library when I bumped into them. Nonny and I were introduced, and I joined them for a stroll across the Quadrangle. I remember that my friends and I chattered away. And that Nonny hadn't said any more than hello. And I remember, as I prepared to take my leave of them, turning to Nonny and asking her specific questions in an effort to know her better. But again, her answers were in words of one syllable.

I walked away feeling a little uneasy. For though she had hardly uttered a word, she had said a great deal. With her face.

I couldn't interpret it well then. But I knew that she was commenting on everything. Little comments, reflected in a tilt of the head, a turn of the lower lip, a funny little muscle moving in her lower right cheek. Of course none of these physical reactions is unique to Nonny. But you are far more keenly aware of them in her because they destroy the startling symmetry of her face. And because they divert you from the steady stare of her eyes — large, dark and as perfectly matched as the handiwork of an ancient Armenian or Assyrian stonecutter. Imagine the full lips on one of those bas-reliefs curling up for just a split second, then resuming their eternal expression, and you have the picture, only slightly exaggerated, of what might well be your impression following a first meeting with Nonny.

Naturally, I remembered her when we met a few years later. As we grew to know each other, I was not too surprised to discover, on the one hand, that Nonny is extremely articulate and, on the other, that she is as far removed from that ancient bas-relief as you would expect the woman to be whose book was featured in Scribner's Fifth Avenue window last February.

Nonny likes music, books, movies, walking, ice-cream cones (which she is allergic to, but eats anyway), big parties, cooking (which she says she has forgotten how to do, but her apple-sauce cake and pheasant say she hasn't), olives (her favorite food), sewing, the mountains and the seashore, big cities and little towns, traveling, exotic foods, and lots of other little things that many other people like.

She does not like pushy saleswomen, deadlines (she is always on them), participating in sports, driving cars, ugly modern architecture (like the Pan Am building), nationalists, subways and other places where people are hemmed in, people who shout at children in public, being pressured or put on the spot regarding her feelings about things. Like most sensitive people, she pays great attention to the shadings.

Her life revolves primarily around her work and secondarily

around a few individuals: her niece, her sister, her parents, and a few close friends. Their comfort and feelings occupy much of her time and thoughts. And though she is not the kind of person who would carry a bowl of chicken soup across the city when one of these people is sick, her patience and desire to help and please them know no limits.

This past Christmas, for instance, she gave birds — exquisite, jewel-like, fantastically imaginative birds, painted in colors that make nature look dull, chose beautiful old frames for them, wrapped them in delicate Japanese hand-blocked papers, and presented them to her coterie of friends.

We were all together at the time. And Nonny insisted that it did not matter who got which. But she was careful about choosing a particular package for each person, and I couldn't help noticing little differences between the designs.

In mentioning a coterie of friends, I hope no Proustian images come to mind. For Nonny is not at all like the Duchesse, who tolerated people as long as they could amuse her — as long as they remained within her highly arbitrary standards of obeisance and aloofness. Far from it. Nonny's friends are for the most part rather complicated people. Or perhaps it would be more accurate to say that they are sensitive people, aware of complications in the world. Not that any of them would get on a soapbox about anything in Nonny's presence. She would abhor it and, I am certain, remove herself quickly from the scene. Though I have seen Nonny in countless situations that would provoke paroxysms from many other people, she rarely exhibits any extremes of emotion. At the sight of a mouse, she becomes terrified, but it is a terror that freezes rather than one that unleashes hysteria. When a sales clerk tries to tell Nonny what she should buy, Nonny quietly insists on seeing what she wants and quietly leaves if it does not appear. She faces most frustrating situations with a Griselda-like patience. Sometimes her patience is rewarded. Sometimes it isn't. But that's life. And that's Nonny.

Though I don't know her family well, their home, as felt in a dozen visits to it, is filled with a gentleness and tranquillity that

I can only characterize as extremely civilized. They are happy people, at peace with life. And whereas one tends to think that artists pursue their call against many odds, such does not seem to be the case with Nonny. Her mother dabbled in painting when Nonny was a child. Her sister was an interior designer before she married. Her father to this day copies Renoir, Homer, Monet and others. (Surely there is no greater expression of love for painting than this!) You can easily imagine, therefore, what a congenial atmosphere the Hogrogian household must have provided for the budding young artist in its midst.

Her present surroundings, the ones in which almost all her books took shape, are deceptively simple. In her three and a half rooms are, among many smaller treasures, a great Dunbar chair covered in nubby blue, an eighteenth-century hiredman's bed, which she uses as a sofa, Knoll dining chairs, a Tanier teak dining table, an unornate Spanish chest which serves as a coffee table. Eclectic, individual, and very tasteful.

The backdrop to this apartment is the Russian Church across the street. Six cupolas, leading up to a dominant seventh, complete with tracery, cherubs, della Robbian-blue tiles, and pigeons. The only view that I know to equal it is the one from the Campanile, looking down on Saint Mark's Cathedral. Of course, the cupolas there are golden. And there are two orchestras in the Piazza below. But Nonny has plenty of imagination. And a great stereo set. And I have seen a misty look in her eyes when she stands by that window.

Nonny pensive at the window, however, is not a frequent sight. The more typical Nonny is looking through the window of her imagination at the evocative pictures that will grace the pages of her books.

Let me tell you what it was like to visit Nonny as she worked on *Always Room for One More.*

Get off the elevator at the fifth floor. Follow the strains of Scottish music — Robert Burns ballads or nippy songs from the Jacobite Wars, providing a cadence for every stroke of Nonny's pen. Ring the bell and wait. There's Nonny, in slacks and a turtle-neck sweater. You see her for a moment; then she's back at the drawing table finishing what you had interrupted, surrounded by studies of odd people with turned-up noses and wispy hair. Books about Scotland lie open on the floor. She puts down her brush and, without turning, asks, "Look at the heather tones — aren't they beautiful? I hope they will do a decent job of reproducing them." Now she turns to you and smiles devilishly. "Would you like some coffee? And some of my mother's cookies! Or would you rather have my Cousin Zaza's chocolate cake?" She knows I'll take both, along with the coffee, and, of course, her delightful asides on the whys and wherefores of her art.

I'm no kid. But I love those drawings. Just as everyone must.

SAM, BANGS & MOONSHINE

illustrated by EVALINE NESS

written by EVALINE NESS

published by HOLT, RINEHART AND WINSTON 1966

BOOK NOTE

This is a story of imagination, or moonshine, and its consequences, as the fisherman's little daughter, Samantha, learns that her tall tales can lead to real trouble. Her young friend Thomas believes it when she tells him she has a baby kangaroo, especially as she sends him everywhere to look for it. When Thomas nearly drowns during a storm as the high tide maroons him on Blue Rock, Sam has to admit to her father just how her imagination has gone astray.

The illustrations make the most of the theme of moonshine versus real through contrast. The figures of Sam, Thomas, Bangs her cat, and her fisherman father are dramatically dark in tone; while the backgrounds of houses, boats, harbor and lighthouse, or mermaid and lion and chariot-pulling dragons are lighter in tone. The artist prepared the work for the black plate with a Japanese pen and wash. The color overlays were done with printer's ink and a rubber roller to achieve the desired texture.

Caldecott Acceptance Speech

by EVALINE NESS

When Augusta Baker called me last January from New Orleans to tell me that I had been awarded the Caldecott Medal, I said, "Wow!" That comment indicates my ready talent as a writer. But since I think of myself as an artist who happens to write, I will get on with the art part.

When I was a child, my interest in art barely revealed itself. My gift then consisted of cutting pictures from magazines to illustrate my older sister's stories, which she wrote profusely and which I admired greatly. (There was always a heroine named Dulcie, trapped in a castle.)

My next attempt as an artist was in high school. The art director of the year book turned down the drawings I submitted.

In my first year of college my muse appeared in the form of of a gentle, middle-aged alcoholic, who had fallen from the position of a top illustrator in Chicago to a photo retoucher in the small college town. He told me that he knew a girl who was a shoe artist and that she was paid five dollars a drawing. To me, this sounded like unheard-of wealth! It took me one second to decide that that was the career for me.

Instead of returning to college the following year, I went to the Chicago Art Institute, where I enrolled in the fine arts department (not knowing the difference between fine arts and commercial art) and studied for two years. During that time I did not learn how to draw shoes, at least any that would sell, and I have not since.

But I did meander into fashion drawing, advertising art, and magazine illustration. The money was lavish, but the strain of short deadlines was terrible. So I took occasional sabbaticals for more study. There were two years at the Corcoran School of Art in Washington, D. C., two more years in Rome at the Accademia di Belle Arti, and little jaunts to the Art Students League in New York.

About nine years ago Mary Silva Cosgrave, who was then children's book editor at Houghton Mifflin Company, asked me if I would illustrate a children's book. I was interested until I heard that the dole was only five hundred dollars with royalties. Royalties! What were they? Certainly not *real* money. And who promised that the book would sell? A risky business. I said no.

But Mary persisted (I will be grateful to her forever for that) and came up with a beautiful story that I wanted to illustrate regardless of those mythical royalties — *The Bridge* by Charlton Ogburn, Jr. During the months of work on the book, I realized the same kind of peace and enjoyment that comes when I paint for myself. There were no changes, no picking at details, no hot breath on my neck because of a deadline, which in advertising is always yesterday. Added to that I worked with a superb art director, Walter Lorraine. It was heaven and I did not want to leave. I was hooked.

After that I accepted almost every manuscript sent to me by publishers. Each one was a new exciting experience. The limitation of color separation, called overlay, fascinated me. In this process each color is drawn or painted in black on a separate paper and the color is indicated in writing for the printer. The name of that game is how to maintain freedom within a limitation. Because printer's ink is flat, my main concern was how to get texture into that flatness.

Some of the methods I have used are woodcut, serigraphy, rubber-roller technique (too complicated to explain here), scratching through black paint on acetate, ink splattering, and sometimes just spitting. Anything goes.

The day that Nancy Quint, at that time children's book editor at Charles Scribner's Sons, called to ask me to illustrate a book, I had just finished a series of woodcuts of Haiti. Nancy suggested that I write a story around these. I did, with enormous help from her. The story was *Josefina February*. Margaret Evans, the art director, designed an elegant book which enhanced my illustrations.

Nancy supported me through four more books that I wrote and illustrated; then she decided to have a baby and quit her job. I was furious! How *could* she think that was more important than being my prop! I hope that the baby has enough sense to realize how lucky he is to have Nancy editing him.

Meantime, over at the Holt, Rinehart and Winston ranch, I had been having some wonderful times working with Ann Durell, who is a rarity.

And this brings me right up to *Sam, Bangs & Moonshine*. One day when I was looking through a portfolio in which I keep drawings I make for no reason at all, I found one of a ragged, displaced-person little girl who was quietly ecstatic over a starfish. In the same portfolio were drawings of fishing boats.

Before I did another thing I telephoned Ann. Busy as she was (and always is), she came to lunch and stayed all afternoon and we talked. We talked about things, both nice and naughty, that we remembered as children.

I remembered me as a liar and a profitable one. My lies had a way of coming true. Three of them got me a piano, a telephone, and ballet lessons.

If I was a liar then, I am a thief today. I steal anything that will help me to resolve a piece of art: sunlight falling across a half-finished drawing, a dirty fingerprint, knots in wood, accidents like spilled ink, broken pens, ripped paper. Even the muddy water I rinse my brushes in can be the answer to a color problem.

Anyway, the shabby misplaced child of my drawing became Sam, who told lies. And what else could she be except a fisherman's daughter, with all those drawings of boats handy? I added the cat because I have a live one to draw from, and I decided to put Thomas under a racy bicyclist's cap I had seen in a photograph. The baby kangaroo got into the story because of a newspaper article. A child had written home from camp saying, "We got gerbils." (The parents were certain that the camp had been stricken by a new and horrible contagious disease.)

I really cannot tell you *how* I wrote the story. All I know is that I sat at the typewriter for four days and nothing happened. On the fifth day it struck.

I sent the story to Ann immediately because she believes a story should stand on its own without illustrations. When she gave me her approval, with suggestions for valid changes, I had a story. But the worst was yet to come: illustrating it!

For some reason or other illustrating my own stories is torture. For days before I start, I generally mutter thoughts such as, "Why in heaven's name did I accept *this* book to do?" and "If the editor thinks it's so important for a story to stand on its own, why not let it stand?" All this, while I do what I call maid's work. I put my bureau drawers in order. I decide to redecorate my apartment. I read minutely the travel section of the newspaper. I get out my sewing machine and make a new suit which I don't need.

Then the art director closes my escape valves. She sends me galleys (text set in type) and the dummy (paper folded into the size and amount of pages the book will be). Actual creative art work can still be put off until I have cut up the galleys and pasted them into the dummy, leaving blank spaces for the illustrations. When this is finished I always think it would be a good idea to publish the book as it is and let the children do their own illustrating. No one agrees with me.

The day that I actually produce my first illustration is the day that I stop muttering and start humming. I am involved. The book will be finished.

Months go by before the first bound book arrives. I have almost forgotten it. So much else has been in the works since then. I open it with a cold and critical eye. I look at all the unsuccessful parts first. This may sound like a negative action, but to me it is positive. I am not interested in what succeeded because that is a *fait accompli*. Things undone and unresolved are my loving antagonists, my agents who keep open paths that lead me to new experiments and experiences — forever expanding and always infinite.

Since receiving the Caldecott Award, I have become fully aware of the professional talent at Holt, Rinehart and Winston, without which *Sam, Bangs & Moonshine* would not have been a reality.

Dear Mr. Edwards, thank you for having the perceptive good taste to hire all that talent.

Muttering again, I ask rhetorical questions: How could I have started the book without Ann Durell's subtle editing or finished it without Jane Byers Brierhorst's impeccable art directing? Where could it have gone without the inexhaustible energy of Beverly Bond in publicizing it and of the salesmen in selling it? And how in the world could this little book have been seen by thousands of children without its acceptance by librarians all over the country?

The biggest words in my vocabulary are thank you. But they seem pitiful when I try to tell all you librarians how happy I am, and will always be, because you found my book worthy of the Caldecott Medal.

Evaline Ness

by ANN DURELL

On a small island, near a large harbor, there once lived a fisherman's little daughter (named Samantha, but always called Sam), who had the reckless habit of lying.

On a small island, near a large harbor, there now lives an artist (named Evaline, but generally called Eve) who has illustrated thirty children's books, some of which she has written herself and one of which has won this year's Caldecott Medal. She is Evaline Ness, and her sun-filled apartment on the island of Manhattan overlooks the East River, where, like Sam, she can see ships with strange cargoes. Like Sam, she tells stories, but hers are put into books for children!

Her father was not a fisherman but a photographer and later a carpenter in Pontiac, Michigan, where she grew up, although she was born in Union City, on the street that divides the Ohio half of the town from the Indiana side. She belongs by birthright to Ohio, but it is perhaps symbolic of the nomadic pattern of her later life that she was practically born in two states at once. The Michelow family — with two sisters and a brother, all older — moved to Pontiac when Evaline was two years old.

Her mother, like the one in *Exactly Alike*, sewed "for the ladies of the town," and Evaline loved clothes and sewing. She still does. She and her closest sister, Josephine, played endless games with the paper dolls they cut out of old copies of *Elite* magazine. Life for these elegant paper ladies, Dulcie, Gloria, Constance, and Consuelo (after the Duchess of Marlborough) was a constant round of changing from negligees to shopping clothes to evening costumes to keep up with the elaborate and varied social engagements invented by their imaginative sponsors. There were also "penny dolls," tiny china dolls with painted faces. Evaline's had one hundred dresses, all carefully sewed and hemmed as well. Even her cat did not escape this passion for dressing up: she made him hats and dresses and wheeled him in her doll carriage. He must have been an unusually cooperative cat, as understanding of a little girl as his imaginary descendant Bangs.

Evaline did not start drawing until she was in high school, but she did "illustrate" by cutting pictures out of magazines and pasting them into her sister's books. The oldest sister, Eloise, was a milliner, and Evaline was enchanted by the long rolls of strong white paper that came from the ribbons used to trim hats. She would spend hours copying stories onto the rolls, and blank paper has never ceased to have an irresistible appeal, from the sketch books that opened out like an accordion that she once found in Japan (particularly pleasing because they reminded her of the ribbon paper!) to the blank books provided by her publisher in which she lays out her illustrations.

The first picture she can remember drawing was an exact copy in pastels of a picture of a ship in a Sears Roebuck catalogue. "I was so proud of it! I couldn't understand why the people I showed it to didn't think it was marvelous too. It wasn't until a long time later that I realized the difference between art and copying." Her talent for drawing continued to be dormant all through high school. She worked summers and part time after school in the children's room of the public library, and her ambition to be a librarian was inspired by Miss Adah Shelley, a librarian whom she dearly admired.

When she was graduated from high school a term early in January, she went to work full time at the library and saved enough money to take a course in library work at Chautauqua, New York.

A promising recruit was lost to the profession, however, by one of the odd chances of fate that she says have affected her destiny all her life: she was told she would have to wear stockings (which sounded stuffy), and a fellow student named Rosalie, whose mother had decreed she would have to live at home in Muncie, Indiana, and attend Ball State Teachers College, asked Eve to live at her house and go there too. So she decided to become a teacher. But again fate stepped in, this time in the form of a commercial artist who told her about a girl he knew who got five dollars for a drawing of shoes. Feeling after a year at the teachers college that she was not cut out to be a teacher, she made up her mind instead to go to Chicago and study art.

Finances were a major barrier, and it was Josephine, who with her seniority of five years had steadily cut a path ahead of Evaline as an outstanding student (Robert Frost wrote her a letter when she had a course with him at the University of Michigan asking her to be sure never to stop writing), who made the move possible by using her own assured standing to get a loan for tuition at the Chicago Art Institute. A job at the architectural library at the Institute paid the rent; modeling paid for the food. Not realizing that the name of the shoe-drawing game was "commercial art," Eve enrolled as a fine arts student (painting, life, anatomy) but took a night course in dress designing because she liked it.

After two years at the Institute, she left and got a job in a fashion studio, a kind of talent pool that produced drawings for all kinds of fashion advertising. Here she modeled, ran errands, and finally got a break, drawing children's fashions for a department-store account. It is probably significant that drawings of children were her entree into making a living as an artist.

New York was the mecca for fashion artists, however, and

after three years at the studio, she made a move there. But since New York was not exactly agog for this particular fashion artist, she kept going by modeling. In New York she met Eliot Ness, then safety director for the city of Cleveland under the reform mayor Harold Burton. She became Evaline Ness and pursued her career in Cleveland, a career that like many, many others was interrupted by the Second World War. Mr. Ness went to Washington as a dollar-a-year man. Although the job he had taken — breaking up centers of vice to protect the servicemen stationed in various cities — entailed a great deal of traveling, they managed to find an apartment in Washington (no easy feat in the war years) and made that their head-quarters. And Eve went to art school at the Corcoran Gallery. This, she feels, was the breakthrough that really shaped her as an artist. She had a brilliant teacher, Richard Lahey, who, with most of his brillant students off to the wars, had all the time possible to recognize and develop the talent that was waiting to flower into artistry. For two years she studied painting and drawing with intensity: the first year she won first prize in painting and also had a painting accepted in the Bi-Ennial (a big American show held every two years in Washington). Lahey gave her a studio separate from the classroom where she could work (and did) after the school closed at four in the afternoon and on Saturdays.

At the National Gallery she passionately absorbed the work of the French Impressionists (Ben Shahn is her favorite "living artist," her other two are Degas and Vuillard); the paintings had been sent from France as a safety measure and "they were there. They were all mine."

It was also in Washington that she got her first taste of book illustration: she entered a competition and did a series of paint-ings for *Look Homeward, Angel* by Thomas Wolfe. She did not win the contest, but she used the pictures as samples when she moved to New York and started free-lancing, after she and Eliot Ness were divorced. And she got the break which started her on her next phase — magazine illustration. *Seventeen* magazine used her illustrations for a story. "All it took was one. The phone started ringing, and there I was in the big time." Almost too big, for she was doing advertising art and fashion drawing for Saks Fifth Avenue as well, and the pressure was enormous. She felt she needed to find painting again and could not in New York, despite the fact that she kept studying at the Art Students League (she was to do that for years whenever her pattern pulled her back to the city).

She decided to go to live in Bangkok where she had friends. Oriental art had always fascinated her; she felt she would find what she needed in the East. Absorbing as she moved, she went the slow way, by the Philippines, Japan, Hong Kong, Taiwan, Saigon. But Bangkok was a disappointment. "It was too small, too social. I couldn't work. And I found I needed Western culture. Oriental culture was so completely alien to me at that time. There was no point of contact, much as I love Japanese and Chinese art in itself."

Like many artists before her, she went to Italy and settled down to study at the Accademia di Belle Arti in Rome, for the two years that seem to have formed a ritual pattern in her life as an art student. She and Rome got along just fine; she loved the Italians, because "they will cheat themselves rather than be rude," although she found this exquisite courtesy had drawbacks. The Accademia was in an ancient building with stone floors, and in winter her feet were agonizingly cold, so, many years ahead of the Paris fashion pundits, she decided boots were the answer and took a pattern for what she wanted to a shoemaker, who politely agreed to make them for her. Winter turned into spring, and whenever she went to collect her boots, the answer was that they would be ready tomorrow. She finally realized that he had no idea of how to make them, but could not bear to hurt her feelings by saying so.

But, sympathetic as she found Italy, she could not at first free herself of the fashion-art syndrome. Unable to paint, she cast about for some medium to free her by chaining her, by presenting a set of technical impositions that would force her to get away from the automatic techniques of what she had been doing. She took some cloth she had picked up in the

Philippines and some yarn and started to do a tapestry. The result was a collection of tapestries worthy of a very successful one-man show when her pattern again finally pulled her back to New York — to more commercial art; to more work at the Art Students League, where she studied woodcutting, lithography, etching; to a call from Mary Silva Cosgrave, who asked her to illustrate *The Bridge* by Charlton Ogburn, Jr. And Evaline Ness entered the world of children's books. Once her work had appeared it was inevitable that the phone should again start ringing, summoning her into this world, and that the manuscripts should start arriving from publishers.

She found the new field altogether satisfactory. The technical demands of modern reproduction did, and still do, for her what the tapestry did for her once in Italy. The serigraphy (a silk-screen technique) she had studied in Oakland, during a San Francisco sojourn between Rome and New York, could come into play, as could everything else she had learned along the way. Study her illustrations and you will find it all — painting, drawing, the endless sketching that filled far more than the Japanese fold-out sketchbook, woodcuts, the quick sure lines of fashion art, tapestry textures — transmuted into her own distinctive style by her need to achieve a particular effect. The art work she prepares for the printer is endlessly fascinating. I asked her once how she got a particular texture effect in *Sam, Bangs & Moonshine* and after a frown of concentration she remembered she had used an inked roller and a wad of string.

So also is everything grist for her writing mill, for which the stones grind very slowly and painfully. She loves and collects words and reads constantly; Vladimir Nabokov and Anthony Powell are her favorite writers. But she finds writing extremely hard work, and there is a great sigh of relief when she and her editor finally decide a story is just right, and she can plunge into illustrating, at which she works in a white heat once she gets started. The things that go into her stories can come from anywhere (a clipping from a Japanese newspaper that her husband, Arnold Bayard, sent her gave her the idea for *Double Discovery* but mostly come out of her own head.

At present, she is taking another one of her "freeing sabbaticals" — this time to "paint things no one else may ever see." While I was at her apartment talking to her about this article, she had a call from an artist friend from whom she wanted information about collage, a technique in which she plans to experiment. The sun poured in the windows, her Siamese cat Nicky made demanding noises, and I sat comfortably and sipped my coffee and watched Eve talking and listening, her voice and face reflecting that vivid intentness which is one of her most outstanding characteristics. I remembered the same expression when I sat in the same apartment and we talked about a little girl named Sam.

I hope it is not true that no one will ever see those collages.

DRUMMER HOFF

illustrated by ED EMBERLEY

adapted by BARBARA EMBERLEY *from a folk verse*

published by PRENTICE-HALL 1967

BOOK NOTE

With the repetitive refrain, "But Drummer Hoff fired it off!", this succinct verse tells how each soldier brings part of the cannon, *Sultan*; then the powder, the rammer and the shot; till at last the general himself brings the order to fire it off. The consequences of the firing are as vivid as the colors printed throughout the book. This very free adaptation was inspired by a folk verse called "John Ball Shot Them All" found in the *Annotated Mother Goose* by William S. and Ceil Baring-Gould.

The woodcut technique used by the artist for the strong black line of the illustrations goes back to the very earliest means of book illustration in black-and-white. However, the sophisticated concept of this book as a whole, and the brilliance of the color, go far beyond the primitive appeal of a simple woodcut.

Caldecott Award Acceptance

by ED EMBERLEY

It was a cold, snowy evening back in January when I received a person-to-person call from Florida. We were entertaining some of our friends, so that in the confusion I missed some of the first part of the conversation. The part I did get was the name Mae Durham. . . . We've met . . . California. . . . I thought to myself . . . Mae Durham . . . Mae Durham. Who is Mae Durham? Then I heard, "I thought you would like to know that *Drummer Hoff* has been chosen as the Caldecott Medal book for 1968." This news came as such a surprise that the only thing I could think of to say was "How do you know?" Needless to say, since then I have found out who Mae Durham is and how she knew.

I am, of course, honored, delighted, grateful — and petrified, — to be up here speaking to you tonight.

Since the announcement of the Caldecott Award, my wife, Barbara, and I have often been asked about the preparation of *Drummer Hoff*. How was the technique developed? What steps were taken to turn a simple folk rhyme into a picture book? How does the adaptation differ from the original? And, surprisingly, what does it mean?

The drawings in *Drummer Hoff* are woodcuts. They were drawn on pine boards, all the white areas were cut away, ink was rolled on the remaining raised areas, and a set of prints was pulled on rice paper. The colors were added by using a technique I first tried in *One Wide River to Cross*. Although only three inks were employed — red, yellow, and blue — we were able to create the impression of thirteen distinct colors. This effect was accomplished by taking advantage of the fact that the inks with which most picture books are printed tend to be transparent. Therefore, by printing one ink over another, or "overprinting," a third color is made. For instance, if blue ink is printed over yellow ink, the yellow ink shows through and turns the blue ink green. Blue ink printed over red makes purple, and so forth. A separate drawing has to be made for each of the three colors, to show which color went over which color to make what color.

Since both the method of making the black line drawings and the method of coloring them seem unnecessarily complicated and time consuming, you may properly ask: Why bother? Why didn't you just draw the pictures instead of carving them and then just color them with water colors and send them to the printer?

Why I cut the pictures in wood instead of using a faster method like pen-and-ink drawings is hard to explain in a few words, but I suppose the most important reasons are that the pictures looked better and the method pleased me. It is easier to explain why we decided to use that particular method of printing the color. The sharpness and brilliance of the color in *Drummer Hoff* cannot be duplicated by any other practical printing process, including any "four color-full color" process.

You may have guessed by now that there is more to illustrating a picture book than knowing how to draw pictures. To an illustrator the picture on the drawing board is merely a means to an end. The end is the printed picture. An illustration could be defined as a picture that can be printed. A good picture is a bad illustration if it cannot be printed well.

And, of course, a bad picture is a bad picture no matter how well suited it is to the printing process.

I work in many different techniques when preparing illustrations — woodcuts, pencil, pen and ink. But as varied as they are in appearance they have one thing in common — the illustrations are meant to be printed. Although I am primarily an artist and not a printing expert, the necessity to be both dreamer and realist is what fascinates me most about picture-book making.

The original rhyme from which *Drummer Hoff* was evolved came from the *Annotated Mother Goose* by William S. and Ceil Baring-Gould. Entitled "John Ball Shot Them All," the verse, which was about the making of a rifle, read as follows:

> John Patch made the match,
> And John Clint made the flint,
> And John Puzzle made the muzzle,
> And John Crowder made the powder,
> And John Block made the stock,
> And John Brammer made the rammer,
> And John Scott made the shot,
> But John Ball shot them all.

In the adaptation, we first turned the rifle into a cannon to provide a more dramatic center of interest. The change led naturally to others. Military titles were substituted for the name John, since the gradations of rank from drummer to general accentuated the cumulative pattern of the book. Also, military uniforms provided the opportunity to make full use of the bright colors which the technique allowed. John Ball shooting them all did not seem an appropriate ending to the tale, so the refrain was changed to "Drummer Hoff fired it off." The name Drummer Hoff was selected (instead of Private Hoff or John Ball) because of its rich sound, and the "KAHBAH-BLOOM" was added just for fun, to give the book a good strong climax. The verse now reads:

> General Border gave the order,
> Major Scott brought the shot,
> Captain Bammer brought the rammer,
> Sergeant Chowder brought the powder,
> Corporal Farrell brought the barrel,
> Private Parriage brought the carriage,
> But Drummer Hoff fired it off.

The book's main theme is a simple one — a group of happy warriors build a cannon that goes "KAHBAHBLOOM." But, there is more to find if you "read" the pictures. They show that men can fall in love with war and, imitating the birds, go to meet it dressed as if to meet their sweethearts. The pictures also show that men can return from war sometimes with medals, and sometimes with wooden legs.

The book can have two endings. Many people prefer to stop at the "KAHBAHBLOOM" page. And for some purposes that is where the story should end. But others prefer to go on to the next page, which shows the cannon destroyed. The men have gone, and the birds and flowers that appear to be merely decorative through the first part of the book are in the process of taking over — again. The picture of the destroyed cannon was purposely put on a half page to keep it in its proper place as a minor theme. The main theme of the book is, I repeat, a group of happy warriors building a cannon that goes "KAHBAHBLOOM." The book's primary purpose is, as it should be, to entertain.

After I had been working less than two years as an artist, I started on my first children's book. I felt at the time that if I could inherit a million dollars on the condition that I stop doing art work of any kind, I could accept it with no regrets. As I started, I thought I was working at merely another job. Little did I know that I really had a tiger by the tail. For here I am, eight years and twenty-seven books later, not knowing who is the master, the art or the artist, and not caring. This change was brought about partially by the work itself and partly by the people I have met along the way.

I speak for Barbara also when I say thank you: first of all to the people at Prentice-Hall, past and present, whose infectious enthusiasm provided us with one thing all creative people need — momentum. And especially to Jean Reynolds, our editor, who gave us assistance, advice, and encouragement when we needed it; to Walter Ott and his staff for turning *Drummer Hoff* into a book — in time — and for giving us their patient cooperation when we needed it; to Bob Verrone and Mimi Kayden, who gave us counsel and friendship when we needed it; and to Eunice Holsaert, who gave us a push when we needed it. I would also like to thank Holt, Rinehart and Winston and Nonny Hogrogian, Thomas Y. Crowell and Elizabeth Riley, and Doubleday and Blanche van Buren for giving me work when I needed it. I would like to thank Little, Brown and Company, Jean Bates, and Helen Jones, who gave me a start when I needed it. Especially Helen Jones, who once said to me, "Don't cheat the children. Give them your best. They deserve it." A piece of advice I have taken to heart and passed on at the slightest provocation. And I would like to thank the rest of you whom we have met in person or through our books for your interest and for your obvious good will. I wish to express my appreciation also to Mrs. Durham and the members of her committee. My personal feelings about the Caldecott Medal and the tradition and the people it represents are best expressed in a poem that has been haunting me since that cold January night. It is Robert Frost's "Stopping by Woods on a Snowy Evening." Especially the last verse.

The woods are lovely, dark and deep,
But I have promises to keep,
And miles to go before I sleep,
And miles to go before I sleep.

⚞   ⚞   ⚞

Ed Emberley's reply to our query about post-medal-winning happenings revealed both interesting and dramatic events. He reported that *Drummer Hoff* has been translated into Braille, so that a blind mother can read to a sighted child. And also that the film of *Drummer Hoff* by Weston Woods was made in Czechoslovakia and finished just before the Russians put down the revolt there at that time. "A woman was shot in front of the studio (interesting since *Drummer Hoff* has an antiwar-military theme). The film was smuggled out by Gene Deitch, the American director, during the height of the conflict."

Ed Emberley continues, "You might be interested to know how 'we' (Prentice-Hall, Barbara and I) felt about *Drummer Hoff.* We had no idea that it would ever become a popular book. It was designed for a very few special (unknown) children. We thought the story line was too simple and naive and the art work too complicated and sophisticated to interest more than a very few. We were wrong. We still don't know why, even with the Caldecott, so many have found it interesting."

Ed Emberley

by BARBARA EMBERLEY

Ed's first instruction concerning this biography was to make it just that — a biography, not an appreciation. So I will do as he requested and "stick to the facts."

To begin, Ed's full name is Edward Randolph Emberley. He was born in Malden, Massachusetts, on October 19, 1931. He was a city boy, raised and schooled in Cambridge, Massachusetts. His maternal grandfather was a coal miner in Nova Scotia, and his paternal grandfather made his living from the sea in Newfoundland. His father left Newfoundland in his twenties and has been a carpenter most of his life. As far as Ed knows, there were no artists among his ancestors.

Ed remembers only one book from his childhood, *Little Black Sambo.* The rest of his library, housed in three orange crates, consisted of funny books and old *Life* magazines. He does not remember going into a library until he went to high school.

Ed and his two brothers were encouraged to draw, he says, "mostly by lack of discouragement and by having pencils and paper in the house at all times for us to use if we wanted to."

Encouraged and supported by his parents and high-school teachers, he went to the Massachusetts School of Art, where he earned a Bachelor of Fine Arts degree in painting and illustration. Ed was serious about his work and was considered one of the better students.

Since I received my Bachelor of Fine Arts degree in fashion design, I think I am qualified to say that he was less than serious about his appearance. He shaved only on weekends, and his "uniform" consisted of one pair of levis encrusted with paint (he had the habit of wiping his brushes on them) and set off by an ancient pair of moccasins and a flannel shirt, similarly decorated. In spite of his appearance we became good friends, dated, and were married a year after graduation.

Ed started working as an artist in 1958. In 1960 he wrote his first book, *The Wing on a Flea*, for Little, Brown. It was well received and became an ALA Notable Book and one of the *New York Times'* ten best illustrated books. He bought thirty copies of *The Wing on a Flea* and sent them to all the publishers he could find, with a letter asking for a chance to illustrate more books. As a result he received work from Holt, Rinehart and Winston; Doubleday; and Thomas Y. Crowell; as well as from Little, Brown.

During the summer of 1962, Ed started experimenting with woodcuts and sent out a mailer to the children's book publishers. It showed a print of Paul Bunyan and Pinocchio, with a note saying that he would like to illustrate Paul Bunyan or Pinocchio in woodcuts. The prints were mailed out at five o'clock one evening and ten o'clock the next morning we received our first and only answer. It was from Eunice Holsaert of Prentice-Hall, who said that she was interested. Could he send some sample pages? Thus began our association with Prentice-Hall, which led to the publishing of *The Story of Paul Bunyan*, 1963; *Yankee Doodle*, 1965; and *One Wide River to Cross*, 1966, sole runner-up for the 1967 Caldecott Award.

The story of *Drummer Hoff*, 1967, and of the part played by Jean Reynolds, the present children's book editor of Prentice-Hall, is told in Ed's acceptance paper.

Perhaps Ed's most outstanding quality, at this time, is his ability to work in many different styles and techniques. An excellent example of this variety can be seen by comparing his two 1967 books, *London Bridge is Falling Down* and *Drummer Hoff*. Ed illustrated these two books at the same time, yet they look like the work of two different artists.

Ed's personality as related to his work is best explained in his own words:

When I am looking for an idea or trying to tie down a concept for a new book, I am restless, tired, fearful, superstitious, withdrawn, and just about the crabbiest person you would ever want to meet. When I settle down to an idea and get a few pages, I feel like a happy, powerful, creative genius destined for greatness! This feeling dwindles slowly, so that by the time I have the final art work ready for the printer I feel that I am a competent, clever illustrator. When I first examine the printed, bound book I am depressed and I see that it is quite obvious that my expectations were not realized and that I must try again.

Which he does.

THE FOOL OF THE WORLD AND THE FLYING SHIP

illustrated by URI SHULEVITZ

retold by ARTHUR RANSOME *from a Russian folk tale*

published by FARRAR, STRAUS & GIROUX   1968

BOOK NOTE

This story full of peasant humor and ridiculous situations has all the elements of the folk tale, from the three sons off to seek their fortune, to the Czar who demands the fulfillment of impossible deeds as the only way to marry his daughter. These elements come craftily together in a totally satisfying story. Through his kindness and simplicity, the third son, who is the Fool of the World, acquires the Flying Ship and the crew of characters who help him outwit the Czar. When at last he marries the princess, there is a traditional happy ending, for he turns out to be handsome and she "loves him to distraction."

This is an extremely well-balanced book, for Uri Shulevitz matches the length, detail and hilarity of the text with full, rich, inventive pictures. The brilliance and purity of the colors is also enhanced by the openness of the pages, where white space is used as effectively as the color of the illustrated portions. The artist used pen and brush with black and colored inks.

Caldecott Award Acceptance

by URI SHULEVITZ

An old Russian folk tale, retold by a British writer and published in America far from its origins in time and in space, has helped bring us together today from different parts of the country. *The Fool of the World and the Flying Ship* has indeed brought many together.

From the story's beginning, there is a distinction between the Fool of the World and his two clever brothers. A division has been established. Their parents accept it. Perhaps it is they who established it. But apparently the two clever brothers do not accomplish much with their cleverness, for they are never heard of again.

I have been asked: Why does the Fool of the World deserve the Flying Ship? What has he done except answer an ancient old man kindly? The Fool of the World makes no distinction between himself and "the ancient old man." Furthermore, he refuses to accept the distinction his mother makes, according to which he is incapable of accomplishing anything except walking "into the arms of a bear." He refuses to be bound by the generally accepted opinion of himself and sets out to find a new world. Therefore, it is he who gets the Flying Ship; it is he who welcomes the varied companions who eventually help him in his task.

The view from the Flying Ship, moving freely in the boundless sky, must be one of splendor and unity. The diverse elements that make up the landscape below blend into a single harmony, enriching each other.

This vision comes to an end when the Flying Ship lands in the palace courtyard, because the Czar insists on making the distinction between himself and a simple peasant. But as the story goes on, the Czar, powerful as he is, cannot maintain artificial differences forever. An army, real or imaginary, finally breaks down the false barrier. The princess and the Fool of the World are united. Now he becomes so clever that all the court repeats everything he says.

May I propose here that the source of the Fool's wisdom is the breaking down of *false distinctions*. The ending of the story is truly happy, because it is the wonderful beginning of a new life.

✓   ✓   ✓

According to Anatole France: "Children have, most of the time, an extreme dislike for reading books that were written especially for them. This is very understandable. They feel, from the first pages, that the writer has forced himself to enter into their world instead of transferring them into his own, that consequently they will not find under his guidance that newness, that unknown, which the human soul, at every age, is thirsty for. . . . They find the writer who binds them in the contemplation of their own childhood a terrible bore. . . . I have read songs from the *Odyssey* to very young children. They were delighted. *Don Quixote*, in a selected version, is the most enjoyable reading a child of twelve could wish for . . . *Robinson Crusoe* was originally written for serious adults, merchants of the city of London, and for sailors of his Majesty. In this tale the author has put all his art, all his resourcefulness, his vast knowledge, his experience. All this was just right to entertain schoolchildren." So wrote Anatole France.

I remember the first book I read, Charles de Coster's *Thyl Eulenspiegel*. I was enchanted. It was not, as far as I know, written for children. The same goes for *Gulliver's Travels*. Even our library of folk tales, as we know, was not originally collected as children's literature. Myths and legends, going back to ancient times in India, reflect, again, the absence of conventional limits and distinctions. Bluebeard, according to some, is the sun; his beard's blueness, the sky; and his seven wives, seven dawns. For every day of the week, the sun, by rising, put an end to another dawn. Cruel Bluebeard possibly might have had a more respected past in a very ancient legend. After all, the sun is more ferocious in hot India than in Alaska. Similarly, the color of Little Red Riding Hood's hat might be an indication of her celestial origin: She emerges from the darkness of the wolf's belly unharmed, just as dawn dies and is reborn afresh after the night's darkness.

It seems to me that some of the magic of fairy tales also consists in the absence of distinction, the distinction between the living and the inanimate. Everything is alive, just as in a child's world. Animals and people, plants and trees, rocks and stones are all alive. They talk to each other, communicate with each other, and are transformed into each other — back and forth. I have read of evidence that plants actually do respond to human feeling. They respond to love by growing and expanding.

Are children foolish to ignore accepted distinctions? Conceivably there is much more to reality than we adults are ready to accept. Perhaps it is the children who are more realistic. They will quickly recognize animals as manifestations of life just as they are themselves. They will immediately recognize that a fur coat is the hide of a slaughtered animal, while the adult wearer of the fur has to kill this connection and pretend that fur grows on trees. He has to make the *distinction* between life and life, between people and animals.

> The wolf also shall dwell with the lamb,
> And the leopard shall lie down with the kid;
> And the calf and the young lion and the fatling together;
> And a little child shall lead them.

Are these words of the prophet Isaiah the words of a wise man or of a fool? There may be a problem, however, that Isaiah did not expect: By the time man is ready for this new world, leopards and lions may be extinct, unless hunters and poachers miss some.

Once while I was petting my cat, she responded by licking my hand, then licked herself. She did not find it necessary to make a distinction between me and herself. She was genuinely practicing Rabbi Hillel's teaching: "And you shall love your fellow man as yourself."

✦   ✦   ✦

I have been asked: "Don't you find it limiting to draw for

children?" Children are people. People are people. To children, even animals are people. As soon as we remove the *false distinction*, drawing for children is a limitless endeavor. I believe, furthermore, that there is an *artificial distinction* between "art" and other human activities. Art is not something special, but only an extension, one more manifestation, of life.

It is not surprising that an ancient Chinese painter has advised: "When drawing a stone, be a stone." This is one way of saying how important it is to open up and lose *binding distinctions* in order to achieve a deeper experience and a more satisfying work of art.

In the West, we have been conditioned to think that the more solid and tangible an element, the more real it is, while in fact the elements indispensable for life stand in a reverse order. There is, first, no life without air, then without water, then without bread, then without stone for defense or shelter. In Chinese painting, air — the empty space around a stone — is as important as the stone. In my own work, I want them both to be equally solid.

There is no real distinction between "art" and illustration, between old art and new art. There is only good art and bad art. While teaching, I have observed that one of the main reasons why students do poor illustration is that they maintain the distinction between "art" and illustration.

As a child I loved Rembrandt. I still do. His etchings are sublime illustrations. I have seen a landscape drawing of his at the Fogg Museum that looks like a Chinese painting. In Rembrandt the distinction between East and West, between child and adult, fades away. He was wise. But again, in his day many considered him a fool.

✏ ✏ ✏

It is by ignoring false distinction, by aiming higher than seems necessary, by keeping an open approach in which the possibility of unlimited interrelations exists, that I have been helped in the past; and therein lies the only hope for furthering my future work. I will not decide how and what to draw or write because more people like such and such better. I have never believed in a statistical approach. I will do what I love. It is the only way to give someone else pleasure. If I do not like what I am doing, no one else will. By getting closer to myself, I can hope to reach others.

Donald Wallace

Uri Shulevitz

by MARJORIE ZAUM K.

Uri Shulevitz was born in Warsaw in 1935. When he was four years old, Warsaw was bombed. He remembers standing in line with his mother, waiting for bread. Shrapnel fell, and when the smoke cleared, one third of the people who had been in the line were lying on the ground. He also recalls that the staircase in his apartment building was destroyed by a bomb while he was at home. He had to walk down a wooden plank that seemed to be balanced over an abyss. Uri has described these memories as having "an over-all color — the grayness of destruction."

In 1939 the family fled. They spent years wandering, and by 1947 they were living in Paris. Uri spent countless hours on the Quai de la Seine, browsing among the bookstalls. He was fascinated by the city, its streets, its architecture. This love of cityscapes is in his picture books; many drawings contain rich details of streets, rooftops, chimneys — the texture of a city.

At this time Uri became very much interested in movies and often sat through the same film two or three times. His books employ cinematic movement. He draws panoramic views and then focuses on portions of them. As a child, he also developed a passion for comic books. He and a friend made their own; the friend supplied the words and Uri drew the pictures. And when Uri was twelve, an art competition was held among all the grammar schools of the district. He won the first prize.

In 1949 his family left Paris and went to live in Israel. Between the ages of fifteen and seventeen, Uri worked at various jobs and went to high school at night. One of his jobs was issuing dog licenses at the Tel Aviv City Hall, where he had plenty of time to read. He loved reading and received the highest grades in literature. Yet, in his later schooling he deliberately chose natural history as a major field of study — botany, zoology, and anatomy, among other subjects. He felt that these would be a counterbalance to his natural inclination toward fantasy.

From 1952 to 1956 Uri studied at the Teachers Institute near Tel Aviv. During this time he also studied painting with Ezekiel Streichman, a semiabstract painter. In 1956 Uri went into the army. After his basic training, he joined the Ein Geddi kibbutz, founded by a group of his friends. He recalls driving out to the kibbutz through the harsh and barren desert, and the moving experience of coming upon the lush green vegetation of Ein Geddi. He lived here for over a year and here made his first attempt at graphic design, as Passover Haggadah. Later he became art director of a youth magazine.

In 1959 Uri came to New York City. He studied painting at the Brooklyn Museum Art School for two years and began making illustrations for a publisher of Hebrew books. The work required of him was rigid and limiting. One day, while speaking on the phone, Uri noticed that his doodles had a fresh, spontaneous quality he had not seen in his drawings before. Convinced that he could develop this approach, he resigned his job, lived on savings, and devoted himself to writing and illustrating his first book, *The Moon in My Room* He has now done fourteen books — all but three with texts by other writers — that range from pure fantasy to complete realism. *Rain Rain Rivers*, which he both wrote and illustrated, exemplifies his realistic approach. Rainwater in its various aspects — pond, stream, river, ocean — derives its strength from being just what it is, and needs no embellishment.

Uri wants to give children stories and pictures that will be meaningful and enjoyable to them. He brings his total experience in art and literature to every book he does and considers the distinction often made between "children" and "people" as false.

He still lives in New York City. For the past year he has been working extensively in etching and lithography, techniques that are a natural development of his style of drawing. When he is not working on children's books, he makes prints, paints, practices Tai Chi Chuan (Chinese exercise), and takes care of Bianca and Fuzzball, his two cats. Bianca can be seen at the window in several of the drawings for *Rain Rain Rivers*.

The Caldecott Award **1970**

SYLVESTER AND THE MAGIC PEBBLE

illustrated by William Steig

written by William Steig

published by Windmill Books
   Simon and Schuster 1969

BOOK NOTE

Sylvester Duncan is an enterprising young donkey who collects pebbles. When he is all alone in a rainstorm, he discovers a shining red pebble and is holding it as he wishes it would stop raining. It does. With a test or two more, Sylvester knows his pebble is magic. But he forgets its powers when he meets a fierce lion and in a panic wishes he were a rock. In an instant, that's just what he is. And of course his poor mother and father, who look everywhere for Sylvester, would never think of looking for a rock. They all have a sad winter — his parents' suffering over the loss of their child, and Sylvester suffering from being rock-bound. But spring and a picnic and the magic pebble bring a joyous ending.

Steig's style of drawing allows characteristic human expressions of concern, curiosity, despair and joy to appear naturally in his animal characters, and his depiction of their humor and pathos is endearing, but it is never cute. The artist used watercolors to enhance the strong line of the pictures, which are well-distributed throughout the text.

Caldecott Acceptance Speech
by WILLIAM STEIG

The last time I spoke formally to a group of people anywhere near this size was over a half-century ago, at P.S. 53 in the Bronx. I very quickly got tongue-tied and forgot what I was supposed to say. I have avoided this kind of confrontation ever since then. I was a poor speaker at age ten, and I've grown rustier with the years. So — to reduce my discomfort, and yours — I shall make this a short speech. Anyway, as a matter of form, it should not be as long as the little book that landed me here.

Among the things that affected me most profoundly as a child — and consequently as an adult — were certain works of art: Grimm's fairy tales, Charlie Chaplin movies, Humperdinck's opera *Hansel and Gretel*, the Katzenjammer Kids, *Pinocchio. Pinocchio* especially. I can still remember after this long stretch of time the turmoil of emotions, the excitement, the fears, the delights, and the wonder with which I followed Pinocchio's adventures.

Often, at work or in everyday living, I do things or have experiences for which I find symbols that somehow derive from Collodi's great book. Recently I had a dream in which I was being led towards a place of judgment by two policemen, each with a firm grip on one of my arms. No doubt I was feeling guilty about something. But the scene was right out of a similar episode in *Pinocchio*, and I am sure that was its derivation. And it is very likely that Sylvester became a rock and then again a live donkey because I had once been so deeply impressed with Pinocchio's longing to have his spirit encased in flesh instead of in wood.

I am well aware not only of the importance of children — whom we naturally cherish and who also embody our hopes for the future — but also of the importance of what we provide for them in the way of art; and I realize that we are competing with a lot of other cultural influences, some of which beguile them in false directions.

Art, including juvenile literature, has the power to make any spot on earth the living center of the universe; and unlike science, which often gives us the illusion of understanding things we really do not understand, it helps us to know life in a way that still keeps before us the mystery of things. It enhances the sense of wonder. And wonder is respect for life. Art also stimulates the adventurousness and the playfulness that keep us moving in a lively way and that lead to useful discovery.

Books for children are something I take very seriously. I am hopeful that more and more the work I do for children, as well as the work I do for adults, will approach the condition of art. I believe that what this award and this ceremony represent is our mutual striving in the same direction, and I feel encouraged by the faith you have expressed in me in honoring my book with the Caldecott Medal.

I want to express my appreciation and gratitude to my friend and publisher, Bob Kraus of Windmill Books, who had the insight that I — and others like me — could make a contribution in this field, and who, because he himself is an artist, recognizes that the artist-publisher relationship is a symbiotic relationship, mutually beneficial not only in terms of monetary reward but in the more lasting reward of producing worthwhile work and being culturally useful.

Finally, I want to say that I still feel the pleasure and the gratitude that I felt when Mary Elizabeth Ledlie telephoned me from Chicago. And I love you all. I love you because you must love me. Anyway, that's how I understand your liking my work, which is a large part of me. Thank you.

✶ ✶ ✶

In a recent letter, William Steig wrote: "It's gratifying and useful to be honored. I still get mail because of the award. Making a speech before so many people is an ordeal for a shy person, and the long wait between the announcement of the awards and the ceremony causes many sleepless nights. Still, I wouldn't mind going through that suffering again."

Nancy Crampton

William Steig

by ROBERT KRAUS

When William Steig asked me write his biography, I was very pleased at the opportunity to tell the world what a wonderful person he is. Bill has not only been a stimulating and fascinating person to work with, but he has been a true friend.

William Steig is part of a remarkably creative family. His parents, Joseph and Laura Steig, were both painters. He has three brothers: Irwin — an artist and writer; Henry — an artist, musician, and writer; and Arthur — a poet and artist.

Bill was born in Manhattan and went to the public schools there. As a small child he showed so much interest in painting and drawing that his eldest brother Irwin, a professional artist, gave him lessons. Later Bill went to the City College of New York and the National Academy of Design. In high school and college he was an all-round athlete, and at CCNY he was on the All-American Water Polo Team.

At a very early age, Bill worked for the old *Life* and *Judge* magazines, and later for *The New Yorker*. Ever since he joined *The New Yorker* he has been delighting Americans with his incisive comments on the human condition. His sympathetic, observant eye has served him well in the production of many adult books — among them *Small Fry* and the brilliant *The Lonely Ones*. And now, his candid, but uncensorious view has been turned to the service of a new medium for Bill — the writing and illustrating of children's books. Children respond immediately to this kindred soul, whose illustrations display an outlook which is as clear and as fresh as their own.

Bill lives and works in Greenwich Village in an apartment off Washington Square. A night person, he prefers to work in the evening and seldom rises before noon — which often creates problems in his being on press for the printing of his books!

Bill Steig is a very private person and rarely sees anyone but old friends and members of his family. A loving and attentive father, he frequently sees his young married son and daughter, who live in the neighborhood. In fact, he often helps his daughter Lucy take care of her first child and his only grand-child.

His children are carrying on the creative tradition of the Steig family. Jeremy is the well-known jazz flautist, and Lucy is a painter. Maggie, his third child by a later marriage, although very young, already shows signs of artistic ability.

Bill Steig's work is central to the man. From his myriad *New Yorker* covers and cartoons to his adult books of symbolic drawings and to — most recently — his books for children, his work displays a superb ease of execution and a grace that transcends mastery of technique. It is evident that, in part, Steig works for the sheer love of producing a beautiful drawing. You can see the playfulness, the ease, and the absolute control, and sense the understandably human delight in the virtuoso skill of his performance. Beyond that he has the ability to comprehend the hitherto unimaginable and to make it plain to the rest of us.

William Steig's award of the distinguished Caldecott Medal for *Sylvester and the Magic Pebble* was exciting and wonderful, and I like to think that Randolph Caldecott (himself a cartoonist for *Punch* before he went into illustrating his marvelous children's books) would have been pleased by the choice.

A STORY, A STORY

illustrated by GAIL E. HALEY

retold by GAIL E. HALEY *from an African folk tale*

published by ATHENEUM PUBLISHERS 1970

BOOK NOTE

Ananse, the Spider Man, wants stories to tell to the children round his knee. But all the stories are kept by Nyame, the Sky God, in a golden box. When Ananse asks if he can buy them, the Sky God laughs at such a weak old man thinking he can meet the price — which is to bring him Osebo the leopard-of-the-terrible-teeth, Mmbora the hornet-who-stings-like-fire, and Mmoatia the fairy-whom-men-never-see. But Ananse knows cleverness means more than strength. He outwits and captures the leopard, the hornet, and the fairy, and hauls them up in a web to the sky. Nyame keeps his promise and gives all his stories to Ananse and to this day in African cultures they are known as "Spider Stories."

Gail Haley has combined a woodcut medium, the African elements of the tale, and a sure sense of design into a visually bold and dramatic book, and the imaginativeness of the illustrations equals the fantasy of the story.

Caldecott Award Acceptance

by GAIL E. HALEY

Members of the American Library Association, distinguished members of the Newbery-Caldecott Committee, Mr. Melcher,

ladies and gentlemen, I am deeply moved by the great honor
you have conferred on me. The very existence of the Randolph
Caldecott Medal is an inspiration to all who choose children's
literature as their life's work. I read many Caldecott Medal
acceptance speeches made in former years, before I wrote my
own. I have the feeling that at this point in my speech, almost
by tradition, I am supposed to say that I am an artist, not a
public speaker, and that if you would just give me my Medal,
I should like to go home now. But I shall break with this
tradition, if it is one. I appreciate and welcome this opportunity to speak to you. But, first, I want to share this award
with those who have helped and encouraged me — my husband Arnold, and my children Marguerite and Geoffrey, on
whose love, strength, and patience I depend; Toni Mendez,
who is also part of our family; Jean Karl (my unerring editor
and loyal friend), Sue Glazer, David Rogers, and all the other
people at Atheneum who make it possible for me to do my
very best.

You — librarians, teachers, parents — and I share a great
community of interests: children and books. None of us can
ignore the fact that our time is hostile to children and that our
culture inhibits literacy. A recent Gallup poll disclosed that
eighty-two percent of the surveyed elementary-grade children
had not read a single book in the preceding month. Projected
nationally, this means that of twenty-four million early-grade
children, twenty million had not used their school or public
libraries, and that their teachers and parents had not supplied
them with any reading material during that time. According
to other reliable statistics, each of these children, during that
same period, had watched between ninety-three and one
hundred and fifty-five hours of television. Even before they
enter the first grade, our children spend more hours watching
television than students spend in class to get a Bachelor of
Arts degree in college.

Konrad Lorenz points out that a society can develop a fatal
culture, just as some species can develop fatal mutations. I fear
that we may be in the process of doing just that. In deperson-

alizing our verbal and literary lore we are creating a culture that inhibits the flowering of literacy. It is a trend that is as unhealthy for children as the destruction of our environment. The audio-visual assault on our children's senses interferes with their spontaneous play with words, ideas, images, and objects. Children are turned into passive consumers of whatever is offered them. It then becomes increasingly difficult for them to use their own faculties; but their spontaneous use is a precondition to literacy.

Live storytelling, reading to preschool and early-grade children, and the discussion of picture books with them are perhaps more important today than at any time since Comenius. In the days before mass literacy, the oral tradition prepared children for later life. The give and take between storyteller and child was a vital educational experience. It provided incentives for speech and for self-expression. This oral tradition has all but vanished; but the book is a natural extension of the storyteller. It takes the place of folk memory. And the picture book, especially, is a bridge from speech to literacy. It allows adults to whet a young child's appetite for finding out about a world that is beyond his experience. No "Right to Read" and no TV program can compensate children for a lack of exposure to stories and books. Instead, they encourage — rather than reverse — the trend toward autism and functional illiteracy, even when they succeed in drilling children to recite letters and numbers.

Deprive a child of love and he will reach for affection or clamor for attention at the expense of all other aspirations. Deprive him of fantasy and he may try, on his own, to make up even for that deficit. But children who are not spoken to by live and responsive adults will not learn to speak properly. Children who are not answered will stop asking questions. They will become incurious. And children who are not told stories and who are not read to will have few reasons for wanting to learn to read.

The advocates of electronic shortcuts to literacy do not understand the storyteller's function. My interest in African folk tales stems in large part from the role they play in the education of children. The African storyteller, like the live reader of children's books, invites questions and he answers them. He adapts his tales to the understanding and experience of his audience, and he repeats or explains what is difficult. He is an imitable example. He is marvelously well informed and he has a prodigious memory. He recalls heroic deeds of whole dynasties of chiefs, back through three or more centuries. He is the keeper of the tribe's traditions, conscience, and identity. He is the poser of riddles and conundrums. He is the spontaneous teacher of the young. He chronicles the exploits of his contemporaries and he adds them to the stories that are memorized by his successors. He plays with the sound of language, and he weaves witticisms, sly barbs, and criticism of tribal members and chiefs into the fabric of the classic stories he tells. No two renditions of the same story are ever alike. Each evokes new contributions from his audience. The African folk tale and the modern children's book are very closely related.

An adult book requires only two participants — the author and the reader. But a picture book, like the folk tale, needs three — the author, the story-reader, and the child. Any live reading of a picture book, like the telling of a folk tale, requires interpretation. The reader must adapt it to the child-listener's experience, and no two versions need ever be the same. This point was dramatized to me when Weston Woods recorded *A Story, A Story*, narrated by Dr. John Akar, Ambassador to the United States from Sierra Leone. I had heard these same words in my mind's ear when I first wrote them. I have since read them many times to children. But Dr. Akar's delightful rendition made my story new even to me. It was like hearing a familiar song played on an unfamiliar instrument. This can and should happen with every rereading of a children's book.

A picture book, like a good toy, invites participation. A mechanical toy may seem very clever to adults. But it is the toy and not the child that plays. The child only watches from the sidelines. None of his faculties are engaged. He is just a spectator. But building blocks, for example, encourage the child's self-expression, inner direction, and skill. They stand in relation to wind-up dolls that weep, wet, and dance, as children's books do to the hysterical animations of children's TV shows.

Our children need shelter from the incessant bombardment of their senses. Television makes them passive and it atrophies their ability to attend, to reflect, and to be active. It kills their curiosity, their imagination, their faculty of play, and their appetite for books.

The first generation of TV-reared children has now reached maturity. It is not too far-fetched to attribute the drug habits of many to an influence that taught them early to rely on hypodermic injections of a pacifying culture. Please do not think that I join those who use today's youth as scapegoats. I am on the side of the young. They are victims and not perpetrators.

I was lucky. In my childhood, in rural North Carolina, I still had the opportunity to escape, to wander through woods and fields, to hide away under a tree, and to curl up with a favorite book. Many of my less-favored contemporaries have turned into nonreaders. Others keep searching for a childhood they missed. They want to be reborn as children, but the fantasies in which they engage are more often childish, rather than childlike. A more encouraging by-product of all this resurgent interest in childhood is that children's literature has been discovered in the colleges. It is becoming a favorite course of study. This reflects a yearning for experiences that were withheld from today's adult students when they were young.

The leisurely daydreams of childhood, stimulated by stories and picture books, are not mere pastimes for children. Children expect, from babyhood onward, human and humane responses from everything with which they come into contact. And they need to be able to respond, actively and spontaneously, to people, animals, objects, and ideas. Seen in this light it becomes obvious that children need anthropomorphic fantasies for proper development. They make it possible for the child to interact with his world. Children live in a world in which they are "so small, so small" — the smallest in the family. Most of their choices are made for them: what they will eat and wear and when they have to go to bed. Their earliest independence is gained only in fantasy. At first, these fantasies may be merely rebellious. But they help children learn to cope. Children's dreams allow them to come to terms with the necessary limitations on their freedom and impulses. Eventually, this sheer resistance to authority is displaced by idealized heroic yearnings. And these permit a child to try out who and what he would like to become. No one who learned to enjoy a rich, imaginative life in childhood need ever lose this faculty. As children mature, their fantasies are converted into ideals and into goals. Such children stand a good chance to turn longings into reality — at least in part. The exercise of a child's fantasies give him foresight and prepare him for a fearless and hopeful future.

Yet, we seem determined to choke learning that is "species specific" to human beings. Laughter, imaginative play, curiosity, self-expression, and language are among the skills that are peculiar to our kind. They cannot flourish unless our young practice them actively. And so the picture book, among other essential early learning experiences, is pitted against the lavishness of the motion, color, imagery, and sound of television — a presentation that makes no demand on the audience. But the picture book's esthetic economy is much more valuable for the child. It demands that he fill in the void between the peaks represented by succeeding spreads. He is required to make his own contribution.

More than a personal catharsis, my work is an effort designed to stimulate verbal and visual responses, and a preparation for literacy. My books are for children. They are also frames of reference for the story-reader who needs to dramatize, explain, and discuss the ideas I express, the pictures I draw, and the words I use. My object is to involve adult and child. Both are my collaborators. Telling stories and illustrating them is my invitation to children to join me in a world of fantasy I envision and to elaborate on what I present to them. My aim is not to manipulate children, but to encourage them to be active, imaginative, whimsical, and curious. These, more than fact gathering or rote memorization, are the specific appetites that lead to learning which is essential for human survival. Chief among such appetites is the hunger to read.

I am happy to have had this chance to share my thoughts and concerns with you and to give you insights into what moves me to write and to illustrate children's books. It is an all-consuming occupation. My husband and I share and live these ideas in our family, in our work, and in the raising of our children. Yet, we often feel isolated when the threats to a joyous and loving future for our children overwhelm us. But here, among you, my optimism is revived. I sense and share your passionate concern for children and for children's books. I feel, like Ray Bradbury's protagonist in *Fahrenheit 451*, that I have discovered my tribe of like-minded survivors, each dedicated to nurturing and keeping alive, not just one author or book, but the very idea of literacy.

❧   ❧   ❧

Three years after she won the Caldecott Medal, Gail Haley wrote: One of the frequent questions asked by librarians, teachers, and children, and now by the editors of this book, has been: "What is it like to be a Caldecott winner?" They might as well ask: "What is it like to become Miss America, a Nobel Laureate, or a winner of the Irish Sweepstakes?" Any of these are wildly happy surprises — frosting on the cake of life; but they also raise certain problems.

The first reaction of a partner of the publishing house that produced *A Story, A Story* on learning that this book had won the award was: "Now you know what it's like to be famous. Next you'll have to learn what it means not to be famous any more." He set the tone for the emotional seesaw on which most award winners find themselves — feeling exhilarated and like a target in a shooting gallery.

The most gratifying experiences resulting from winning this medal are purely professional. You know that your work will reach the largest possible audience of children; that you will be published and read and that you have the chance to remain productive for the rest of your life. You receive immediate feedback from large numbers of librarians, teachers, parents and children. Authorship and illustration are solitary occupations. The Caldecott Medal gives an artist many opportunities to be in direct contact with his or her audience.

The celebration at the annual ALA meeting is a unique event in the life of an award-winning author. Aside from the weeks of preparation and speech writing, there's the dinner, an audience of more than two thousand eager faces, the long line of people who want their books autographed, and the publisher's breakfasts, lunches and suppers. It's a week-long "high" without benefit of drugs. Then there's the inevitable anticlimax.

It must be kept in mind that parallel to the hooplah run the mundane concerns of everyday life — husband, children, paying the bills, and doing your work. And so the many gratifications, obligations, and responsibilities connected with winning these awards must be viewed in context with the normal stresses of an author's life, especially if he or she has a family. Mine survived, but only just; and after considerable turmoil and heartache. This is due in no small measure to my husband's love and firm convictions that helped see us through the worst personal crises. There were also librarians and children whose faith and steadfast confidence gave me the courage to carry on.

Professionally, there can be problems with academic sharp-shooters who want the free right to include your work in their text books and to convert it to videotape. Winning the Caldecott Medal, especially in this day of reduced library budgets, rising production costs and a shrinking children's book market, is not the way to get rich. It does provide a small steady income after the first rush of sales and it gives you the opportunity to stay in print. But authorship is always speculative and risky. The initial and main investment is the author's own, and perhaps it is larger in proportion to the publisher's part, since he can spread his financial risk over many authors and books.

Finally, there are the book critics, and I wonder whether all Caldecott winners have been subjected to a similar amount of carping.

You survive this kind of thing — or you don't. I have survived. On re-reading this, I seem to have harped excessively on the painful consequences. Despite them, these awards are eminently worthwhile. Winning the Caldecott Medal is a beginning and not an end. I look back on it as a high point in my life, on a par with giving birth to my two beautiful children and to my books. I savor the experience and relive it every time I receive the first copy of each new book I write and illustrate.

Gail E. Haley

by ARNOLD ARNOLD

Gail and I first met six years ago, at New York's annual toy fair. She mistook me for a toy buyer and I thought she was a shill — one of the provocative girls hired by exhibitors to lure customers into their showrooms. It was the first and only time we have been wrong about each other. Gail was autographing one of her books.

Twenty-four hours later we had agreed to marry, to have two babies; and we had agreed on how to bring them up, on how to live and work together. We have done and are doing all we promised one another, so I feel qualified to write about Gail. My account may not be entirely unbiased, but it is accurate.

Gail is several people, each interesting and complicated. She looks like a girl little boys dream about, but one who makes them clammy and tongue-tied when they meet her. If you do not know her, she may at first sight seem a nothing-on-my-mind-but-fun-and-games creature. If you know her slightly, she can be intimidating. But if you know her well, you are more likely to see her elbow deep in printer's ink, in paint; or immersed in whatever idea interests her; making something with our children, or baking a loaf of bread. She can transform herself at a moment's notice into a whacky, dancing, carefree girl, into a responsible mother, or into a regally aloof young matron.

Gail is immensely curious and intellectually alert. She learns and works at a prodigious rate. She converts words and images into a new context — one that reflects diligent study and research as well as her original outlook. She has a lively grace about everything she does and she is quite unself-conscious despite her many-faceted gifts. She is internally turned on to life and to her work without any need for artificial stimuli. She is given to speaking her mind and she has a foul temper when aroused. She indignantly rejects untruth and injustice, but she is also more loving and lovable than anyone I have ever known.

She was born in Shuffletown, deep in the rolling hills of North Carolina. Her ancestry is a slice of genuine Americana; on one side, a German student who fled across the Atlantic to escape prosecution for his part in the antiauthoritarian revolution of 1848; and on the other side, red-bearded Scotchmen whose offsprings still speak with a remnant of brogue. Gail's earliest memories consist of being rocked to sleep in the overhead luggage rack of a troop train onto which her mother had smuggled the two of them to accompany her G.I. father to the West Coast during World War II. Gail grew into a slightly awkward, dreamy girl who did not learn to read until she was seven years old. Then her father sat her down and taught her in one day and she has not stopped devouring books since.

I would say that Gail invented herself. She had decided very early that she wanted to write and draw. But, like many little girls of her generation, she spent a large part of her childhood fighting off attempts to turn her into a tap-dancing and marimba-playing prodigy. Those were the days of Major Bowes, and Gail's marimba still clutters up our basement.

On graduation from high school, Gail attended the Richmond Professional Institute, where she majored in art. Later, she studied at the University of Virginia in Charlottesville, where her first husband, a mathematician, completed his doctoral dissertation. Here she worked with Charles Smith, the graphic artist, who taught her wood cutting and printmaking and who encouraged her to try her hand at the writing and illustrating of children's books.

White-gloved and hatted, portfolio in hand, Gail came to New York to storm the publishing world. But her first attempts to break into print were unsuccessful. It is perhaps difficult for anyone who has not made the tiring round of publishers to understand the frustration of being told that you show a lot of promise, that you will soon be given a book to illustrate; and then having to wait for a call that somehow never materializes. This kind of experience, after art school and college, is the second great weeding out of female (or male) would-be artists or writers. A very few hold on tenaciously. The rest fall by the wayside forever — to do paste-ups and mechanicals in art departments, or to cook meals and wash diapers, or to join Women's Lib.

Gail returned to Charlottesville to publish her own first slender children's book herself. She managed to sell enough copies to the Washington, D. C., buyer of Brentano's to pay for the production, and then used the rest to besiege juvenile-book editors anew. Eventually one took a chance on her. Others followed, each gaining confidence from the courage of the last. A year before I met her, the first children's book Gail wrote and illustrated in its entirety was published. It was not exactly a howling commercial success; but it proved her writing and illustrating skills, and from then on she flowered into professional maturity.

Some time after our fateful getting together, Gail and I were induced by the United States Government into developing a research project on early childhood education. It required our living in the Caribbean. After a year in the tropics, we were left high and dry, our personal funds totally exhausted as a result of bureaucratic treachery and the heating up of the disaster in Vietnam. Gail was seven-months-pregnant with our first baby and we had no redress. Though the research project was scrapped, it was not a wasted year. We had learnt a great deal about Caribbean culture and about each other. Each of us had done work that eventually enabled us to right ourselves. Meanwhile the germ for Gail's book, *A Story, A Story; An African Tale* had been planted.

After our return to New York with sixty-five cents in our pockets, our baby happily born and perfect, Gail began to trace Caribbean folklore back to its origins. She immersed herself in African art, music, dance, and oral traditions. One year later, on the basis of her manuscript and rough sketches, Atheneum agreed to publish *A Story, A Story*. It took Gail another year to cut and print the final wood blocks.

A close, creative, and trusting relationship between author and editor is as rare today as it is essential for the production of good books. But Gail was fortunate in developing just such a rapport with Jean Karl, who is — without question — a most discerning and sensitive juvenile editor. Gail, in addition to being enormously gifted, has been lucky. Both talent and luck are required for success in the publishing world. Either one without the other just is not enough.

It is extremely tempting for a successful young author to become uncritical of her work or to rest on her laurels. Neither of these things has happened to Gail. Her self-discipline, her intellect, her warm and loving nature, and the direction of her life and work remain unchanged. Since the publication of *A Story, A Story*, we have had our second baby, Geoffrey; and Gail works as hard and as enthusiastically as ever, and continues to be totally devoted to child culture and children's literature — as she always will be.

ONE FINE DAY

illustrated by NONNY HOGROGIAN

adapted by NONNY HOGROGIAN *from an Armenian folk tale*

published by THE MACMILLAN COMPANY 1971

BOOK NOTE

When the fox steals the old woman's milk, she angrily cuts off his tail. Because he is ashamed before his friends, he asks her to sew it on again. But she will not, until he brings her milk from the cow, who will only give him milk if he brings her grass; and so the story goes on and on, until the fox completes all the requests and can return with the milk for the old woman — who carefully sews his tail back on. The cumulative tale, where one situation leads to another and the suspense builds along with the repetition of the situations, is a favorite in the folklore of many countries. This adaptation of an Armenian story also adds to the wealth of fox tales in folk literature.

Nonny Hogrogian's illustrations are as simple and unadorned as the story, with the content of each doublespread composed to carry along the rhythm of the text. The stylized drawing of fox, animals, and people keeps to the spirit of the story, and the color range of the oil paintings gives a pleasing sense of background atmosphere.

Caldecott Award Acceptance: How the Caldecott Changed My Life—Twice

by NONNY HOGROGIAN

Somewhere around the end of 1965 I began to feel discontent. I loved illustrating children's books, but only half of my time was given to that. The other half was spent designing and art directing other artists' work for a publishing house. As you probably know, most artists are very possessive of their time and creative energy, and I wanted to spend more of mine on my own work. I made some inquiries and had an interview with Jim Van Dyck, then in the Art Department of the University of Pennsylvania, where I had hoped to get a scholarship to work for a master's degree in painting. I had followed through with preparation of a portfolio and had done everything but send in the final forms when I received the news that *Always Room for One More* had won the Caldecott award. The forms were never sent. I decided the Fates had stepped in, and I was not about to challenge them.

I did feel at that time that the award was not quite deserved, that I was not ready to receive such honor. Nevertheless, and needless to say, I was very grateful. The 1966 Caldecott award enabled me to devote all of my time to art work — to illustrating children's books on a full-time basis, and to have some time left to paint and sketch. In addition, it changed my personality just a little. I used to be terribly shy and overly humble, and perhaps a bit self-deprecating. Well, after a few receptions and speeches I was forced to get over the shyness, and when so many people respond favorably to one's work, humility seems foolish and even insulting to their judgment. In fact, a little arrogance is a good thing for an artist or writer to possess when receiving an award, because this is the time when all those not in favor of the award attack and reject and criticize, and pomposity becomes a shield. And in the natural course of events I became a little pompous and a great deal more demanding of myself and of my publishers. The book that I was beginning to work on when I heard the news of my first Caldecott was a book of Armenian folk tales, and after the first few weeks' excitement had worn away, I found I had gained a new sense of responsibility about my work, and that I could not allow myself to do a single illustration that I didn't consider as good as any other in the book. The result was that *Once There Was and Was Not* was probably my best book up to that time, and certainly the most even in quality. My husband, who did not know me in 1966, found the book in a shop in Santa Fe, where it would not have been if I hadn't been a Caldecott winner, and although we did not meet until early last year, you can see that the medal was at least in part responsible for my marriage.

I like to think that each new work I do is better than the last, for I work very hard to grow as an artist with each new project. There were times in the last six years when I felt the struggle and devotion to the work were not reward enough to sustain me, since in order to earn enough money to live I was forced to illustrate about four books a year, which left no time for my own painting. Once again, at the end of 1971, I decided to change the way I was living in order to have enough time to paint. I began making calls to find out about teaching jobs, which I thought would allow me more time, but by the end of January of this year you know what happened. Fate decided I should not leave children's books.

During the stormy New Hampshire evening of January 25th, as I worked on a new deadline, our electricity went out. My husband and I were trying to keep warm by the fire with wraps and brandy, and trying to figure out how we would survive if I only illustrated one book a year and saved the rest of my time for my own painting. With a touch more brandy than I needed I found myself suggesting that it would be wonderful if I won the Caldecott Medal. David said I was being silly, and 1 protested (and here's what I mean about pomposity) that I deserved it, and so the conversation went until the heat and lights went on to sober us back to work for another hour, and just as I closed shop for the night Anne Izard called with the wonderful news.

So now in 1972 the Caldecott hopefully will enable me to do fewer but better books in the future, and to have time left over to paint and to garden and to keep house now and then.

I would like to thank all of my friends at Macmillan — Libby and Susan, Ada and Doris, Ava and Janet, and all their assistants, for accepting, then guiding and struggling with me through the production of *One Fine Day*. And I thank all of you who, with the Caldecott Medal, have helped change the direction of my life once again.

Nonny Hogrogian

by DAVID KHERIDAN

The first time I saw Nonny Hogrogian was in her home town — New York — to where I had come from 3,000 miles away to attend a reception in my honor as the new editor of *Ararat* magazine. We had previously exchanged a few letters, and had spoken once on the phone, out of which came an agreement, or rather, her acceptance to do the cover drawing of my new book of poems.

She was talking to a mutual friend across a long room, and as I approached her, we were informed of each other's identity by the people we were with. If I am a smiler, too often naively and foolishly open to all new experience and people, Nonny is at least somewhat the opposite. All greetings are registered first in the eyes, and in the beginning, at least, they tell us all we need to know about the person we are meeting. In the days that became months and that are now more than one year since that meeting, I have spoken often to Nonny about her eyes, and I have often tried to write in poetry their meaning and truth. Certain deep conflicts leave their trace: in the hands of some, in the mouth of others, and in those who consume their rage — and in the case of Nonny, *also* control their demon, or pain — it comes to rest finally in the eyes, where all of it is held and burns. If in every other way she is serene, contained and noble — and I know of no one more so — her eyes continue to speak of an earlier struggle and war, that each artist in the beginning must wage: against society and the mistaken exigencies of time.

It was in her eyes that I first saw her — and their penetration into my own was the only introduction I needed to her character, for they told me she could only be a great artist, because all endeavor is built on will, and here was a person, I was certain, who was indomitable, courageous and unconquerable. I took her then on those terms, and I do still.

✓ ✓ ✓

When I watch Nonny work I am struck each time anew by the mystery of art and its strange, unknowable processes. The ruminating, the furtive flipping through book after book, the long walks, blank stares, tantrums, and the final declaration that nothing nothing is possible — before the swift outpouring and then the long hours of concentrated work, with the panic slowly subsiding as the work begins to emerge, as I once wrote in a poem to her:

> You are murmuring and sighing and
> I am imagining the drawing that is
> moving down thru the tributaries of
> your body into your arm and down thru
> your fingertips onto the paper that
> is lit by your face.

Art is swift, life is not, and the sources of art are twofold or twice occurring: from the beginning chaotic years, when the will we impose on our art is the outgrowth of the will that others exercised upon us when we were young and the self was only becoming; and the years past manhood, when the quality of our art is dependent totally on the quality of our lives. That few, especially in children's books, escape the claims of childhood in their art, and instead seek refuge in its nomenclature and neurosis in an effort to certify what they deify, is too self-evident to go into here — juvenile adults creating for captive children. That few humans become truly adult, and fewer yet men or women, needn't be my concern here: only that work that is both true and mature *is* occasionally honored and valued.

But to give you Nonny in words such as these — which inevitably reflect my own preoccupation with life and art, living and making, achieving and surviving — is, if not misleading, certainly a case of rolling the ball to you in words, whereas her element is paint: another medium, another dimension, and finally another person and life. She speaks for herself and always in her own language — paint; and she never lies. The precision that knows and honors the value of imperfection; the clear and calligraphic line; a flawless sense of color and design; compassionate characterization of the real — her imagination is *always* fed by life; and the lack of trickery, fakery, gimmickry, or device. And finally, the deep commitment to her art, because she long ago assumed the responsibility of everything she signed her name to, as she has always assumed the responsibility of every act of her life.

I am a poet, she is a painter, we live in an old farm house and have our garden and animals and family and friends. Anything further is redundant, I can only ask you to see it with your own eyes.

THE FUNNY LITTLE WOMAN

illustrated by BLAIR LENT

retold by ARLENE MOSEL *from a Japanese folk tale*

published by E. P. DUTTON

BOOK NOTE

A jolly little Japanese woman loses a dumpling down a hole. She chases it as it rolls along a strange underground road. It rolls past statues of the gods who warn her to let it go, for at the end of the road live the wicked *oni*. But the jolly lady keeps on giggling "Tee-hee-hee" and chasing the dumpling, until she is indeed caught by a wicked *oni*, who takes her home to cook for him and all the other wicked *oni*. Which she does, using a magic paddle the *oni* give her so she can turn one grain of rice into a potful. But at last she becomes lonely, and taking the magic paddle, she runs away and escapes from the *oni*, even though they try a very ingenious way of stopping her. Back in her little house, she becomes famous for her rice dumplings and becomes the richest woman in Japan. The tale of the rolling pancake, or dumpling, is well-known in folklore around the world, but this Japanese version has both humor and suspense, as well as a quite different flavor.

Blair Lent has used color built up with acrylic paints, along with pen-and-ink line drawings printed in gray. When the funny little woman is in her house, the house and garden are in color; when she is underground, the cavernous world of the gods and the *oni* is in color — while aboveground, the gardens and house are lightly sketched in gray and show the passage of time as the seasons change. It is a complicated scheme, but it proves effective. It also combines some traditional Japanese imagery with the artist's own inventive detail.

Caldecott Award Acceptance

by BLAIR LENT

The first time I saw a Caldecott Medal, it was made of metal foil, and it was on the jacket of one of my favorite picture books, Virginia Lee Burton's *The Little House*. I used to pick at the edges and run my fingers over the embossed horse, the geese, and the dogs that ran across it.

When I first found out I was going to be given a real Caldecott Medal, I felt very depressed. I sensed eyes studying every line and analyzing every page to find out why this particular book should be singled out, perhaps overlooking the experience I had tried to help create with my pictures. In a way, I felt like the young Saint-Exupéry when he showed grownups his drawing of a boa constrictor that had swallowed an elephant, and they saw it as a hat, while children could imagine the elephant inside the snake. Many children, when they are looking through one of the picture books I have illustrated, seem to be experiencing so much of it. Grownups often consume things too quickly. That is why I enjoy it most when a child looks at one of my books, or when an adult does who can see things in a similar way.

But if my books were made *only* for children, I would be creating something artificial, because it can often be what a grownup brings to work for children that makes it unique. After all, children can draw fantastic pictures and make up good stories for themselves. Children don't need adults to imitate what children can do, but rather an older person with his own particular skills to create pictures a child cannot make for himself.

On the other hand, I feel that if I, as an illustrator, should find myself making a picture book more for the adult in myself than for the child in myself, it might be time to get back to my painting for a while. There are all kinds of kids who like all kinds of books, but I feel that my work for children would fail if it were more for the parents than for the child.

Picture books are a very special medium for me. They are unlike other books. Picture books are a unique combination of words and pictures. Sometimes a picture book can be successful without words, and the reader can make up his own story. But all the books I have worked on have been with words, because I like working with the sounds of words and seeing them set in type. I find it challenging to interrelate the words and the pictures, with both the words and the pictures moving at about the same rate on every page, each element telling its own part of the story. I think of the picture book, especially, as a shared experience: An older person reads aloud from it and talks with a child about it. It is a unique medium that can adapt itself completely to the reader; you can skip pages, go backwards, study one page endlessly. A good picture book lasts a long time, with pages full of details to explore again and again. Through time, picture books can even take on a nice patina; old books don't necessarily become illegible. They are like old friends, perhaps reminding you, with that water stain, of a day you were reading on the beach or, with that smear of gravy, of the day you couldn't even stop reading for dinner. You can even take a book to bed with you and read it under the blankets.

And something else about picture books, especially, is so very important; picture books are the first books a child will read; and if he doesn't read them, there is little chance he will want to go on and read other books.

At a time when what we see around us gets uglier and uglier, a picture book can be one of the first things of quality a child can have, and it may influence his attitude toward how he feels about what he sees. Regrettably, high production costs have made books expensive, but since they are expensive, they should be well-made. It can be disappointing to look at a picture book and sense that the colors have been reproduced incorrectly, the line drawings have lost their character, a book with paper so thin that you can see through one page to the next, or with ugly, clumsy, side-stitched bindings that make it a struggle to hold the book open. I wish people who buy and write about books would be aware of these flaws and let publishers know they are aware of them.

The first time I saw a paperback picture book I shuddered. But after the initial shock and after more paperback picture books appeared, I realized that they could also be well-produced, and that it would even be interesting to design some picture books from the very beginning with only the paperback format in mind. Of course, there still is a place for picture books with rich cloth covers and a feeling of permanence about them, but there is no question that books are in the process of change.

Alvin Toffler, in *Future Shock*, writes about the acceleration of change in contemporary life. There was a time when change was slow, barely noticeable in a lifetime. But failure now to face the rapid technological and social changes can leave a man behind. What will books be like ten years from now? Or even one year from now? Think about it. Most of us here like books and believe in books. But I believe there might be a danger in thinking they should stay exactly the same.

For these are worrisome times for books, worrisome because of high production costs and unfavorable economic conditions. But these can also be challenging times. They can be imaginative times for everyone involved — to explore new ways to make and distribute books, whether they are cloth-bound or carefully printed paperbacks.

🙻   🙻   🙻

Anyway, right now, it does feel good to be doing what I have always wanted to do — making picture books; but there was a time when I thought I might never begin, and a dark time when I had trouble going on.

Ann Durell sent me Arlene Mosel's spirited words during that dark time in my life. Mrs. Mosel's comical adventures of the Funny Little Woman lifted my spirits. It is an important book for me because I finished it — after many years of not being happy with, or able to complete, any work at all. Ann Durell was the right editor at the right time, and her friendship and involvement with the growth of the book was vital to its completion and to my being able to work again.

Not all of the books I have worked on have moved as well as *The Funny Little Woman*. There are still books lurking in my studio that I have been unable to come to grips with, just like some of the paintings, with their faces to the wall, that I have yet to finish.

Other books that I have been able to finish have been almost unrecognizable to me after they have been printed. One of the greatest difficulties for an illustrator is that his work is interpreted by photographic processes and machines, and either the people who run the apparatus enhance the work or come near to destroying it. That is why when I am not illustrating, but painting or making a print, I sometimes feel relieved, because I myself am responsible for my completed work, and often I prefer this because so often the work of an illustrator is in the hands of others — and I worry.

But whenever I have worked with Hilda Scott, who was the art director for *The Funny Little Woman*, I haven't worried. It is hard to say what part of the design of the book is Hilda's and what is mine, because I have worked with her before and her ideas have strongly influenced my own. Her influence and her reputation as a really fine designer have been very much apparent in all the field.

I feel picture books can gain or fail depending upon the people involved. There really should be a list somewhere in a book naming all the people who are part of that book, especially when you feel happy about the contributions they have made. Mimi Kayden, whom so many of you know, and Dave Zable should be counted among the people I worked with at Dutton. I'll never forget the time when Dave, who was the production manager, shouted for the presses to be stopped and a large monster of a press was halted, and the book delayed for a long time because it wasn't printing the right way. That's the sort of production-manager illustrators dream about working with.

Although I have been making picture books almost all my life — ever since I was little — this year marks the first decade during which my work has been published. It was ten years ago this summer that Emilie McLeod of Atlantic Monthly Press saw something in my work, encouraged me, then published my first picture book. That same summer Walter Lorraine gave me a chance to illustrate a picture book for Houghton Mifflin. My Boston friends, Emilie and Walter — they were part of the beginning, and they have been part of many of my books ever since.

✦ ✦ ✦

It has been good to have been able to express with my work the way I feel about things. And it is good to be able to try to express these feelings to children, just when they are beginning to think about the world around them. Sometimes I feel a little guilty because I'm not more involved in some of the changes I would like to see taking place in the world; but, in another sense, I am involved, for I feel that picture books can be a way of showing a child some of the things an artist thinks are important in life, a way of getting ideas to children in their formative years. I am happy if one part of a book I have illustrated has affected the reader, if one idea has perhaps begun to form from it, so that he will see beyond the illustrations, perhaps to things I haven't even shown. I have received drawings from children that they have made after experiencing a picture of mine, and the ones I like best are those that look nothing at all like my illustration.

I guess what I really want to do is tickle the imagination. I talk about the acceleration of change and keeping up with it, but I also believe in trying to keep alive some of the magic in a world that has less and less magic.

Sometimes it is difficult to know if there really is *anyone* looking at your work. Very often after I finish illustrating a book I wonder if I'm communicating with anyone at all out there. So at a time like this I want to thank Priscilla Moulton, and the Caldecott Committee, and the librarians, and the children who have responded to my work, for helping me to know that what I have been trying to do has been noticed. I can feel happy knowing that there are many who do see and understand the potential in my work. It makes me want to do a book that is far better than anything I have ever done, not only for myself, but for them as well.

Editor's Note: This version of his Caldecott Award Acceptance is printed as Mr. Lent gave it in Las Vegas, Nevada, at the meeting of the American Library Association on June 26, 1973.

✦ ✦ ✦

Recently, Blair Lent wrote: In the acceptance speech I gave in Las Vegas, I spoke about an impasse I had reached with my work. There were many reasons for the impasse — one was that I was not working well in a city environment. The studio in my apartment had become crowded; a once residential area had become congested, noisy and ugly. The sun was hidden more and more by new luxury apartment towers and office buildings were growing up all around my studio.

I had been looking for a house or a piece of land in the country; the kind of property that once could be found for relatively little, but has now become more and more expensive. However, I was better able to buy twelve acres of land in Northeastern Connecticut once I had received my first royalty check for the Caldecott winning book. I then built myself a small workshop beside the pond that is on my land.

One might be disturbed that *an award* brought recognition and increased income to a book faster than a book having to make it on its own. But I feel the award enabled me to do something about my environment and embark upon what I feel will be my best work.

Blair Lent

by WILLIAM SLEATOR

Blair Lent grew up in a small suburb of Boston. He was fat, awkward, and shy, an only child; and, as his father was putting himself through M.I.T., Blair's family was noticeably less affluent than most of the families in his community. As one might expect, other children excluded him, and he was aware of having less, and of being alone. He escaped into the books his mother and father gave him, which provided other worlds for him to indulge in. His father, who became a successful electrical engineer, enjoyed exploring all the second-hand book shops on Cornhill in Boston and started Blair on his large collection of illustrated books. Reading books, making his own to give to his parents, an activity which they encouraged, and visiting his uncle Harlow, a painter, on his farm in Vermont relieved in part the pain of being an outsider. When he was a teenager, another uncle gave him a copy of *Babbitt;* the book was a revelation to him, for he had never before realized that perhaps it wasn't only his fault that he had never fit in or that there might be other worlds that would suit him better than the one in which he had grown up.

After a brief and unsuccessful attempt to study economics, Blair turned to odd jobs. He worked in a chicken eviscerator factory, and as a short-order cook at Howard Johnson's (where he even invented a drink, the "orange freeze," that is still on the menu today). Finally, he began studying art at the Boston Museum School. This was the world he had been looking for, and his life took on an excitement and a direction that did not waver for many years. With the encouragement of Ben Nason, the designer, who was his teacher and friend, he majored in graphics and design and was awarded a traveling scholarship at the end of his senior year. He used it for spending a year in Europe, where he met artists such as Rowland Emmet, Ronald Searle, Alois Carigict, and Hans Falk. He visited their studios, talking to them and learning everything he possibly could in preparation for his career as a graphic artist, which he was sure was about to begin.

Back in the States he found, after a long search, a job dressing manikins in a Boston department store. He took out his frustration on the manikins themselves, by putting their dresses on backwards, their hats upside down, and carrying them through the store with their limbs twisted into distorted, surrealistic poses. He was quickly relieved of these duties and given others, such as the care and feeding of the penguins that were part of a window display. And once, at Christmas, he had to stand guard over a cage of monkeys that had been set up near Santa Claus's throne and cover the cage at certain moments to hide the monkeys' activities from the fascinated children waiting in line, who had forgotten all about Santa. Everything but designing.

He never stopped looking for another job and, at last, found one as creative designer at the Bresnick Advertising Agency, then one of the top advertising agencies in the country. It was a good job, which involved designing TV commercials and high-fashion ads. With his limited experience, it was necessary for him to lie his way into the job, to insist that he had had experience turning out all kinds of layouts, and then spend his free time teaching himself how to do layouts. He later discovered that Lennie Karsakov, the art director, had suspected that he had been lying all along and had hired him anyway. Blair learned a good deal about design from Karsakov, who eventually made it possible for him to work only three days a week at the agency, so that he would have the rest of his time for painting. Finally, he left the security of a steady-income job altogether, to devote full time to his own work. It was the kind of risky move that has characterized Blair ever since — to gamble what he has achieved in an attempt to prevent stagnation and to keep freshness in his work.

And though his painting was successful (both of his one-man shows, in Provincetown and New York, nearly sold out), it wasn't the only thing he was doing. Ever since his first job at the department store, he had been putting together book after book and sending them to publishers. Making picture books was what he had always wanted to do, and he had never allowed the piles of rejection slips to intimidate him. Finally, Emilie McLeod at the Atlantic Monthly Press responded to a story he had written ("I like it! I like it! I LIKE IT!" said her excited letter), and his first book, *Pistachio*, was the result. He had also submitted his portfolio to Houghton Mifflin, for he was an admirer of the illustrations of Walter Lorraine, the art director there, who told him that if the right book came along he would give Blair the chance to illustrate it. The right book did come, Walter Lorraine did call, and Margaret Hodges' *The Wave* subsequently became a Caldecott Honor Book. Blair began to concentrate more on picture books than on painting; once again, to the astonishment of those who could not understand how a "serious" painter could actually prefer making books for children, he turned away from success in one means of expression to start as a beginner in another. He has never been without a book to work on since then.

During the time he was painting, and also when his first books were being published, he worked in an old carriage house on Beacon Hill with Theo Wolfe, the artist and teacher. It was a stimulating atmosphere for him; not only did he enjoy the old neighborhood, but Theo Wolfe's influence helped him to achieve a greater freedom in his paintings, a freedom that developed into the wild and rhythmical quality of some of his early books, such as *Baba Yaga*, which, under a pseudonym, he also wrote.

Environment has always been important to him, and he has had studios not only on Beacon Hill but also in Gloucester, Massachusetts, and in Maine. His love for the sea — as well as the sights and sounds of the small harbor towns — drew him to these places. His great grandfather was the captain of a clipper ship, and it was the atmosphere of ocean and boats and fishing villages that he set out to express in the words and pictures for *John Tabor's Ride*, which, of all his books, remains his favorite.

But, as always, there was the need for further development, and Blair Lent's style has changed several times. At first, there were the cardboard-cut books — bold, primitive, and stylized — but eventually he began to feel that this technique was not appropriate for the ideas he wanted to express. He began to draw the pictures for his books freehand, which was difficult, at first, because painting and graphics had always been his media; and not until he had drawn several books and reached *The Little Matchgirl* did he feel that his drawings were really drawings, rather than designs for prints. During this time, there was also a development in his sense of color and texture, until he felt that color separations were preventing him from putting down the illustrations he now had in mind. So, with *The Angry Moon*, he went on to full color — painting once again; but painting abstract canvases is quite different from painting illustrations, and he has continued struggling to improve not only his drawing, but his painting as well.

This development in style and technique has never been just for its own sake but is part of the most important aspect of Blair Lent's approach to picture books: Every book must have a basic, underlying concept. In each book, there is a problem to solve that involves all the separate components — words, pictures, type, colors, and paper; and what technique he uses and how the pictures move from page to page have to relate to everything else. In *Why the Sun and the Moon Live in the Sky*, he wanted to portray the elements as people enacting a pageant. In *The Little Matchgirl* he focused on the village, showing all of it at first and then zeroing in on different locations as the girl, tiny and overwhelmed by her surroundings, makes her way through the village. And in *The Funny Little Woman*, the small black-and-white drawings tell their own everyday kind of story, emphasizing, by contrast, the fantastic yet ridiculous quality of the Little Woman's more unusual adventures under ground.

It would have been much easier (and perhaps more lucrative) if he had kept on turning out book after book in an earlier, comfortable style, for constant development takes its toll. Throwing away drawing after drawing, painting after painting, trying to make his hand discard familiar patterns and work in new and difficult ways, Blair, once able to finish as many as three books a year, became unable to finish even one. To someone whose work is practically his life, such a creative slump can be hopelessly discouraging, and there were some very bleak years. But they are coming to an end. Working with Ann Durell and Hilda Scott on *The Funny Little Woman* helped to break the spell; and now, whether it is due to the stimulation of new media, or just to the basic fact that his survival depends on it, his work is gaining new momentum.

Recently, he won another scholarship from the Boston Museum of Fine Arts, which he used for traveling extensively in the Soviet Union, where he sketched small villages and met Russian illustrators. (In Russia, though there is restriction in most of the arts, picture-book illustration is especially imaginative.) Since then, he has been making animated films, has begun an exploration of sculpture, and is still working to develop as an illustrator.

For, even now, he is not satisfied with his illustrations. His teacher Ben Nason once said that Blair Lent would never be satisfied, and, taking into account all the changes he's put himself through, one might be tempted to agree. But Blair does not. If he ever does the right book, he insists, he will be satisfied with it. And when he does do that book, then, perhaps, we will see, as he has seen all along, the goal that all his changing and developing have been leading up to.

DUFFY AND THE DEVIL

illustrated by MARGOT ZEMACH

retold by HARVE ZEMACH *from a Cornish tale*

published by FARRAR, STRAUS & GIROUX   1973

BOOK NOTE

The Rumplestiltskin story, where the maid who has been aided in accomplishing miracles of industriousness must guess the name of her supernatural helper, is at its most rambunctious in this Cornish version, often given as a play during Christmas festivities. The maid is bumpkin Duffy, a lazy lout who claims she spins like a saint and knits like an angel, and so is hired by Squire Lovel to help his housekeeper, Old June. But when Duffy, who can spin nary a thread nor knit nary a stitch, cries "The devil can make Squire Lovel's stockings for all I care!", the devil appears and does just that and more. Squire Lovel is soon the best-apparelled man in the county and in appreciation makes Duffy his wife — Lady Duffy Lovel of Trove. But the three years in which the devil has given Duffy to discover his name fly by, and in fright Duffy tells the Squire what a devilish situation she's in. With an unusual twist to the tale, it is the Squire who stumbles on the answer — and who pays for it.

Margot Zemach has put sophisticated wit into portraying country bumpkins, which in itself produces sly humor. Her devil is engagingly nasty. She can handle a crowd scene or an individual smirk with deftness. While the effect of her watercolor combined with pen-and-ink drawings is muted, the illustrations are full of action and complexity of detail. The seeming sophistication of the whole book is mocked at the end by Squire Lovel's unapparelled predicament. There is a good balance of text and picture throughout the book.

Caldecott Award Acceptance

by MARGOT ZEMACH

"I stand here before you to sit down behind you to tell you of something I know nothing about." I would much rather be sitting down behind you than standing here before you, since the way I express myself is by drawing pictures. I worked nearly a year on the pictures for *Duffy and the Devil*, and I can tell you some of the thinking behind them.

At the beginning of the story the Squire is riding to town to find a helper for his old servant, Jone. He is bouncing along on his rickety horse on a country road on a hot dusty day. He is a self-indulgent old ruffian, with his tummy before him, buttons popping off his coat. He has seen better times. Nowadays he spills egg on his vest, drops food on the floor, feeds his dogs behind his chair, kicks off his boots first thing when he gets in the house — and doesn't bother to take off his hat. He's harmless. Good for a cheerful country romp, which is how I saw the story.

Then you meet Duffy. She's a match for the Squire. A simple-minded girl. Look at her hat, look at her stockings falling down. A lazy, overgrown girl, addled from eating too much and sitting too long in the sun. Certainly the spinning wheel will be too much for her. She's one of those people constitutionally unable to make anything work. And furthermore, it doesn't bother her. She'll get by somehow. That is the morality of the folk tale: a little luck, a little magic, and a laugh at fate. And look at how far she comes up in the world. From drudgery to splendor, with a silk bathrobe and jewels, dancing on the village green with the ladies.

But first she has to get past the lecherous devil. He looked lewder in my preliminary drawings, but I thought if people are going to paint diapers on Maurice Sendak's little fellow, I had best keep my devil clean. He still looks slightly lewd, I hope. One problem in drawing the devil pictures was to capture the quality of magic happening, trying to make him suddenly appear on the paper and later really stomp himself out of existence. But here one comes up against the limitations of the picture book, and the results are never what one wished for.

It is old Jone who gets Duffy out of trouble. I think she offers to help Duffy out of fellow feeling for a fellow female and servant. Or maybe she is looking for a good time, a night out with the girls — her fellow witches, who are the servant women, the old pensioners, and the fishermen's wives. The grand ladies of the town, the crew joined by Duffy when she marries the Squire, own tea sets and best shoes and clothes to be seen in and dancing lap dogs and have time to cultivate the finer things in life. Duffy thinks it bliss to be one of them. But the witches in the fuggy hole have no pretensions to grandeur. The main thing about them — apart from their bawdiness — is their ability to defy gravity. And also the hats they wear as their badges of witchdom. The hats have a squashed look, as if they are hastily taken out of the trunk when there's going to be a big night. These witches have to be up early next morning. When they chase the Squire out of the cavern, waving their broomsticks, the party is already over. They still have their hats on, but they can't fly any more. They turn into a pack of angry fat ladies in hot pursuit.

Meanwhile Duffy, stolidly cow-like, waits up for the Squire. Today she'd be chewing gum and reading a movie magazine. When the Squire arrives and discloses the devil's name, they both have a good laugh. They are affectionate friends, and will be for a long time. Duffy sends the devil packing, but there is still a bit of bother for the Squire when his clothes disappear and even his dogs laugh at him. And then it is over, another day, old Jone sweeping up the debris of magic, winter in the air, a good time had by all. With no more nor less than a little luck and a little magic the tale ends happily, as it was meant to from the beginning, because how could we live without knowing that some stories do have happy endings.

And now I want to thank my husband, Harve, for his excellent adaptation of the story; Michael di Capua, my editor, for his help and friendship; Atha Tehon, who designed the book; Millicent Fairhurst and all the others at Farrar, Straus and Giroux; and my special thanks to the printer, Joe Matlack. Finally, I thank the members of the American Library Association who have chosen to give me this award.

Margot Zemach

by A. L. LLOYD

Margot Zemach was born in Los Angeles in 1931. Her mother was an actress and her father a man of roving disposition whom Margot never really knew. Until she was five years old, she was cared for by her grandparents, strait-laced doctors in Oklahoma City.

Meanwhile, her mother had married Benjamin Zemach, a dancer and director, who had come to America from Moscow with the celebrated Habima Hebrew Theater Company. The company went on to settle in Israel, but Zemach stayed behind to direct ballets in New York. The five-year-old Margot joined her mother and the two Gentile ladies settled into an intensely Jewish — though highly unorthodox — household.

Till that time, Margot had been a little recluse, kept in an Oklahoma City back yard, seldom seeing other children, knowing none of their games or the rhymes with which they accompanied their ball bouncing and rope skipping. For a long time she was frightened in New York, and her unease was added to because her parents moved around the city a lot, which meant constant changes of school for the little girl (in all, she attended thirteen schools).

Life in the household ran strictly according to Benjamin Zemach's timetable: so many minutes for rehearsal, so many for eating, so many for rest. Margot remembers lots of foreign books in the house, telephone calls galore, and the endless lugging of suitcases at night to get to where Zemach was giving his recitals. Particularly she remembers the fuss of getting an old Russian tin trunk through the subway turnstiles of a freezing night.

At an early age, left by herself while her parents were at rehearsal, Margot would make herself hard-boiled eggs and settle down to painting pictures, mostly illustrations of fairy tales. When, from the age of eleven, she was allowed to play with the costumes from her stepfather's shows (a beautiful wedding dress still haunts her memory), she was inspired to draw dancers. Everyone had to be dancing, leaping, whirling, going in all directions at once. Everything was colorful, and a strong flavor of Jewishness crept into her work, derived from her stepfather's art.

On weekends, Benjamin Zemach would take her to picture galleries, the Museum of Modern Art, the Metropolitan. He would talk to her about pictures, and even when she was small, he would ask her opinion. "What do you think of this?" "Do you think that one would be better if it were changed a bit?" Also, he would seek her advice about sets and costumes. "I felt very dignified about that," she says.

By the time she was twelve or so, Margot — a street roller-skating virtuoso, because it was something a loner could do — was drawing cartoons making fun of life, of adolescent sufferings and such. Her stepfather thought that painting in oils was the important art, and Margot did try to copy Michelangelo out of a book, but she couldn't manage it. However, she was privately consoled because people laughed at her cartoons. She found *The New Yorker* more stimulating than the Old Masters, and an early ambition was to make the *New Yorker* cover. "Central Park at Night," she recalls it was to be.

After Margot left school, her stepfather got a job in Hollywood, but it was at the peak of the McCarthy time, and within six months he found himself blacklisted. Margot entered the Los Angeles County Art Institute, which had an excellent drawing department, and between the ages of eighteen and twenty-two she can't remember doing anything but draw all the time. There was a big split in her mind. On the one hand she wanted to draw funny things, à la Steinberg and André François, and on the other hand she felt she ought to be drawing pictures with social significance, à la Käthe Kollwitz and Ben Shahn. But who was she, a young muddlehead with a comic sense of life, to set about depicting the sufferings of the world?

In 1955–56 she was in Vienna on a Fulbright Scholarship. The city was in a bad way, dark, full of ruins; it was like living under water. To Margot everyone seemed to resemble George Grosz drawings, with congested blood vessels. She enrolled in the Academy of Fine Art, but on the first day, at the sight of two hundred students drawing plaster casts, she left. She felt it more profitable to spend her time drawing market people, bus conductors, artistes, bombed buildings. There were few Jews in Vienna, but the museums were nice. Margot's companion during those days was Harvey Fischtrom, a fellow Fulbrighter, in Vienna to study European history.

Returning home from Vienna, she found herself in Boston, married to Harve, who was then a graduate student at Brandeis, studying the history of ideas under Marcuse. Their first child, Kaethe, was born in 1958, and in that same year Margot illustrated her first children's book, *Small Boy Is Listening*. The text was written by her husband, and it concerned the musical life of Vienna, a city Margot felt she could draw convincingly. Later she began to illustrate folk tales adapted by her husband, who uses the name Harve Zemach when collaborating with her. Most of the tales chosen were European, such as *Nail Soup* (Swedish) and *Salt* (Russian). The only American book was

Mommy, Buy Me a China Doll, based on a ballad in the repertory of the fine Ozark folk singer Almeda Riddle, of Heber Springs, Arkansas. In all, Margot Zemach has made thirteen books in collaboration with her husband.

At the start, the Zemachs would send publishers a finished dummy which they could see as a complete book. Then in 1966 Michael di Capua of Farrar, Straus and Giroux invited Margot to illustrate *The King of the Hermits,* a collection of stories by Jack Sendak. This was the beginning of the Zemachs' lasting connection with Farrar, Straus and Giroux. "They have high and exacting standards," Margot says, "and because they expect so much, one does so much." For the first time she was able to work in full color without separation — that is, without having to paint, color by color, on a series of acetate sheets. Working without separation makes the printing more expensive, but it allows for infinitely more subtlety in the coloring of one's pictures.

Also, with Farrar, Straus and Giroux, Margot Zemach has the chance to do black-and-white illustrations, and that, she says, is really laying it on the line where drawing is concerned, for then "you can't hide behind color or make people happy with it. You have to do it all with a pen or pencil." Choosing from a large output, she names the books that have given her most pleasure to illustrate: *Salt* and *Nail Soup* among the earlier books, and among the latter ones *The Judge, A Penny a Look,* and some stories by Isaac Bashevis Singer, *When Shlemiel Went to Warsaw* and *Mazel and Shlimazel.*

After living awhile in Italy and Denmark, the Zemachs moved to London in 1971, where they now reside in Greenwich, in a curious, rambling house within sight of a handsome park laid out in the seventeenth century by the landscape designer of Versailles. They have four children, the oldest sixteen, the youngest three. In the last few years, the children have been closely involved in the making of the books. Margot has never had a studio or a place to retire to, but works on the living-room table, with the children running around, so the pictures are produced right in the midst of family life. It means a certain chaos, but it has its pluses as well as its minuses. The childen pick up the words in the books, and some of the expressions become family jokes — as good a way as any for testing the effectiveness of a text designed for children. They use the stories as a basis for plays and have drawn their own versions of the illustrations. They constantly exercise their right of criticism, both of the use of words and of the manner of picture making. Indeed, to the children it almost seems they're personally responsible for the books.

Pressed for her views on what makes an effective children's book illustration, Margot Zemach says: "The modern trend of oversimplification is impossible; it's merely foisting designers' ideas on children. Children are fascinated by detail. Take a child to the zoo and you may well find that amid all the exotic beasts, it's the pigeon walking around the child's feet that catches the attention. In the most elaborate picture, the chances are that what gives special delight is a little fly or a dropped glove. Children need detail, color, excellence — the best a person can do. I always think, when I'm drawing the view of a town or the inside of a hut: 'Would *I* have liked to live there?' One doesn't need meticulous authenticity of costume or architecture; to a certain extent, one can invent one's own styles of dress and house shapes. But things have to be made real. The food has to be what you'd want to eat, the bed has to be what you'd want to get into right away. But, all in all, I'm not sure that one should consciously bear in mind that the drawings are meant for the gaze of children. If I make a book for children, I draw it the same as I'd draw for grownups."

The Caldecott Award **1975**

ARROW TO THE SUN

illustrated by GERALD MCDERMOTT

adapted by GERALD MCDERMOTT *from a Pueblo Indian tale*

published by THE VIKING PRESS 1974

BOOK NOTE

When the Lord of the Sun shot the spark of life to earth and it reached the dwelling of a young maiden, the Boy came into the world. But as he had no father, other boys mocked him until the Boy left home to seek his father. Neither Corn Planter nor Pot Maker would help him; but Arrowmaker turned the Boy into an arrow and sent him to the sun. The Lord of the Sun would not acknowledge him, however, until he endured four trials — passing through the Kiva of Lions, the Kiva of Serpents, the Kiva of Bees, and the Kiva of Lightning. The Boy survived them all, and rejoicing in his father's favor, full of the power of the sun, he returned to celebrate a Dance of Life with his people.

This tale of the Pueblo Indians has been adapted in a spare, straightforward manner which makes the energy and excitement of the illustrations even more intense. Though the Boy, the Maiden, the Corn Planter, Pot Maker, Arrowmaker, and the Lord of the Sun are all presented as boldly stylized figures, inspired by figures and motifs found in Pueblo Indian art, they have a strong and surprisingly moving impact. The universal dimension of the myth is emphasized by its abstract treatment.

Caldecott Award Acceptance

by GERALD MCDERMOTT

Imagine an ancient and mysterious figure who sits alone on the desert plain. He wears a dark ceremonial mask, and he is robed in desert hues of ocher, gold, and brown. By his side is a clay pot, decorated with magic symbols, and filled with bits of wood, feather, and stone. From these materials, he will create the feathered shaft that releases a spirit into solar flight.

This is the Arrowmaker, a pivotal figure in the drama of *Arrow to the Sun*. Of all the mythic characters who act out their roles in my books and films, he is the one who especially intrigues and interests me. He is a shaman who possesses the ability to see where others fail to see. He can penetrate the unyielding surface of reality with what has been called the open eye. Wordlessly gazing, the Arrowmaker perceives an essential truth and is inspired to action. He gives his vision tangible form by creating a special arrow that will send the hero on his transcendent journey to the sun. The Arrowmaker has thus acted as a liaison between the everyday world and the realm of dreams. He connects the sphere of the intellect with the sphere of intuition.

Many people believe that the role of the artist is like that of the shaman and, in fact, this role has grown directly from our archaic need for an interpreter of the image world obscured by common sight. The artist must attempt the shamanic task of penetrating surface reality to perceive a universal truth; that is, he draws out the essence of the idea. In transforming this vision into powerful graphic shape, he hopes to communicate it to others. In the process, he can expand our visual sense and enhance our ability to see with an open eye. The artist, like the Arrowmaker, assists in releasing the imagination.

Imagination. Image-ination. The ability to call up spontaneously the visual forms of our inner life. Children seem to possess the open eye, a direct access to "the unpolluted rivers of perception and imagination."* But early in childhood, swiftly, almost inexorably, our natural perceptual responses, instead of being cultivated, are eradicated. Other sensibilities are crushed as well, but visual perception seems particularly susceptible to debasement. As Herbert Read has described it, "Somewhere in the process of upbringing, in the environment we have made for ourselves, there exists a corroding influence [that] . . . prevents the development of aesthetic consciousness."**

We have all flailed impotently at the most obvious of these corroding factors: an environment cluttered with synthetic junk, the cheapening influence of advertising stereotypes, the banal imagery of television. We continually bemoan their pervasiveness and lament their trivializing influence upon our sensibilities. We have almost ritualized our complaints against these massive realities which are largely beyond our control.

Meanwhile, what about the area of visual experience that we as professionals can control — the picture book. Have we brought to our task as broad a knowledge of art as we have of the written word? Do we encourage illustrators and designers to experiment and to push forward beyond conventional solutions? Do we insist that contemporary artists be true to their artistic age? If we have closed ourselves off from the larger field of the fine arts, if we have established a hermetic world, then we limit our ability to distinguish bad art from good art. This is a crucial distinction, and I refer those who minimize its importance to John Rowe Townsend, who has offered what he feels is "[o]ne incontrovertible truth . . . to those who think serious artistic endeavor is wasted on a child audience: namely, that even if children do not always appreciate the best when they see it, they will have no chance of appreciating it if they never see it."

A picture book of artistic integrity will often be the only place where a child can expand his imagination and direct his gaze toward beauty. In this medium, it is possible to create a dynamic relationship between the visual and the verbal. The

* Herbert Read, *Icon and Idea*. Schocken. 1965, p. 139.
** *Ibid.*, p. 138.

techniques of storytelling and the compelling serial imagery together convey the force of exciting ideas. In form and content, the picture book can become an essential element in the child's evolving aesthetic consciousness, and the artist creating a picture book has an opportunity — and a special responsibility — to nurture the development of his young audience's visual perception.

This certainly sounds like a heavy burden for that cloistered breed, the picture book artist, separated as he is from the dynamism of modern art. Often shunned by his brethren in other graphic disciplines, he is looked upon as a thumb-sucking regressive, re-creating his nursery fantasies in pastel hues. Can the picture book artist really be expected to devote himself to raising the art consciousness of a new generation? Perhaps he would, if we demanded that he undertake this responsibility. Yet in our sometimes desperate need to be sentimental about childhood, we ask that the picture book artist produce an art that is easily accessible and realistic in the most trivial sense, reality being the lowest level of cognition.

Often the only expectation of the picture book is that it provide pretty settings for an easy vocabulary or comic-strip clichés that can divert and entertain as they lure the neophyte reader into the realm of words. Once the truly serious task of acquiring reading skills is accomplished, the images cease to be valuable — if indeed they ever were valuable — and they are dispensed with. The reader has now graduated from the precisely designated picture book category. There is no mistaking it, it is printed on the flap — Ages 5-8 — and must be so. The powerful potential of art to communicate what cannot be expressed in words is dismissed and consigned to the nursery along with toys that have been outgrown.

Our language is rich and powerful. We strive to learn it, to master it, to put it at our service as a means of communication and expression. But in our intense effort to verbalize, analyze, and categorize all experience, we tend to overlook the importance of the visual as a means of personal communi-

cation and personal expression. This has resulted in a dichot-
omy between the values we assign to our word-sense and
those we assign to our image-sense. We set a goal to acquire
a vocabulary, a grammar, and — if we are ultimately to enjoy
the riches of our language — a knowledge of literary tradition
and contemporary writing. Yet we have no such aspirations
for the development of our visual sense. This faculty is held in
such low esteem, deemed so expendable, that few of us even
have the equivalent of an alphabet. As a result, our natural,
spontaneous, child-response to form and color is left untended,
to wither away.

What remains is a kind of art-blindness that makes us ill
at ease with any but the most banal and representational
imagery — that is, those images that can be narrowly defined
or put into words. To the extent an image is representational,
it narrows interpretation. To the extent an image cancels out
interpretation, it sterilizes the imagination. We all know many
adults who feel uncomfortable with, if not actually hostile
to, images that communicate in an interpretive, stylized, or
abstract manner. Yet children, with their open eye, initially
feel no such hostility. Indeed, it has been my experience that
even the youngest children respond in a direct and receptive
manner to the most stylized of images. I believe this quality
is manifested in the magic and symbolism of their own
paintings.

Our childhood ease with the symbolic can be seen in graphic
ways. For example, when I've had the opportunity to share the
story of *Arrow to the Sun* with small children, they often react through their art. This Pueblo tale culminates, with the
masked celebrants moving rhythmically, in an exultant "Dance
of Life." We pretend that the children have also been invited
to join in the dance. In order to participate, they are to imagine
masks and costumes for themselves — not realistic self-por-
traits but abstract designs that will serve as symbolic representations. From the hands of eight- and nine-year-olds,
gripping fat brushes heavy with paint, come exciting and
stylized images. Most of the children can make the leap of

imagination to this rather abstract concept — to represent themselves in a graphic and symbolic way. They have felt the force of the symbols on the pages of the book and eagerly express themselves in a similar manner. They plunge with delight into a world of color and form and emerge with images of meaning and beauty.

Within a brief time, however, this balance of perception and imagination will be upset. The expression of ideas will become narrowed, and the art will become contrived and awkward. The child's ability to receive the messages of symbolic form will rapidly diminish. This will happen because visual expression and communication will be dismissed as invalid. The child's spontaneous image sense will be underestimated and left undeveloped. Eventually, it will be submerged in the deadening tide of inferior visual representation. We cannot hope to reverse this stultifying process until we overcome our denial of the force and value of art and make it an integral part of our lives.

How can we begin to salvage and develop the visual sensibilities of a new generation — and our own as well? In the broadest sense, we have already begun. The people gathered here have been working toward this goal most of their professional lives by creating and selecting fine picture books and by spreading them open before the eyes of the young. In a specific sense, in awarding the Caldecott Medal, you not only honor the artist for a singular achievement, but you also commission that artist to pierce the screen of convention. You challenge the individual to explore and experiment in future graphic work. I am especially grateful that this honor should now come to me, and I will try to respond to your challenge.

Beyond what we have all accomplished, it is our task, as artists, publishers, librarians, and teachers, to expand our awareness of the larger world of the fine arts and to recognize the potential force of art in our lives — to honor art as it opens the human spirit to infinite domains of possibility and fulfillment. To reduce the art in a picture book to a word-prop or to dismiss the art in our lives as merely ornament is to sterilize our sensibility. Art is "an energy of the senses, that must continually convert the dead rain of matter into the radiant images of life."* Instead of devaluing our visual sense, we should develop it. It requires active support, not in a fragmentary way, but through a comprehensive new program that forms an integral part of our education. I hope to be able to make a personal contribution in the design of such a program. We must strive to sustain an organic continuity of imaginative freedom beginning with the poetic and spontaneous vision of childhood and growing into a fully developed aesthetic consciousness.

---

* *Ibid.*, p. 140.

Beverly McDermott

Gerald McDermott

by PRISCILLA MOULTON

The awarding of the Caldecott Medal for *Arrow to the Sun* concludes a critical period for Gerald McDermott, a period begun two years earlier when *Anansi the Spider* was designated a Caldecott Honor Book. Gerald then realized that his work as a book illustrator was valued by children's librarians, even though he was at first a film artist. Gerald originally produced *Anansi the Spider* as an animated film; and since he knew of no precedent for transforming a film into a picture book, he made it his responsibility to solve the technical problems involved.

We met in 1973 at the Newbery-Caldecott announcement reception. In my town of Brookline, Massachusetts, Gerald began speaking about his work as a filmmaker and as a book illustrator, giving *Arrow to the Sun* its initial public showings. It was Gerald's first opportunity to learn how children reacted to his art. "I was tremendously excited," he wrote afterward, "by the sessions at the various schools. Until recently I'd spent so much time working in my 'monk's cell' that I rarely had contact with the real world — with the people . . . who see the films and the books. . . . There was . . . joy . . . in meeting the children and in watching their faces as they watched the films and listened to my stories." At those sessions, children seemed to see more in Gerald's films and books than adults did. But both listened to Gerald describe how he works with story, folk art, and music. The audiences began to sense the discipline required: the extensive reading, the self-searching, the weeks and months of meticulous effort — all to produce the thousands of separate drawings needed for a ten- or twelve-minute film.

Gerald McDermott grew up in a family in which no one was associated with the arts. When, as a very young child, he began to draw, his parents wondered at it. Realizing the boy had a special interest, they enrolled him in Saturday classes for children at the Detroit Institute of Arts. He was only four, but he derived so much enjoyment from these sessions that his mother and father continued to encourage and support him in the classes for over ten years. Thus Gerald spent every Saturday of his childhood immersed in the images of the museum, absorbing their variety and richness, storing up inspiration for later life.

Of his elementary-school art experiences, Gerald remembers nothing. He does recall, however, the importance of winning a poster contest in a school competition when he was about ten. This was his first award — the first of several which stimulated and motivated him. About this time he auditioned successfully for a part in a local radio show dramatizing Detroit's two hundred and fiftieth anniversary. This led to small parts in other programs and subsequently to his becoming a member of the regular cast of a Saturday morning show called "Storyland." For a couple of years, Gerald read for these programs; he learned about music and timing and sound effects and gained invaluable experience.

For Gerald his high school days were a most significant part of his training to be an artist. He attended a special public school which focused on the artistically talented with a student body from all over Detroit. A rigidly designed curriculum was based on Bauhaus principles. Here was the formal approach to drawing and painting — in fact, the whole systematic organization which underlies Gerald's work today. In addition, Gerald studied music for four years and classical ballet for two. School was totally consuming. Gerald developed an intense interest in producing live-action films and worked at this on his own time, alone or with friends. In his senior year he began experimenting with graphics on film. During this period, his parents were enthusiastically supportive.

A Scholastic Publications scholarship offered the means for art training at Pratt Institute. He expected to devote himself to his studies as he had done in high school, but the Pratt program proved disappointing. He felt that it failed to carry him forward, so he left and went to work in television. He had spent his summer vacation making a film, *The Stonecutter*, and because of this production he was hired as a graphic designer for New York's public television station, Channel 13. Here Gerald did all kinds of film work, learning as he went; the following fall he submitted this work for Institute credit and returned to Pratt with permission to engage in independent study — a privilege not usually granted at this time.

Between his junior and senior year at Pratt, Gerald made his first trip to Europe. *The Stonecutter* served as entrée to film studios in England, Yugoslavia, and France. Visiting and making friends in these studios, Gerald experienced for the first time a sense of kinship with those who saw their own film work as art. He was greatly stimulated by the excitement pervading this field in Europe.

After graduating from Pratt, Gerald moved to Manhattan and pursued his work as a filmmaker. He spent most of his time trying to interest someone in producing his films, but he met with little success and became discouraged. During this period, however, his work began to assume a shape. He was making *Flight of Icarus* when he met the Jungian mythologist, Joseph Campbell. Gerald had been reading Campbell's writings and had found in them a great source of inspiration. Now, through a growing knowledge of Campbell's ideas, Gerald began to focus on the theme of the hero quest as the subject of his animated films. At this time, Gerald met a particularly interesting young woman, with whom he shared many interests. She was a painter, recently graduated from Brooklyn College, where she had studied under Ad Reinhardt. Beverly Brodsky and Gerald McDermott were married in 1969. Gerald was at work on his films, *Anansi the Spider* and *The Magic Tree*, but there seemed to be little support for his work, and the newlyweds sought a change of environment. They moved to southern France where they fell in love with the quality and the pace of Mediterranean life.

Just before they left New York, however, Gerald had met George Nicholson, who was to be an important figure in Gerald's professional career. George made Gerald aware of the world of children's book publishing and offered him a multi-book contract. Gerald then left for France, where he set to work transforming his first films into picture books. These two years in Southern France were active, stimulating, and wonderfully satisfying for the McDermotts. *Anansi the Spider* was cited as a Caldecott Honor Book. Back in the United States to receive the plaudits, Gerald was encouraged by the recognition of his work. The warmth of this reception suggested new possibilities for his future so he and Beverly returned to this country. Gerald went to work simultaneously on the book and the film, *Arrow to the Sun*.

Gerald is now a recognized illustrator and filmmaker. He is satisfied that within the last couple of years people have begun to look at his work differently and to accept it as a departure from familiar styles of illustration. He speaks to us visually, this reteller of myth, firing our imaginations and arousing our wonder.

Picture Books, Art and Illustration

by BARBARA BADER

Ten years, ten books. Ten books that, one by one, have been put forth as the best of the year's picture books, by inference the best that America could produce.

This is the burden of the Newbery and Caldecott awards. As a means of focusing attention on children's books, the awards have been singularly successful. Once a year children's books are news. The choices arouse interest; people seek them out. On the basis of the awards, moreover, the winners are preserved in perpetuity. They acquire a permanent standing.

For assorted reasons, this is especially true of the Caldecott winners. Anyone who frequents a library has seen students of children's literature assembling a pile of Caldecott Medal books and diligently examining them in the belief that they represent a touchstone of quality, in particular of artistic quality.

From the past ten years, this is the body of work they will find.

✓ ✓ ✓

Always Room for One More, Sorche Nic Leodhas's adaptation of a rhyming Scottish tale, is ingeniously pictured by Nonny Hogrogian as a shadow play rising out of the mists. Texture and silhouette are the basic components; or atmosphere and gesture — best seen perhaps when Lachie MacLachlan stands by his door hailing the first passing cart. The heather sweeps over the horizon; the house sits squat and low, hugging the hill; his upraised hand says "Welcome"; the wayfarer is the weary traveler incarnate.

When the figures cease being striped or cross-hatched shadows, however, and become individuals, persons with faces, one discovers that they all look alike. They not only have the same sharp-nosed long-lipped faces, they have the same looks on those faces. And they strike the same poses; they're all striking poses. By the end there's no more big-hearted Lachie MacLachlan — or tinker or tailor or sailor — but a passel of performers putting on a good show.

This was Hogrogian's first full-fledged picture book and it seemed fresh — a new approach. Whether that approach has the appeal for children that it had for adults is questionable. Whether a more personalized, anecdotal approach could have turned a long rhyme in Scots dialect into a successful children's picture book is open to question, too. But the book suffers most in retrospect because it has come to look mannered. As accomplished as the illustration is, the pictures have very little content. The point is made, but it doesn't matter as it should.

Sam, Bangs & Moonshine, written and pictured by Evaline Ness, is a classy book, as high-class an object as a Gucci bag or a Hermès scarf. This is not a matter of mere surface glitter. Just before the double page spread illustrated in this volume, with its first line smartly set in larger type, its evocative pattern of boats, its picturesque peaked house, its small musing child, are two pages that are almost blank. The left-hand page is the copyright page, and its obligatory data is printed in sea-green; to the right is a half-title printed in black with the ampersand in green. Even when no one is looking, *Sam, Bangs & Moonshine* keeps up appearances.

The story is about a child "named Samantha but always called Sam" whose fanciful tales (called moonshine) endanger both the little boy who believes them and her beloved cat, known as Bangs. It is a story complete in words; there is no need for pictures. Nor do the pictures *tell* the story. Most of them, in fact, are static. Only once does something really happen before your eyes, something that you can't wait to find out about: Sam sees hopping toward her on its long hind legs a tiny, funny-looking animal. (A gerbil, her father insists, not, as Sam would have it, a baby giraffe.)

Overall, *Sam, Bangs & Moonshine* is a conventional story,

One of the prints popularly known as Images d'Epinals from *Les Maitres Graveurs Populaires 1800-1850* by Jean-Marie Dumont, L'Imageries Pellerin, Epinal (Vosges)

with pictures, gotten up as a picture book. This is not a cardinal sin, but neither is it cause for celebration. Moreover the illustrations contain little of direct interest to a child, and their interest to an adult is chiefly in their technique and design. Characteristic are the pinwheel of slat fences and the file of twisted tree trunks, elements that have no bearing on the story and no meaning in themselves; they say nothing. Here as elsewhere Ness is not so much an illustrator as a set designer, and she seems to me an illustrator for children only by happenstance.

On to *Drummer Hoff,* adapted by Barbara Emberley, pictured by Ed Emberley, an old cumulative rhyme made into a heavy-treading, high-keyed picture book. Anything so lacking in variety and inflection can either be praised for its plainness or faulted for its obviousness, depending on one's point of view. But it is difficult to imagine a plausible defense of the worked-up woodcuts that form the basis of its humor.

278

One of the prints popularly known as Images d'Epinals from *Les Maitres Graveurs Populaires 1800-1850* by Jean-Marie Dumont, L'Imageries Pellerin, Epinal (Vosges)

Their antecedents, the crude woodcuts that once appeared in chapbooks and on broadsides, have served as models for many an artist. They have vigor, directness, concision, and withal a certain stiffness that, to our eyes, gives a stagey, sportive look to the matter at hand. The stiffness is archaic, a throwback to beginnings, but the clear-cut crisp quality derives from the very language of woodcut — the bounding line, the parallel strokes, the solid black.

Emberley cuts this way, that way, every which way. Far from defining form, all that wild cutting effaces it; and the arbitrary application of patches and stripes of garish color serves only to increase the disjunction between form and design. The simple, direct manner of the popular woodcut and its value as illustration are sabotaged by superficial elaboration.

A certain cachet attaches in picture books to the use of woodcuts, and derivative modes and techniques are much in evidence in books based on traditional rhymes and tales. It is as if a woodcut were *ipso facto* "art" — a higher form of creation than mere drawing, and as if a period or folk style somehow conferred authenticity. But a model can easily become a crutch, and an imitation can be a travesty.

To take up *The Fool of the World and the Flying Ship* as pictured by Uri Shulevitz, is to bite gratefully into a loaf of honest bread. Here is the Fool, looking simple and guileless; here are his brothers, looking gross and devious; here is an unconcerned cow and an attentive dog. The Fool sets out to seek his fortune and marry the Czar's daughter. Does he know how to make a flying ship and win her? the ancient old man asks him. No, he doesn't know. Then what is he going to do? "God knows," says the Fool of the World.

They eat, they drink and make merry; then the ancient says to the Fool . . . that one must turn the page to find out. And there, on the crest of a golden road, is a flying ship. A ship all ready to fly, with its square sail billowing and its pennant flapping and its bowsprit pointed up and away. When you have taken your fill of the little ship, you spot the Fool stretched on the ground asleep, and while the story proceeds you have a page to anticipate his delight when he wakes to find it.

Next comes an exultant wordless doublespread, the Fool of the World sailing over the countryside, vast and minute, and there are other good pictorial moments, as well as some in the second half that seem feeble or clumsy. In concept and design the book is less distinctive than Shulevitz's earlier *One Monday Morning*. But it has two great attributes that the preceding winners lack, memorable imagery and a sense of conviction.

The same can be said of William Steig's masterly *Sylvester and the Magic Pebble*. *Sylvester* is an original story conceived in terms of images that constantly renew one's interest in it. At its core is the most excruciating of all situations — ceasing to be. Donkey Sylvester, holding the magic pebble, wishes he were a rock; and he is a rock. Who then will ever pick up the pebble and wish that Sylvester was there? His parents, of course, because it reminds them of his penchant for collecting stones.

Steig's characters are individuals and his pictures are lovely. Few picture book artists except for Beatrix Potter and Edward Ardizzone have used watercolor so felicitously. He has made lovely, touching pictures of a donkey who turns into a rock. The rock, for its part, lies on the hill through the seasons and each becomes a poetic metaphor for Sylvester's condition and prospects. Come spring, he, too, must return to life.

This is pictorial storytelling of a high order, beyond the reach of most illustrators. The idea that children's taste in art is formed by what they see is to my mind overworked, and a poor excuse for exalting much artifice. But Steig has conceived nobly and, through his art, made his conception real. He has made us feel what it's like to be a donkey become a rock on a hill in the snow.

The five remaining books, like three of the foregoing, are based upon traditional material; but there the similarity ends.

Gail Haley's *A Story, A Story*, the pictorial rendering of one of the African Anansi tales, is an unexceptionable book — effective for reading to a group, commonplace as art. The spread represented in this volume perfectly illustrates its utility — the large scale, the clear-cut flat forms, the manifest action, the vivid coloring — and, equally, its deficiencies. What exists in African art as expressive simplification is here facile stylization, without meaning or force. The tree, for instance, is not an idea of a tree but a wallpaper pattern; and a similar lack of precise observation, variety or modulation is marked throughout. It needn't be so. Janina Domanska's drawings for *The Coconut Thieves* and Marcia Brown's woodcuts for *Once a Mouse* are demonstrations, in their different ways, of creative as against rubber-stamp stylization.

The phenomenon of the deserving artist honored for something less than his or her best work is a familiar one, and examples turn up in this group, too. The first is Blair Lent — another illustrator who, like Domanska, might be called a creative borrower (and who scrupulously disclaims authenticity). *The Funny Little Woman*, a tale of "Old Japan," is as likeable as can be but not in a class with *The Wave* or *Tikki*

Tikki Tembo as an artistic and dramatic entity, or with some of Lent's others for sheer illustrative verve.

A hallmark of Lent's books is the cunning way he plots the action pictorially from the title page forward, and that we see here, too. On the title page, framed by the Japanese chrysanthemum motif, is the funny little woman holding her talisman, a small rice paddle. Next we take in her little house, the nearby river and bridge, and the approach of her elderly neighbor — the setting and circumstance of the story to come. Then with the turn of a page, the wall of the house opens up and we see her inside, making rice dumplings and laughing her first "Tee-he-he-he."

But we also see, where part of the garden has fallen away, a tell-tale crack in the floor and, at the next moment, a dumpling about to roll into it. In a thrice the funny little woman is down the hole, too, running along an underground river, talking with statues, being seized by a wicked *oni*, while back at the little house her elderly neighbor knocks at the door, peers in the window, and starts back over the bridge.

The side action isn't part of the story and in this case it doesn't contribute directly to it (as, for instance, the stillness of the Old Man With The Ladder does in *Tikki Tikki Tembo*). But besides pleasing a child, it makes more graphic the passage of time and brings us to the heart-warming climax, the funny little woman's return to her little house where her neighbor waits to help her up from the hole and trees, flowers, birds break out in welcoming array.

Lent has not simply pictured a story, he has made *The Funny Little Woman* a pictorial adventure, and consequential.

The one merit of *One Fine Day* — a not inconsiderable merit — is that it tells a simple cumulative story clearly to small children. It has momentum, and at every opening something happens. On the debit side the old woman is grotesque; the animals by and large are ungainly; and the afflicted fox, the focal figure, is neither a real fox nor a real character — that is to say he has neither verisimilitude (like the animals of Rojankovsky, Sendak and Garth Williams) nor personality (for which see Petunia, the silly goose, or Ferdinand, the peaceable bull). Altogether the treatment is ambitious; the execution is thin.

Margot Zemach, who has to her credit *The Judge*, *A Penny a Look* and others of uncommon interest, is another splendid artist honored for a weak book — in this case the decidedly inferior *Duffy and the Devil*. A basic function of illustration is to make the meaning of the story plain; but if anything *Duffy and the Devil* is more easily understood paragraph by paragraph than picture by picture. Some of the compositions are crowded and chaotic, but there are other reasons, too, for the book's difficulty.

The story is a Cornish variant of Rumpelstiltskin, the tale of a man of means who marries a poor girl under the misapprehension that she can "spin like a saint and knit like an angel," while she has pledged herself to the devil who does it for her. She finds a way to extricate herself, predictably, but one could not say that the story ends happily. Rather, ironically and amusingly; happiness is not an issue.

Happiness is not an issue because, one and all, the characters are buffoons. This may be true to the original; the illustration accentuates it. The girl, Duffy, is crude and gross, a carbon-copy of the squire; in pigtails she can pass as his daughter. The old crone who keeps house for the squire is indistinguishable from Duffy's termagant mother. The local folk, witches included, are so many more slatterns and louts. Which is witch? one might ask. One could certainly ask who's who. Dramatically, psychologically, what are these people to one another?

Cornwall or not, this is Rowlandson country, a caricature of society. In *The Judge*, which pays homage to Rowlandson, too, we have a persecutor and victims (never mind that they're not as innocent as they pretend); in *A Penny a Look*, one of the two brothers has his doubts about the freak-show scheme, and the one-eyed men put a deserving end to it. Zemach is adept at nuance; she can portray character by the twist of a foot, but *Duffy and the Devil* draws no distinctions. In everyday terms the characters are all foolish, fat and funny, and what is particularly suspect, funny because they're fat.

Arrow to the Sun, Gerald McDermott's picturization of a Pueblo Indian myth, may be the most problematic of the lot. Contained within a thirty-two-page picture book — and the film that was made concurrently — is an epic quest in outline. A boy born to the Lord of the Sun and an Indian maiden goes to seek his father, passes the trials set him, and transformed, returns to earth bearing his father's spirit to the world of men. "The people celebrated his return in the Dance of Life," the book concludes.

To me this is meaningless. We are given to understand that the sun has power, but what power (apart from the ability to transmit a "spark of life") and for what purpose? Light, heat, fire — none of these attributes of the sun are invoked. Nor is the Lord of the Sun portrayed as a broadly generative or beneficent spirit. In what altogether does the boy's transformation consist? What is the spirit of his father that he brings back to earth?

The boy, the villagers, and the Lord of the Sun are all depicted as animated kachina dolls, an ostensible Pueblo touch that is also a good device for an animated film. An animated doll can be manipulated to broadcast action or emotion far more readily than a man — mouth down, he's glum; mouth up, he's glad — and, come what may, an animated doll is amusing. But in actuality kachina dolls represent supernatural beings, rain spirits and the like, not human figures. To blur the distinction is to rob the kachina-image of its point and to suggest, wrongly, that geometric dolls represent the Pueblo image of people. (From early times the Pueblos have drawn human beings realistically.)

Moreover, while some of the kachinas are genuinely, intentionally funny, many are stylized abstractions only; the same is true of other Indian spirit-figures. When such forms are used indiscriminately, the onlooker fails to realize "how few of the frequent distortions or exaggerations of human or animal likenesses are meant to be grotesque."* They all take on a comic (or horrific) aspect, to the detriment of a true perception of tribal art.

It is just because tribal art — Indian, African, Oceanic — has been widely misconstrued and misapplied that discretion is called for. This is all the more so when a book, like *Arrow to the Sun*, takes on an allover "Pueblo" look — the consequence also of the patterned forms made from Pueblo patterns and the lush coloring broadly suggestive of the Southwest. On Pueblo pottery, however, the geometric patterns are applied with close attention to form, with discipline and restraint. Indeed, these are hallmarks of Pueblo art as a whole, which Miguel Covarrubias went so far as to characterize as "sober, formalistic and conservative."**

In short, there is no basis in Pueblo art for this highly theatrical treatment, visually arresting though it may be. To what extent it is dramatically compelling is the next question.

Prospectively, the most dramatic passages are the four trials — the lions reduced to a frazzle, the serpents tied in knots, the bees put to rout, the lightning shaken-up. There is no real contest, the boy has so much the better of it; but in the film (where the passages crackle) there is action and duration — a period of time in which boy meets beast. On the book-page he triumphs instanteously, *ping*.

The triumph is mechanical and abstract. This is not to disparage symbolic abstraction. Leo Lionni's *Little Blue and Little Yellow*, the most abstract picture book extant, is one of the most moving. Blair Lent fills a hut with symbolic figures in *Why the Sun and the Moon Live in the Sky*, and convinces us that they represent the sea and its creatures. But Lionni's blobs of blue and yellow, for all that they are blobs, have individuality. This is a small thing but enormously important: the book would not have nearly the same impact if they were circles. Lent's symbolic personages have individuality too, as

---

* Douglas, Frederic H., and Rene d'Harnoncourt, *Indian Art of the United States*, New York, The Museum of Modern Art, 1941, p. 11.
** Covarrubias, Miguel, *The Eagle, the Jaguar and the Serpent: Indian Art of the Americas*, New York, Alfred A. Knopf, 1954, p. 224.

Illustration by Blair Lent from *Why the Sun and the Moon Live in the Sky* by Elphinstone Dayrell (Houghton Mifflin)

do the masked figures they're based upon. In contrast, McDermott's symbolic representations of man or beast are formalized designs. Two or more designs can play out a comedy, briefly; it happens in television commercials all the time. But high drama is beyond them. And in fact the effect of the trials is comedic. They're funny.

The trials are also done in pantomime. Indeed, the book as a whole is pantomime, whether or not there's an accompany-

286

Illustration by Blair Lent from *Why the Sun and the Moon Live in the Sky* by Elphinstone Dayrell (Houghton Mifflin)

ing text. The depersonalized gesticulating figures are the essence of pantomime (to efface themselves similarly, professional mimes dress in black or white); and so is the concision. Jean-Louis Barrault, a student and master of the art, once observed that pantomime "is an action which takes place exclusively in the present; it contains neither narrative nor explanation."* *Macbeth*, he noted, "could be reduced to a pantomime of forty minutes."

* Barrault, Jean-Louis, *The Theatre of Jean-Louis Barrault*, London, Barrie & Rockliff, 1959, p. 29.

287

Arrow to the Sun is a myth of divine birth and transfiguration become a brief spectacle — eye-filling, transitory, and to me, empty.

⸱   ⸱   ⸱

These, then, are the ten prize-winners. Some are effective picture books, very few merit applause as art or illustration. Since an award must be given each year, it is fair to ask what might have won instead. Were these as good as any or were other, better books passed by?

Some come to mind immediately. In the year of *Drummer Hoff*, a banner year, either *One Monday Morning* or *The Wedding Procession of the Rag Doll*, pictured by Harriet Pincus, or Tomi Ungerer's *Moon Man*. (None of these was an Honor Book.) In the year of *A Story, A Story*, Maurice Sendak's cartoon triumph *In the Night Kitchen*, followed by the Lore Segal-Harriet Pincus collaboration *Tell Me a Mitzi*. (The first was an Honor Book.) In the year of *One Fine Day*, William Pène du Bois's *Bear Circus* foremost, but also *Look Again!* by Tana Hoban; *Changes, Changes* by Pat Hutchins; and *If All the Seas Were One Sea*, pictured by Janina Domanska. (Only the last was an Honor Book.)

Because the choices of these years are among the most deficient of the ten, the alternatives are particularly striking. The citation of *One Fine Day*, for instance, and the total neglect of such a richly imagined and brilliantly executed book as *Bear Circus* is hard to fathom.

Pène du Bois has never won the Caldecott, however, and neither has Tomi Ungerer. Very few books based on original material have won, even fewer in recent years. Pène du Bois and Ungerer are also original creative talents: the two often go together. Jean Charlot, Leo Lionni, Crockett Johnson, Garth Williams . . . what they have in common is a body of unusual, skillful, uncited work — books that stand on their own.

By the large the prize books are imposing editions of folk and fairy tales, or splashy ones. Other ethnic and folk material is well represented on the list of Honor Books. Such books lend themselves to artistic effects and artistic referrals (Indian or antiquarian or whatever). They have setting, décor, costumes: more art per square inch. They look like art.

It's an illusion, the consequences of equating art with artiness. Art is a line that talks, an averted head that speaks volumes. Art is a single tulip growing on a curve of the world in Esphyr Slobodkina's *Caps for Sale*, to take an example out of the blue. Artists are the source of art; subject and style, as such are immaterial. Bernard Waber, defining Lyle by an outline, is more the artist than many who aspire to paint murals in picture books. Art is substance, not appearance. It has character.

Picture books that qualify are not lacking. Were they given their due, there might be more.

The Honor Books

1966-1975

Honoring the Honor Books

by ELIZABETH JOHNSON

The best of children's books brings great pleasure to those who create them and to those who read them. People who have the responsibility of helping children find books have an exhilarating task that has its annual climax with the announcement of the Newbery and Caldecott Medal and Honor Books. These books, the winners and those so nearly winners, are truly the most distinguished books of each year's publications.

The Honor Books serve to enlarge the recognition of important books, thus making it possible for more than just the two prize-winners to be honored each year. With the staggering number of books published every year many a good book can easily be lost without the publicity which comes to an Honor Book. Often there has been complaint from people who work with children that the Medal and Honor Books are not the most popular with young readers. It was never the intent of the founder of the awards, Frederic G. Melcher, or the Newbery-Caldecott Committees, to have a popularity contest. Instead this is the chance to point out each year's prestigious books: the ones which would seem to be of the most durable quality.

Studying the ten-year span of Honor Books is rather like putting a kaleidoscope to one's eye and twisting it now this way, now that, to see if any pattern will emerge. Within a kaleidoscope there is not always a striking pattern; but there is always something fascinating to see. In this survey of Honor Books, 1966-1975, there is no clear pattern of what Honor Books are chosen or why, but rather a shifting display of interesting facts, surmises and ideas. There is also sheer pleasure in a second look at this collection of good books.

In the early years of Newbery-Caldecott Awards, Honor Books were called Runners-Up. In recent years, to focus well-deserved attention on these fine books, the members of the Newbery-Caldecott Committee have changed the designation, thus highlighting this recognition of honor. This change has apparently worked out well, because, according to the *Publishers' Weekly* of February 26, 1973, it is a fact established by the publishers that Honor Books double in sales volume, and "In addition to the immediate impact on book sales, winning a medal or being cited as an Honor Book adds to the life span of the title."

There has been discussion as to the reason why in some years there are several Honor Books and in some years only one. While the voting procedure may be changed in the future, if a less complicated system can be made as valid, an understanding of the present system might be useful.

The Newbery-Caldecott Awards Committee is made up of twenty-three members of the Children's Services Division of the American Library Association. Having carefully considered the year's output of books for nomination, the committee meets for approximately twelve hours of deliberation at the American Library Association Midwinter Meeting. Following a long, lively and often heated discussion of the titles which are nominated by the committee and by the membership of the Children's Services Division, the vote is called for and the balloting begins. In voting, each committee member must give a first, a second, and a third choice. A first choice receives a count of four points, second choice three points, and third choice two points. Although a medal winner is occasionally chosen on the first ballot, such is not usually the case.

To be a winner a book must receive at least twelve first-choice votes, or a count of forty-eight. It must also be at least twelve points ahead of its nearest contender. If no winner is found on the first ballot, the discussion starts all over again, with members arguing for or against certain titles on the slate, and with titles no longer receiving sufficient support being dropped. Then there is again a ballot with first, second, and third choices being given by each member. This procedure of discussion and then balloting continues until a winner clearly emerges. The committee then turns to the other titles on the final ballot which, while below the necessary twelve-point spread, are still strong contenders, close enough in points to the winner and to each other, to be designated an Honor Book or Honor Books.

What kind of book becomes an Honor Book? Among the Newbery awards, fiction has received the greatest number of honors. Seventeen of the books in this period between 1966 and 1975 belong in that category. This includes some historical fiction, such as Scott O'Dell's *The King's Fifth*, 1967,* about the Spanish Southwest, and *Sing Down the Moon*, 1971, about the Navajo Indians. *My Brother Sam Is Dead*, by James Lincoln Collier and Christopher Collier, 1975, is a strong and moving story of the Revolutionary War and its effect on a divided family.

There are a few examples of realism. *Our Eddie* by Sulamith Ish-Kishor, 1970, presents not only Jewish problems, but also the problems of illness and death, with a haunting quality in the characters that is not easily forgotten. *The Jazz Man* by Mary Hays Weik, 1967, an emotionally understated but powerfully written story, is a portrayal of a small boy deserted by his family. *The Planet of Junior Brown* by Virginia Hamilton, 1972, is a novel of black inner city children, written realistically but not sordidly, with unexpected dimensions. *Incident at Hawk's Hill* by Allen W. Eckert, 1972, is a fully believable story of a small boy who, lost in the wilderness, lives with a badger until he is finally found. It is most interesting to note that this story was not published as a juvenile book. This points out the understanding of Newbery-Caldecott Committees from the beginning that to win an award a book need not be written for children: any book that a child might read may be considered.

Fantasy is very popular. Books like *The Black Cauldron* by Lloyd Alexander, 1966, and *The Dark Is Rising* by Susan Cooper, 1974, are part of a series depicting whole new worlds and people with legend-like qualities; yet each is so well done

---

* All the dates given in this article are for the year of the award, not the year of publication.

that it could stand as a single book and thus be honored. *The Perilous Gard* by Elizabeth Marie Pope, 1975, has much the same feeling, in an enthralling tale of the sinister forces of Pre-Druid magic that surround an Elizabethan castle and its inhabitants.

Other titles among the fantasies are imaginative, highly original books that deserve to be brought to the attention of readers. *Enchantress from the Stars* by Sylvia Louise Engdahl, 1971, is for the more advanced readers in the science fiction field. *Kneeknock Rise* by Natalie Babbitt, 1971, explains the cause of a mysterious moaning sound; but the villagers refuse to accept this, preferring their own monster illusion. *The Fearsome Inn* by Isaac Bashevis Singer, 1968, concerns an inn run by a witch and a devil until a young man saves the inn and the people caught in its spell with his magic chalk. *The Journey Outside* by Mary Q. Steele, 1970, is a compelling strange story of a boy's search for wisdom. *The Animal Family* by Randall Jarrell, 1966, is a poetic mood fantasy showing the need of earth's creatures for each other.

In only two years, 1971 and 1966, has there been more than one fantasy in the honors, and in those years the Newbery prize itself was not given to fantasy. But in 1972 four of the five Honor Books were fiction and one was fantasy; moreover, a fantasy, *Mrs. Frisby and the Rats of NIMH* by Robert O'Brien won the Newbery. In 1975 three fiction titles and one fantasy were Honor Books, while *M.C. Higgins, the Great,* by Virginia Hamilton, which might be called fantastic fiction, won the Newbery.

Since the Newbery Award was established, there have never been many non-fiction books winning honors or medals. This period was no exception. There are only three, but they show great variety. *The Upstairs Room* by Johanna Reiss, 1973, is the true story of Annie, a Jewish girl, living in secret on the second floor of a Dutch farmhouse during Hitler's invasion of Holland. It is a day-by-day account, interestingly effective in its quiet way. *To Be a Slave* by Julius Lester, 1969, is a collection of reminiscences and experiences of ex-slaves, skillfully put together as a running commentary on the history of Black Americans. *The Many Ways of Seeing: An Introduction to the Pleasures of Art* by Janet Gaylord Moore, 1970, is an exploration of the relationship between art and life, and how the two constantly influence each other. It is a successful attempt to heighten visual perception and awareness.

Can it be that Newbery-Caldecott Committees are more inclined to fantasy and fiction? There would be no way of proving any preferences since the membership of the Com mittee changes each year so that different backgrounds, tastes, and opinions are available; and, of course, the books published in each year vary in many ways. Undoubtedly creativity and excellent writing in fiction and fantasy are easier to spot. Perhaps excellence in non-fiction has not been truly recognized because of the special requirements inherent in the writing of such books. As each book usually deals with one subject, there is less opportunity for a book to have universal appeal. Whatever the reason, non-fiction winners have been few.

Caldecott Honor Books show even greater variety than the Newbery Honor Books. The range is wide, the only rule being that it must be a distinguished picture book, with text worthy of the illustrations. In this decade being surveyed there are many different categories.

Not often have there been "factual" picture books receiving honors. *Cathedral* by David Macaulay, 1974, has a clear but brief text that sustains the meticulously detailed drawings of the building of a Gothic cathedral in the thirteenth century. *When Clay Sings*, 1973, illustrated by Tom Bahti and written by Byrd Baylor, tells simply of Indian children of today searching for bits of ancient pottery which would help them to learn about the earlier life of their people. The authentic motifs in browns and tans make a beautiful book about the Indian art that is now preserved in museums.

Many of the Caldecott Honor Books are created around a story line. Some of them are traditional fairy stories such as *Tom Tit Tot* by Evaline Ness, 1966, and *Snow White and the*

Seven Dwarfs by Nancy Ekholm Burkert, 1973. Some are African folk tales, such as Gerald McDermott's colorful version of *Anansi the Spider*, 1973, and *Why the Sun and the Moon Live in the Sky*, 1969, by Elphinstone Dayrell, with illustrations by Blair Lent, who also illustrated a Tlingit Tribe story, *Angry Moon*, 1971, retold by William Sleator.

Two books of this period have the feeling of being traditional, yet they are original both in the writing of the stories and in the art. *The Emperor and the Kite*, 1968, by Jane Yolen with full-color pictures by Ed Young, has impressive illustrations adapting the ancient Chinese paper-cut art form. *Hildilid's Night*, 1972, by Cheli Durán Ryan and illustrated by Arnold Lobel has deft line drawings that help to create the humor and strength of the book.

Folk songs and rhymes have been the inspiration for some of the Honor Books. *One Wide River to Cross*, 1967, adapted by Barbara Emberley and illustrated by Ed Emberley, can serve also as a counting book as the animals, portrayed in handsome woodcuts, go across the Jordan River; the music of the song is included at the end. *Pop Corn and Ma Goodness*, 1970, by Edna Mitchell Preston, illustrated by Robert Andrew Parker, has folk-like verses that bring out the character of the watercolor paintings used as illustration. *The Three Jovial Huntsmen*, 1974, illustrated by Susan Jeffers, is the Mother Goose rhyme extended and enlarged by her imaginative artwork.

Alphabet books and counting books are always welcome in the picture book world. In this period there are three that are quite different and deserve to be especially honored. *Moja Means One: Swahili Counting Book*, 1972, by Muriel Feelings, illustrated by Tom Feelings, has as background the beauty of rural Africa shown in shades of brown and smoke-grey with the Swahili name for each number in bright red, all of which makes a striking book. *Jambo Means Hello: Swahili Alphabet Book*, 1975, by Muriel Feelings, illustrated by Tom Feelings, gives twenty-four simple words, one for each letter of the Swahili alphabet, with majestic illustrations that catch the beauty and heat of Africa. *Hosie's Alphabet*, 1973, by Hosea, Tobias and Lisa Baskin, illustrated by their father, Leonard Baskin, is a handsome creative picture book with stunning colors and new concepts for alphabet words.

The sea lends itself as a beautiful backdrop for two of the Honor Books. In *Hide and Seek Fog*, 1966, written by Alvin Tresselt and illustrated by Roger Duvoisin, the reader and looker can all but feel the fog as it creeps in and then recedes. It is a truly atmospheric book. *Seashore Story*, 1968, by Taro Yashima is also a mood book about a day at the seashore, done in muted but rich colors with an interesting combination of wide spaces and fine details in the drawings. Picture books for the very young are recognized, too. *Just Me* by Marie Hall Ets, 1966; *Goggles* by Ezra Jack Keats, 1970; *In the Night Kitchen* by Maurice Sendak, 1971; and *Thy Friend Obadiah* by Brinton Turkle, 1970, have children as their subjects. They also use detailed drawings full of details that small children enjoy studying. *Frederick*, 1968, *Alexander and the Wind-Up Mouse*, 1970, by Leo Lionni, and *Frog and Toad Are Friends* by Arnold Lobel, 1971, prove that picture books can be fun as well as full of fine artwork and thus win honors.

One pattern this kaleidoscopic survey yielded is the number of honor winners who have also been medal winners. In the Newbery field Lloyd Alexander's *The Black Cauldron* was an Honor Book in 1966; he won the Newbery prize in 1969 for *The High King*, the last in the series of Prydain stories. Virginia Hamilton's *The Planet of Junior Brown* was an Honor Book in 1972; in 1975 she won the Newbery prize for *M.C. Higgins, the Great*. Scott O'Dell has been a most consistent honor winner. After having won the Newbery in 1961 for *Island of the Blue Dolphins*, he has received honors for *The King's Fifth* in 1967, for *The Black Pearl* in 1968 and for *Sing Down the Moon* in 1971. Although they have not yet been medal winners, two other authors have received Honor awards three times in this ten-year period: Isaac Bashevis Singer was honored for *Zlateh the Goat* in 1967, *The Fearsome Inn* in 1968, and *When Shlemiel Went to Warsaw and Other Stories* in

1969; and Zilpha Keatley Snyder in 1968 for *The Egypt Game*, in 1972 for *The Headless Cupid*, and *The Witches of Worm* in 1973. The miracle of all Medal and Honor Books came in 1968 when E. L. Konigsburg not only won the Newbery for her *From the Mixed-Up Files of Mrs. Basil E. Frankweiler* but also received an Honor Book award for *Jennifer, Hecate, Macbeth, William McKinley and Me, Elizabeth*. (Had there been prizes for longest titles, she would have won those too.)

In the Caldecott field several artists have been recognized with honors many times within this ten-year period. Evaline Ness had Honor Books in *Tom Tit Tot*, 1966, *All in the Morning Early*, 1964, and *A Pocketful of Cricket*, 1965. *Sam, Bangs & Moonshine*, 1967, won her the Caldecott Medal. Ed Emberley was an honor winner in 1967 for *One Wide River to Cross* and won the Caldecott for *Drummer Hoff* in 1968. Blair Lent received an Honor Book award in 1965 for *The Wave*; then in this ten-year period his Honor Books were *Why the Sun and the Moon Live in the Sky*, 1969, and *The Angry Moon*, 1971. With *The Funny Little Woman* the Caldecott Medal became his in 1973.

Leo Lionni has consistently created notable art. Before this period, in 1961, he was honored for *Inch by Inch* and in 1964 for *Swimmy*. In the decade covered by this survey he had Honor Books for *Frederick* in 1968 and in 1970 for *Alexander and the Wind-Up Mouse*. In an interesting exchange of emphasis, Arnold Lobel was on the list of Caldecott Honor Books for *Frog and Toad Are Friends*, 1971; yet a continuation of these same stories with the same type of fine artwork brought *Frog and Toad Together* a Newbery Honor in 1973. In between, Mr. Lobel won another Caldecott Honor Book for *Hildilid's Night* in 1972. Besides an Honor for *Seashore Story* in 1968, Taro Yashima had two previous Honors for *Crow Boy* in 1956 and *Umbrella* in 1959. Tom Feelings had two Honor Books in this period: *Moja Means One: Swahili Counting Book*, 1972, and *Jambo Means Hello: Swahili Alphabet Book* in 1975.

An impressive note is the number of artists who repeat winning honors *after* having won the Caldecott Prize. Marie Hall Ets did so in 1966 for *Just Me*. She had previously won the Caldecott prize in 1960 for *Nine Days to Christmas* as well as having received Honor Books in 1945 for *In the Forest*, in 1952 for *Mr. T. W. Anthony Woo*, in 1956 for *Play With Me* and in 1957 for *Mr. Penny's Race Horse*.

Roger Duvoisin, a Caldecott winner in 1948 for *White Snow, Bright Snow*, won an Honor Book in 1966 for *Hide and Seek Fog*. Ezra Jack Keats, the Caldecott winner in 1963 for *The Snowy Day*, received an Honor in 1970 for *Goggles*. Maurice Sendak is the champion repeater of them all. He won the Caldecott in 1964 with *Where the Wild Things Are*. His Honor Book in this decade was in 1971 for *In the Night Kitchen*. Previous Honor Books were *A Very Special House*, 1954; *What Do You Say, Dear?*, 1959; *The Moon Jumpers*, 1960; *Little Bear's Visit*, 1962; and *Mr. Rabbit and the Lovely Present*, 1963. This brings out the fact that the prize itself and the Honor Book awards truly recognize the consistent high standards of children's book artists. Good artists we have with us for a long time.

All of the foregoing listing seems to indicate that only artists and writers who have worked in the children's book field for some time are recognized. Fortunately, this is not so. There are constantly new names appearing in the fields of art and writing. In the Newbery area, of the thirty-one Honor Books in this period, twenty-two were by authors who were so honored for the first time. Of the twenty-six Caldecott Honor Books, thirteen artists were so honored for the first time.

This collection of Honor Books does show that recognition is given to new ideas and treatments in art and writing. That is exciting, for children's books must accept and use the new. It indicates that not only are authors and artists aware of changing times and of the necessity of producing really creative work, but also librarians are willing to watch for the new and unusual as well as to recognize the traditional.

The nominating and awarding of the Newbery-Caldecott Medal and Honor Books throughout the years have given all librarians the stimulating challenge of examining each year's publications and deciding which books are the best. For those librarians who are fortunate enough to serve on the Committee, it is a responsibility that is seriously undertaken. Almost all who have served consider the task one of the most exciting and instructive experiences in their professional careers. It is felt that one of the great values in making the awards is the opportunity for discussion of books at the national level; not in the terms of expense, social relevance, or relation to curriculum, but for those qualities in the Medal and Honor Books that help children and adults recognize excellence wherever they may look for it.

A mark of the living quality of any book is in the pleasure of rereading it. Often there is a new discovery of riches, as well as enjoyment of favorite parts. This retrospective examination of the 1966-1975 Honor Books has proven that here is lasting quality and here, indeed, are books worthy of being honored.

The Newbery Medal Honor Books

1966 *The Animal Family*
   Written by RANDALL JARRELL
   Decorated by Maurice Sendak
   Published *(1965)* by PANTHEON

   The Black Cauldron
   Written by LLOYD ALEXANDER
   Published *(1965)* by HOLT

   The Noonday Friends
   Written by MARY STOLZ
   Illustrated by Louis S. Glanzman
   Published *(1965)* by HARPER

1967 *The Jazz Man*
   Written by MARY HAYS WEIK
   Illustrated by Ann Grifalconi
   Published *(1966)* by ATHENEUM

   The King's Fifth
   Written by SCOTT O'DELL
   Maps and decorations by Samuel Bryant
   Published *(1966)* by HOUGHTON MIFFLIN

   Zlateh the Goat and Other Stories
   Written by ISAAC BASHEVIS SINGER
   Illustrated by Maurice Sendak
   Published *(1966)* by HARPER

1968 *Jennifer, Hecate, Macbeth, William McKinley, and Me, Elizabeth*
   Written by E. L. KONIGSBURG
   Illustrated by E. L. Konigsburg
   Published *(1967)* by ATHENEUM

   The Black Pearl
   Written by SCOTT O'DELL
   Illustrated by Milton Johnson
   Published *(1967)* by HOUGHTON MIFFLIN

The Egypt Game
>Written by ZILPHA KEATLEY SNYDER
>Illustrated by Alton Raible
>Published *(1967)* by ATHENEUM

The Fearsome Inn
>Written by ISAAC BASHEVIS SINGER
>Illustrated by Nonny Hogrogian
>Published *(1967)* by SCRIBNER

1969   *To Be a Slave*
>Written by JULIUS LESTER
>Illustrated by Tom Feelings
>Published *(1968)* by DIAL

When Shlemiel Went to Warsaw and Other Stories
>Written by ISAAC BASHEVIS SINGER
>Illustrated by Margot Zemach
>Published *(1968)* by FARRAR, STRAUS

1970   *Journey Outside*
>Written by MARY Q. STEELE
>Illustrated by Rocco Negri
>Published *(1969)* by VIKING

Our Eddie
>Written by SULAMITH ISH-KISHOR
>Published *(1969)* by PANTHEON

The Many Ways of Seeing: An Introduction to the Pleasures of Art
>Written by JANET GAYLORD MOORE
>Published *(1969)* by WORLD

1971   *Enchantress from the Stars*
>Written by SYLVIA LOUISE ENGDAHL
>Illustrated by Rodney Shackell
>Published *(1970)* by ATHENEUM

Kneeknock Rise
>Written by NATALIE BABBITT
>Illustrated by Natalie Babbitt
>Published *(1970)* by FARRAR, STRAUS

Sing Down the Moon
>Written by SCOTT O'DELL
>Published *(1970)* by HOUGHTON MIFFLIN

1972   *Annie and the Old One*
Written by MISKA MILES
Illustrated by Peter Parnall
Published *(1971)* by ATLANTIC-LITTLE

Incident at Hawk's Hill
Written by ALLAN W. ECKERT
Published *(1971)* by LITTLE, BROWN

The Headless Cupid
Written by ZILPHA KEATLEY SNYDER
Illustrated by Alton Raible
Published *(1971)* by ATHENEUM

The Planet of Junior Brown
Written by VIRGINIA HAMILTON
Published *(1971)* by MACMILLAN

The Tombs of Atuan
Written by URSULA K. LE GUIN
Illustrated by Gail Garraty
Published *(1971)* by ATHENEUM

1973   *Frog and Toad Together*
Written by ARNOLD LOBEL
Illustrated by Arnold Lobel
Published *(1972)* by HARPER

The Upstairs Room
Written by JOHANNA REISS
Published *(1972)* by CROWELL

The Witches of Worm
Written by ZILPHA KEATLEY SNYDER
Illustrated by Alton Raible
Published *(1972)* by ATHENEUM

1974   *The Dark Is Rising*
Written by SUSAN COOPER
Illustrated by Alan E. Cober
Published *(1972)* by ATHENEUM/McELDERRY

1975   *Figgs and Phantoms*
Written by ELLEN RASKIN
Illustrated by Ellen Raskin
Published *(1974)* by DUTTON

My Brother Sam Is Dead
> Written by JAMES LINCOLN COLLIER AND
> CHRISTOPHER COLLIER
> Published *(1974)* by FOUR WINDS

Philip Hall Likes Me, I Reckon Maybe
> Written by BETTE GREENE
> Illustrated by Charles Lilly
> Published *(1974)* by DIAL

The Perilous Gard
> Written by ELIZABETH MARIE POPE
> Illustrated by Richard Cuffari
> Published *(1974)* by HOUGHTON MIFFLIN

The Caldecott Medal Honor Books

1966   *Hide and Seek Fog*
        Illustrated by ROGER DUVOISIN
        Written by Alvin Tresselt
        Published *(1965)* by LOTHROP

      Just Me
        Illustrated by MARIE HALL ETS
        Written by Marie Hall Ets
        Published *(1965)* by VIKING

      Tom Tit Tot
        Illustrated by EVALINE NESS
        Edited by Joseph Jacobs
        Published *(1965)* by SCRIBNER

1967   *One Wide River to Cross*
        Illustrated by ED EMBERLEY
        Adapted by Barbara Emberley
        Published *(1966)* by PRENTICE-HALL

1968   *Frederick*
        Illustrated by LEO LIONNI
        Written by Leo Lionni
        Published *(1967)* by PANTHEON

      Seashore Story
        Illustrated by TARO YASHIMA
        Written by Taro Yashima
        Published *(1967)* by VIKING

      The Emperor and the Kite
        Illustrated by ED YOUNG
        Written by Jane Yolen
        Published *(1967)* by WORLD

1969   *Why the Sun and the Moon Live in the Sky:*
      An African Folktale
        Illustrated by BLAIR LENT
        Written by Elphinstone Dayrell
        Published *(1968)* by HOUGHTON MIFFLIN

1970 *Alexander and the Wind-Up Mouse*
   Illustrated by LEO LIONNI
   Written by Leo Lionni
   Published *(1969)* by PANTHEON

 Goggles!
   Illustrated by EZRA JACK KEATS
   Written by Ezra Jack Keats
   Published *(1969)* by MACMILLAN

 Pop Corn & Ma Goodness
   Illustrated by ROBERT ANDREW PARKER
   Written by Edna Mitchell Preston
   Published *(1969)* by VIKING

 The Judge: an untrue tale
   Illustrated by MARGOT ZEMACH
   Written by Harve Zemach
   Published *(1969)* by FARRAR, STRAUS

 Thy Friend, Obadiah
   Illustrated by BRINTON TURKLE
   Written by Brinton Turkle
   Published *(1969)* by VIKING

1971 *The Angry Moon*
   Illustrated by BLAIR LENT
   Retold by William Sleator
   Published *(1970)* by ATLANTIC-LITTLE

 Frog and Toad Are Friends
   Illustrated by ARNOLD LOBEL
   Written by Arnold Lobel
   Published *(1970)* by HARPER

 In the Night Kitchen
   Illustrated by MAURICE SENDAK
   Written by Maurice Sendak
   Published *(1970)* by HARPER

1972 *Hildilid's Night*
   Illustrated by ARNOLD LOBEL
   Written by Cheli Durán Ryan
   Published *(1971)* by MACMILLLAN

If All the Seas Were One Sea
   Illustrated by JANINA DOMANSKA
   Written by Janina Domanska
   Published *(1971)* by MACMILLAN

Moja Means One: Swahili Counting Book
   Illustrated by TOM FEELINGS
   Written by Muriel Feelings
   Published *(1971)* by DIAL

1973 *Hosie's Alphabet*
   Illustrated by LEONARD BASKIN
   Written by Hosea, Tobias and Lisa Baskin
   Published *(1972)* by VIKING

Snow-White and the Seven Dwarfs
   Illustrated by NANCY EKHOLM BURKERT
   Translated by Randall Jarrell from The Brothers Grimm
   Published *(1972)* by FARRAR, STRAUS

When Clay Sings
   Illustrated by TOM BAHTI
   Written by Byrd Baylor
   Published *(1972)* by SCRIBNER

Anansi the Spider
   Illustrated by GERALD McDERMOTT
   Written by Gerald McDermott
   Published *(1972)* by HOLT

1974 *Cathedral: The Story of Its Construction*
   Illustrated by DAVID MACAULAY
   Written by David Macaulay
   Published *(1973)* by HOUGHTON MIFFLIN

The Three Jovial Huntsmen
   Illustrated by SUSAN JEFFERS
   Adapted by Susan Jeffers
   Published *(1973)* by BRADBURY

1975 *Jambo Means Hello: A Swahili Alphabet Book*
   Illustrated by TOM FEELINGS
   Written by Muriel Feelings
   Published *(1974)* by DIAL

Index of Titles Mentioned

Index by Author of Titles Mentioned*

---

* This list is confined to juvenile titles and books pertaining to children's
literature